Globalization: Key Thinkers

GLOBALIZATION: KEY THINKERS

ANDREW JONES

polity

First published in 2010 by Polity Press
Reprinted 2011

Polity Press
65 Bridge Street
Cambridge CB2 1UR, UK

Polity Press
350 Main Street
Malden, MA 02148, USA

ISBN-13: 978-0-7456-4321-2
ISBN-13: 978-0-7456-4322-9(pb)

A catalogue record for this book is available from the British Library.

Typeset in 10.5 on 12 pt Times New Roman
by Toppan Best-set Premedia Limited
Printed and bound in Great Britain by the MPG Books Group

For further information on Polity, visit our website: www.politybooks.com

CONTENTS

1 INTRODUCTION: THINKING ABOUT GLOBALIZATION

Globalization, and other objects of thought

Much has been written about globalization. Too much, in all probability. The concept is now so well established in the popular imagination that few schoolchildren are oblivious too it, pop stars include it in their lyrics and a whole range of people from politicians to poets variously hail or blame 'it' for all manner of changes in the contemporary world. Globalization has become so pervasively 'known' that it is becoming taken for granted, and few people question what it really means or even why 'it' is important. And in terms of the academic study of globalization, the literature is now so vast, diverse and (periodically) impenetrable that to read every thought written on the topic would require a lifetime in a library. It is therefore hardly surprising that several of my students on the course I teach about it told me they were 'getting a bit bored' with having to start another book on globalization. As with all overused, over-hyped concepts, globalization has reached a concept 'life-cycle' stage where it risks becoming *passé*. In such a situation, given the sheer number and range of academic social science books published on the subject, the publication of yet another one such as this might appear superfluous. One might be forgiven for thinking that all there is to write about globalization has been written already.

The premise of this book is that this is not so, and that – what is more – there is a need to stem the deluge of ideas about globalization (many increasingly repetitive) with a broad 'stocktaking' intervention that both reassesses the state of the debate, and makes a series of evaluative arguments about *which ideas* have greater or lesser value. The further premise for writing this book, therefore, is that much which *has* been written about globalization is lacking in important respects – analytically, theoretically and empirically – and that the so-called globalization 'debate' has to some considerable degree fractured into multiple *confused* and *inconsistent* strands. The purpose of this book thus corresponds to the second stage of a project that emerged when I wrote my *Dictionary of Globalization* (Jones 2006). In the process of compiling that critical overview and reference guide to the debate, my perspective on a number of concepts, theoretical contentions and propositions across the globalization literature became further developed. The *Dictionary* neither claimed nor sought to provide a neutral guide to the globalization literature, but it did confine its critical engagements to an (often very cursory) identification of potential strengths and weaknesses with concepts and thinkers. As is appropriate for that kind of text, it did not adopt a certain overarching position nor develop an overarching argument.

This book does both of these things, if incrementally. In writing a critical guide to the so-called 'key thinkers' on globalization, I am seeking in this book to pursue two simultaneous and interrelated objectives. The first is to take the reader on a much more detailed critical journey through many (but inevitably by no means all) of the most influential and significant contributions to thinking about globalization than could be achieved in the *Dictionary*. The goal is to furnish the reader with a detailed overview of the main arguments made by a series of thinkers organized around different *themes* within the globalization debate. Through the book I tackle eleven different kinds of thinking about globalization organized in this thematic approach. There are clear advantages to organizing the book in this way. For a start, it permits an analysis of how an individual thinker or small group of thinkers sits in relation to others who have engaged with a similar theme as well as to the wider debate. It also allows me to develop an overarching typology for understanding current thinking about globalization rather than merely listing the key ideas of a string of thinkers that have been assembled arbitrarily.

This leads to a second objective which is to make a series of overarching arguments about the nature of globalization thinking, the relative strengths and weakness of different perspectives and the implications for the future direction of thinking about globalization. To do this, the book builds up a set of arguments in an incremental and cumulative fashion. As I assess the major ideas of each thinker or small group of thinkers, each chapter also spends time evaluating both the critical reception to that specific thinker or group of thinkers' ideas, and also potential lines of critical engagement with their work. However, and simultaneously, these critical appraisals provide the basis for developing the overarching arguments that are drawn together in the concluding chapter. This then is not a reference book, for whilst the chapters can be read as 'stand-alone' critical guides to the ideas of a respective thinker or group of thinkers, the arguments articulated develop with each successive chapter which themselves are cross-referenced and arranged in a deliberate order related to the wider arguments of the book about the state of thinking about globalization.

An undertaking such as this inevitably has involved taking decisions about *who* to include as a 'key thinker'. Such decisions are by their very nature subjective and consequently controversial. In asking anyone who teaches, researches or commentates on globalization – or indeed those who regard themselves as front-line activists – I have no doubt I would get a wide variety of answers. Which contributors represent 'key thinkers' on globalization depends very much on who, what and where you are. That could be said of many subjects of analysis, but when it comes to the topic of 'globalization' I suspect the diversity of opinion would be greater than most. In that respect, the thinkers included in this book can in no way represent a definitive group. Where I have chosen to focus on one thinker on a particular theme, others might have chosen someone different. Likewise, the themes themselves do not represent an exhaustive framework for conceptualizing the globalization debate. Other themes doubtless warrant attention, and no doubt will emerge in the future. If the scope for extending the length of this book had been greater, additional thinkers could have been included specifically around, for example, the themes of environment or regulation. The list of themes has to stop somewhere though.

The thinkers included in this book must therefore be seen as key exemplifiers of the major themes within the globalization debate, and the overarching arguments developed address a wider constituency than just those specific thinkers identified. The book in this respect maps a journey that will equip the reader with a detailed understanding of each thematic dimension to thinking about globalization in the context of wider conceptual and theoretical issues that resonate across the whole globalization debate. However, before we can begin this journey, and introduce the specific themes and thinkers themselves, it is necessary first to traverse what (hopefully for many readers) will be in part familiar ground in relation to the definitional, theoretical and conceptual parameters of globalization as our object of analysis.

Defining and theorizing globalization

The question of definition remains a contentious one in the globalization debate. Taken at its most general level, we can reiterate the most broad-ranging definition of globalization as 'the growing interconnectedness and interrelatedness of all aspects of society'. Yet beyond this very broad conception – and notwithstanding a decade and a half of discussion – it is still true that there remains a significant range of competing definitions of globalization at large in the literature. In part, as Nick Bisley (2007) bemoans in his recent appraisal of the debate, this is a consequence of sloppy thinking. However, it is also a consequence of remaining and significant differences in the philosophical perspectives that underpin different thinkers' disciplinary positions and contexts. As Bisley also points out, quite correctly, 'in consideration of globalization, context is all' (ibid.: 2). I want therefore to make three propositions in relation to the definitional landscape that surrounds globalization.

First, across academic thinking there are fundamental issues of epistemological difference that shape thinkers' definitions of globalization. Epistemology refers in simple terms to the framework of assumptions in which concepts and knowledge are constructed. A Marxist framework, for example, represents one kind of social science epistemology. With regard to the globalization debate, the major differential epistemological issue relates to the contrast between more 'modern' and structuralist approaches to social scientific ones derived from classical social and economic theories, and the 'postmodern' and poststructuralist approaches. The former approach tends to assume that coherent systems, processes and structures can be used as units for analysing the social world, whilst the latter doubts that such entities exist and focuses its theoretical attention on flows, networks, relations and interactions. There is, however, much diversity in the specific articulation of this broad division.

Second, and related, is the issue of disciplinary context. Different social science disciplines or strands within those disciplines (economics, sociology, political science, international relations, etc.) are largely characterized by common epistemological characteristics. Furthermore, different disciplines have different objects of interest which lead to a different emphasis in the arguments that emerge, and the use of different empirical approaches. The consequence for definitions of globalization is that segments of the literature often focus on the narrower definition of globalization that has been the focus of attention within one specific discipline.

Third, and finally, there remains an ongoing tension within the globalization debate (largely as a consequence of these two preceding issues) as to whether or not the concept of 'globalization' captures a singular, identifiable phenomenon which is relevant and applicable to the multitude of transformations with which it is associated. On the one hand, there are academic thinkers like Anthony Giddens (discussed in the third chapter) who argue that globalization can be understood as a generalized process linked to modernity, and that it can be identified in almost every dimension of contemporary life. In this way, whilst in no sense a novel development in human history, it has become considerably more pronounced since the mid-twentieth century. On the other hand, many of the 'popular' pro- and anti-globalization thinkers this book will consider – such as Thomas Friedman, Martin Wolf and Naomi Klein – use a much narrower definition that sees globalization as a post-world war political–economic phenomenon.

If there is no agreement apart from at the very general level on a definition of globalization, then the situation is little better when it comes to globalization theory. The epistemological and disciplinary differences identified have also produced a wide range of different theoretical frameworks for understanding globalization. We will encounter a significant number in the coming chapters but it is worth here again reiterating my previous proposition that contemporary globalization theories are underpinned by four major underlying philosophical couplets (Jones 2006). Whilst different thinkers emphasize these four dimensions to varying degrees, they represent the main underlying philosophical 'building blocks' around which theories of globalization as a phenomenon in the world are being constructed

The first, and most important, concerns space and time. Many of the thinkers discussed in this book argue that globalization amounts at its most elementary level to a transformation in the nature of our own and other people's experience of space and time. Anthony Giddens has made one of the most important contributions in this respect. He argues that modern life is characterized by the stretching of our experience of space and time – a process he calls 'time–space distanciation'. Social relations are becoming 'stretched' in all their forms, facilitated by information and communications technology, the global media and transportation. This is a feature of contemporary modernity in

Giddens's view and it represents a fundamental shift in the nature of social systems. In effect, globalization is a process involving the radical reorganizing and reconfiguration of relationships between individuals, groups and organizations so that regardless or not of whether individuals become more globally mobile, multiple distant influences affect their lives. Giddens's conception of globalization's time–space composition position strongly influences the thinking of David Held and Anthony McGrew (chapter 5). Manuel Castells's theories of the global information economy (chapter 4) are also firmly grounded in arguments concerning the impact of information and communications technologies on the experience of time and space.

Second, the concern with globalization as a spatio-temporal phenomenon also relates to two spatial concepts that globalization theorists use as theoretical building blocks: territory and scale. In the case of the former, theorists such as Giddens have argued that the experience of globalization processes is characterized by what he terms 'deterritorialization'. This is where social relations become 'detached' from their places of origin and transferred to new locales (reterritorialized). Arjun Appadurai (chapter 12) and other cultural thinkers about globalization also make extensive use of this concept of deterritorialization. However, issues of territory also run through the more explicitly spatial thinking of theorists like Saskia Sassen (chapter 7) who see globalization as being generically characterized by 'transborderness'. Furthermore, this transformation of the relationship between social practices and territory is often conceptualized as now being constituted at different scales. Considerable debate about globalization in the abstract has sought to use a multi-scalar (local, national, regional, global) framework to try to understand the transformation of social relations in a globalized world.

A third conceptual couplet in globalization theories is that of system and structure. In developing a unified theorization of globalization, various thinkers have argued that globalization is a world systemic phenomenon and is occurring at a structural level in the contemporary world. Growing interconnectedness in this sense is a feature of global society that is occurring beyond the scale of individuals or small groups and is related to meso-scale interactions in the world – by which theorists often mean nation-states in the international state system or market forces in the global trading system. Immanuel Wallerstein's work which is considered in the next chapter is an important example of such thinking. Whilst individual people in their multitude make up this system, organizations and wider collective interactions are (more) important in explaining contemporary globalization.

Fourth, and finally, are the concepts of process and agency. Globalization is widely argued to be processual in nature, although not one process but many in the view of Giddens and Castells. Held, McGrew and their co-authors go so far as to specify globalization as corresponding to four major spatio-temporal processes: the stretching of social relations (extensification), the increasing intensity of exchanges, (intensification), the speeding up of global flows (velocity) and the impact propensity of global interconnectedness (impact). These are the key processes that they argue characterize both the contemporary phase of globalization and earlier historical phases. Not all theorists agree, however, that globalization is one (or many) processes. The underlying disagreement to a large extent depends on how power and agency are understood. For those who draw upon post-structuralist philosophical traditions like the radical thinkers Michael Hardt and Antonio Negri (chapter 11), a processual conceptualization of globalization implies a coherence and rigidity in agency in the contemporary world that does not exist in reality. The power relations and social agency driving global interconnectedness in this viewpoint are inconsistent, contradictory and sometimes work to produce disconnection.

The still evolving globalization debate

The origins of the globalization debate are now well documented. Whilst arguments about globalization 'appeared to flower rather suddenly in the early 1990s' (Bisley 2007: 11), it is clear this academic usage had distinct antecedents back to the 1960s or even earlier. The coining of the word itself is the subject of some debate, but references in English-speaking publications can be found in the late 1950s (Herod 2009). However, for our purpose, as I have previously outlined (Jones 2006), three distinct academic origins of the current usage can be identified. The first is in business and management theory dating back to the early 1960s. Amongst a number of management gurus and within US business schools a number of commentators published what were initially business manuals concerned with how to run and improve the competitiveness of large US multinational firms. This represented a new, 'cutting-edge' area of management science at the time as US firms sought to expand their operations into more countries around the world. By the 1970s, a number of theorists began to argue that firms needed to become global in the scope of their operations rather than replicating multiple national-scale operations. Key management thinkers began to refer to this process as 'globalization' and by the 1980s this was already becoming one of the key vogue concepts pushed in both the academic literature on management and in the popular business literature.

Second is a diverse set of academic contributions across social and cultural theory which again stem back to the 1960s. Most notable amongst these are Marshall McCluhan's idea of the 'global village' which sought to capture the way in which modernity was increasing integrated global society through new forms of communication. Also important are concepts that emerged from the burgeoning environmental movement which began to propagate a conceptual understanding of the earth and its natural resources as a finite entity. The first pictures of earth from space, along with subsequent pictures taken from moon orbit of a distant and small earth, provided substantial impetus behind the idea that all human society existed together in close and inevitably entwined proximity. Likewise, James Lovelock's ecological-based 'Gaia' thesis (Lovelock 1979) presented a set of arguments about the nature of the global environment and the potentially negative impacts of human society and development on the environment. The idea of 'Spaceship Earth' undoubtedly continues to resonate in debates around the global environment today.

Third, but no less important than the others, is a series of academic literatures across political economy and the social sciences that were more specifically concerned with post-Second World War international economic development and politics. During the 1960s, a number of different strands of academic theory were engaging with a 'development-as-modernization' paradigm which had characterized the new Bretton Woods institutions approach to the developing world. Many drew on classical social, political and philosophical theories, including Marx, Weber and Durkheim. Notable predecessors to globalization theories include Andre Gunder Frank (Frank 1966) and others' theories of 'dependent development', contending that the Third World was held in a state of underdevelopment by the capitalist First World. Our first key thinker – Immanuel Wallerstein – emerges from this approach, proposing his Marxian 'world systems theory', characterized by core–periphery relations, and positing that a capitalist world system had become 'global in scope' during the twentieth century (Wallerstein 1979).

It is only since the late 1980s that globalization has become common coinage to these various literatures and spheres of discussion. Crossover between academic disciplines began to occur, and journalists started to use the word. This was certainly catalysed by the end of the

Cold War and the 'triumph of free-market capitalism'. This process accelerated through the 1990s as globalization usage 'took off, first measurable in the number of academic articles, then quickly in book titles and newspapers. By the mid-1990s the word had ceased to be obscure jargon and could be found across the web and popular media. Its entrance into all major global languages and everyday usage probably became assured when mass protests at G8 summits began to be attributed to the 'anti-globalization' movement in the later 1990s.

Not surprisingly, academic writing since the 1990s has abounded with thinkers seeking to provide a history or commentary on the evolution of the debate. The most influential remains David Held and his co-authors' (1999) now classic characterization of three 'schools of thinking': the hyperglobalizer, sceptic and transformationalist positions. We will examine this typology in depth in chapter 5 but, in brief, they argue that *hyperglobalists* regard globalization as the key concept that defines a new epoch in human history, and propose the emergence of a borderless world where economic activity becomes denationalized. In contrast, Held et al. point to the response of what they see as a *sceptical school*, who argue that the concept has been enormously overstated and is largely a myth – at least in the extreme form described by the *hyperglobalists*. Two important thinkers characterized in this school are Paul Hirst and Grahame Thompson whose work we examine in chapter 6. At this initial stage, however, it is sufficient to point out that Held et al. seek to transcend these polarized positions in the 1990s' globalization debate with a development of a third school of thinking which they term the *transformationalist school*. This school of thought is grounded heavily in the thinking of Anthony Giddens whose ideas we examine in chapter 3. This essentially posits that globalization is a central driving force behind the rapid social, political and economic changes that are reshaping modern societies and the world order. It acknowledges some of the criticism raised by the sceptics, but suggests there is considerable empirical evidence to support the idea that globalization processes are historically unprecedented and that globalization is a powerful transformative force.

As I will argue in chapter 5, and contrary to a number of critical engagements with Held et al.'s typology, their position corresponds to more a 'post-transformationalist' position than a simple adoption of the main features of the transformationalist school they identify. However, attempts to fit the globalization debate into a typological framework have not stopped with Held et al.'s contribution. Of particular use is Nick Bisley's (2007) more recent view of the evolving debate – shown in Figure 1.1 – that differentiates chronological phases of the debate by how they characterize globalization. It has significant common ground with Held et al. in phases one to four, but situates their schools in a wider context. Bisley is also critical of what he argues is the tendency within Held et al.'s approach to 'blur the line between scholars' assessments of the nature of globalization, the causes of change and their effects' (ibid.: 18). Furthermore, in Bisley's conception Held et al. are themselves identified as part of a fourth phase that shares common ground with Manuel Castells (chapter 4) and Jan Arte Scholte (see Scholte 2004), as well as the more journalistic contributions of Naomi Klein (chapter 10) and Joseph Stiglitz (chapter 9). Bisley suggests that this has been followed over the last decade by a fifth phase dominated by contributions seeking to defend globalization from its critics. He includes as examples of this phase the journalistic contributions of Martin Wolf and Thomas Friedman which we will consider in chapter 8.

Phase of debate	Characteristics	Examples
1. Late 1980s	Globalization identified as a process driving radical change in the social realm	Giddens (1990), Harvey (1989), Featherstone (1990), Luard (1990)
2. Early to mid 1990s	Claims about globalization amplified, they become increasingly mainstream and key lines of contestation emerge	Ohmae (1995), Giddens (1994), Camilleri and Falk (1992), Albrow (1996), McGrew and Lewis (1992), Scholte (1993)
3. Late 1990s	Central claims about globalization are theoretically, empirically and politically challenged	Weiss (1998), Garrett (1998), Hirst and Thompson (1996), Rodrik (1997), Hoogvelt (1997)
4. Early 2000s	Consolidation of globalization through parameter setting studies and as a site of political contestation	Held et al. (1999), Scholte (2000), Castells (1996, 1997, 1998), Klein (2000), Stiglitz (2002)
5. Mid 2000s	Merits of globalization overtly defended in the face of the critics	Bhagwati (2004), Wolf (2004), Legrain (2002), Friedman (2005)

Figure 1.1 Evolution of the globalization debate
Source: N. Bisley (2007), *Rethinking Globalization*, Palgrave Macmillan.

Chronological classification of the 'phases' to the debate is undoubtedly useful to an extent, as is the differentiation of schools of thinking, but there remains a need to be cautious in carrying such typologies too far. The argument I will develop through this book is that the globalization debate remains more fractured than these attempts at classification often suggest, and that there is a need for a more nuanced critical engagement with many of the thinkers that have been slotted into one or another 'school' or 'phase'. Although elements of consensus across the debate are undoubtedly identifiable, differences of opinion – underpinned by important epistemological differences – still abound in thinking about globalization. It is therefore useful as a last introductory step to consider where some agreement exists, and where differences remain. This should provide some kind of conceptual map as we navigate the landscape of different thinkers in the coming chapters.

The current state of thinking about globalization

The globalization debate thus remains very much alive and well. If the most recent 'phase' has been characterized by a vigorous defence of globalization as Bisley suggests, then this 'defence' has become only ever more the subject of debate since the global economic downturn that began in 2007. Recent popular contributions to the debate have even (once again) begun to suggest that 'globalization is over' as protectionist tendencies amongst nation-states threaten its 'progress'. Such a proposition remains as problematic as similar previous claims, but may be helpful in focusing the future debate more coherently on areas of consensus and continued disagreement respectively. For our purposes in this book, however, it is useful to consider these two issues here.

Despite the typologies that emphasize differences between various schools of thought, I want to argue that the state of the debate around globalization is characterized by at least three areas of consensus where several key thinkers are in broad agreement on an issue (or at least are very similar in their arguments). The first concerns the historical development of globalization. Whilst the early phases of the globalization 'hyperglobalist' literature in the 1980s and 1990s presented globalization as an unprecedented shift in the nature of the economy and human society, most key thinkers on globalization agree now that globalization is part of a much longer process of societal integration. Wallerstein's world system approach provides an important and powerful basis for seeing contemporary globalization as a continuation of much longer-standing trends but thinkers including Giddens and Held et al. also trace back forms of interconnectedness at the planetary scale of some form to the Roman period and earlier. Importantly, the sceptical response of thinkers such as Hirst and Thompson to the economic-centred account of globalization developed by the hyperglobalists has made it very hard to continue to argue that the global economy of the last thirty years did not have its roots in earlier incarnations of the world capitalist economy.

Second, and conversely, a wide number of key thinkers either argue or appear at least to accept that, however defined, contemporary globalization does amount to something 'new'. The issue of 'what' is novel about the contemporary era of globalization remains a moot point, but in a variety of ways across the literature there is a growing consensus that the concept is warranted in order to distinguish a different form of societal integration in recent decades. In that sense, whilst many might question the very general claims of Giddens or Held et al. that this is a common novel transformation spanning all aspects of human life, most of the key thinkers in this book subscribe to the view that some property of contemporary globalization is qualitatively different from earlier periods. For Castells, for example, this lies with the implications of technological change associated with the informational revolution whereas Friedman's emphasis is much more on the key differences that have emerged from firms, their operation and organization (even if that is also about technology). Whatever the perspective, however, there appears diminishing appetite in the globalization debate (in comparison to the 1990s) for the argument articulated most effectively by Hirst and Thompson that the concept of globalization is only a relabelling of already existing forms of societal interconnectedness.

Third, and finally, in the often heated debate about the interaction between contemporary globalization and political structures and entities, there appears to be a growing consensus that globalization has a complex impact on nation-states and other political units. Whilst both the sceptics and the transformationalists criticized hyperglobalist claims in the literature about the end of nation-states and the borderless world in the 1990s, few thinkers now continue to adhere to this position. Political science thinkers like Giddens, Held and McGrew argue that globalization is leading to a wide variety of changes in the context that nation-states find themselves which produces the need for a changed role for states in the twenty-first century. Both Dicken's and

Sassen's work on transnational firms and city regions only serves to further reinforce this point. And even the pro-globalization thinkers like Wolf or Friedman – who have to some extent inherited some of the hyperglobalist mantle – accept that states remain important actors as global interconnectedness develops.

If everyone agreed, however, discussion about globalization would not be a debate and this is far from the case. In terms of the analysis in the rest of this book, seeking to identify key areas of disagreement and ongoing problematic issues in the globalization debate is crucial. There are many, and in our journey we will encounter many vigorous areas of disagreement where thinkers share little or no common ground. However, for our purposes here, it is helpful to point to three key problematic areas in the debate that represent some of the most significant differences between the key thinkers we will consider.

The first area of difference is the (almost) obvious question of whether globalization is 'a single thing', and the related issue of whether it can be understood as being 'systemic' or 'processual'. This issue runs to the epistemological heart of any discussion of globalization theory. For many of the modernist and structuralist key thinkers we will encounter, the answer to this is in the affirmative. Wallerstein's work provides the forerunner for framing globalization as a phenomenon developing within a singular global system in his argument that 'one world system has become global in scope.' Such a conceptual foundation arguably has echoes in the later work of Giddens, who is perhaps boldest in this position in seeing globalization as a singular transformative process or set of processes (Giddens 1999) but Held et al.'s position is one which essentially expands and develops a theoretical framework based on the same premise. However, a variety of key thinkers are more evasive or overtly critical of this idea of globalization being a single thing. Aside from the substantive critiques of Giddens's work as the foundation for some kind of globalization theory, I will also argue that whilst Castells is concerned with different processes of interconnectedness, his thinking is more evasive on the extent to which this corresponds to a single coherent system, or a single phenomenon that can be fully captured in the idea of globalization. Likewise the arguments of Dicken and Sassen, whilst making use of systemic ideas to some extent, also emphasize the complexity of dynamism of economic or urban development. Perhaps most problematic of all for globalization 'meta-theories' though is the thinking of cultural theorists like Appadurai, whose work on cultural interconnectedness destabilizes any simplistic conception of globalization as one kind of common process.

A second key area of disagreement in the ongoing globalization debate is whether or not globalization is a positive or negative phenomenon. Clearly this depends heavily on the politics of knowledge, and the situated position from which various thinkers approach the subject. However, it is interesting that both Held et al.'s and Bisley's classification of the globalization debate – around both schools of thought and phases – partially reflecting whichever perspective is dominant. For example, the hyperglobalizers and the second phase are essentially dominated by positive views of globalization whilst the sceptics and third phase are more dominated by negative views. Bisley's fifth phase is characterized by thinkers including Wolf and Friedman whose work corresponds to a further wave of 'positive thinking' about globalization. What should be clear, therefore, is that much key thinking about globalization struggles to be objective or value free. Held et al. make a significant attempt to create some kind of objective theoretical framework for understanding globalization within a tradition of political science, but a large number of thinkers – both academic and 'popular' – continue to argue from a subjective position. If Wolf and Friedman see globalization as in general a good thing, then undoubtedly radical thinkers like Klein, Hardt or Negri are of the opposite opinion. I will argue in this respect that of particular significance, therefore, is the politically engaged work of Stiglitz, who is probably most successful at developing a middle road between the still largely polarized character of much of the debate.

Third, there remains much disagreement between various key thinkers as to what the key drivers of globalization are. The debate continues (sometimes almost by default) to remain economic-centric. Clearly most thinkers accept that global economic integration has been an important factor in producing globalization, and its undoubted centrality is well substantiated by the work of Dicken, Sassen, Held et al. or Friedman. Yet differences of opinion abound as to the relative importance of politics, institutions, technology or culture in producing greater societal interconnectedness. Globalization theorists such as Giddens or Held et al. see the process as driven by multiple transformations in human life, such that it is difficult to unpick one factor which alone is a key driver. Other political scientists like Hirst and Thompson place more emphasis on the role of political institutions including nation-states in fostering interconnectedness (or otherwise). In contrast, for Castells it is clear that technological change – and notably information and communications technologies – is regarded as the crucial factor. Furthermore, for some of the Marxian radical thinkers like Klein, Hardt or Negri, there is an underlying argument that globalization is a manifestation of an unjust exploitation endemic in the global capitalist system. Hardt's and Negri's argument that globalization largely equates to a new form of (stateless) imperialism is strongly at odds with many of the other key thinkers we will consider.

The journey ahead in this book

Having identified the major features of the globalization debate along with cross-cutting issues, we are now ready to turn to examine the ideas of the various key thinkers in depth. The remainder of the book is thus organized into eleven thematic 'thinker' chapters followed by a conclusion. In the next chapter I begin by considering 'systemic thinking'. The focus here is on one of the earliest globalization thinkers in the form of the sociologist Immanuel Wallerstein, and in particular his Marxian 'world systems approach' developed since the early 1970s. The chapter argues that Wallerstein's approach represents an important antecedent to the more explicit globalization theories that have developed since the late 1980s. Moreover, it also suggests that his work remains important for opening up a series of fundamental questions concerning whether or not it is possible to develop a systemic and generalized theory of globalization. This discussion sets the scene for the analysis of the important 'conceptual thinking' of the sociologist Anthony Giddens to globalization thinking. The chapter examines the way in which Giddens outlines his argument that modernity is 'inherently globalizing' and how he goes on to argue that globalization represent a spatio-temporal process that can be identified in every major aspect of contemporary social life. It argues that this is the single most ambitious claim for the concept made by any thinker and is, not surprisingly, also problematic.

Chapter 4 on 'sociological thinking' then moves on to consider the ideas of another influential sociologist, Manuel Castells, and his concepts of the global informational economy, the network society and the 'space of flows'. It argues that Castells's work is important for its development of these useful concepts but that the main limitation of his thinking is his reliance on technological change – manifest primarily as the information revolution – as a central explanatory tool for understanding globalization. The chapter suggests that, in the end, it does not provide the basis for a comprehensive explanation for the nature of contemporary global interconnectedness. Such a theme persists into the fifth chapter which takes as its central focus two thinkers

– David Held and Anthony McGrew – whose 'revised transformational thinking' about globalization represents one of the most ambitious and comprehensive attempts to develop a general theory of globalization. The chapter outlines in depth their widely cited characterization of the 1990s' globalization debate around three schools of thinking: (hyper)globalist, sceptical and transformationalist. It also assesses their arguments for the 'revised transformationalist approach' to theorizing globalization. However, in so doing, it suggests that, whilst their framework for conceptualizing globalization may overcome some of the problems of other 'meta-theorists' of globalization, it still has limits and should not be regarded as a panacea.

Following on from this, the sixth chapter takes up the question of 'sceptical thinking' about globalization in greater depth as it considers the work of Paul Hirst and Grahame Thompson. One of the central arguments developed here is that the categorization of Hirst and Thompson as part of the 'sceptical school' by Held et al. represents a simplification and partial misrepresentation of their contribution. Rather, it contends that Hirst and Thompson's analysis continues to provide an empirical critique of the very validity of developing globalization theory and that, whilst aspects of their argument might be overstated, many components of their detailed exposition of the continued importance of national-level institutions and organization cast doubt on Held et al.'s revised transformationalist meta-theoretical approach to globalization as they did on the hyperglobalist rhetoric of the early 1990s.

The seventh chapter then shifts to a different strand of the globalization literature in examining two 'spatial thinkers' – Peter Dicken and Saskia Sassen – whose work has focused on the global economy and global urban system respectively. In examining their ideas about the globalized geo-economy and global city networks, the chapter argues that these thinkers have brought a set of spatial concepts and theories to the discussion that – aside from Castells – was certainly oddly lacking in the mainstream of the literature. Their concepts of networks, circuits and embeddedness represent important attempts to develop in depth the theoretical ideas concerning time–space distanciation that thinkers like Giddens, Held, McGrew and even Castells only outline in the broadest of terms.

Chapter 8 broadens the scope of the globalization literature under consideration as it turns to more 'popular' or journalistic 'positive thinking'. This chapter examines the ideas of two leading journalists – Thomas Friedman and Martin Wolf – who have made major interventions in the globalization debate, arguing vigorously that contemporary economic globalization is a broadly beneficial and desirable phenomenon. The contention here is that the US-based Friedman's arguments about 'the flat world', whilst influential and empirically rich, lack any clear conception of the role for social actors beyond his anecdotal accounts. Likewise, whilst Wolf's thinking is often persuasive about some of the benefits that have arisen from neoliberal economic globalization, the chapter suggests his thinking may place too much faith in classic market theories and their arguments about the market's ability to produce progressive social outcomes. Furthermore, it contends that Wolf caricatures radical critics of globalization in a manner that glosses over some of their more substantive criticisms.

In light of these arguments, the ninth chapter's consideration of the 'reformist thinking' of the Nobel prize-winning economist Joseph Stiglitz is a logical next step. Here I examine each of his significant contributions to the globalization debate and in so doing argue that Stiglitz's analysis – more than any other thinker's – has pushed the globalization debate towards a new stage of sophistication that transcends the more simplistic polarized 'pro-' or 'anti-' positions that much of the literature has struggled to escape from. It thus argues that his balanced critique of both the neoliberal free-market ideology behind (economic) globalization, and the anti-globalization response, represents one of the most comprehensive assessments of the nature of contemporary globalization and how it can and should be reformed. This leads directly to thematic focus on the tenth chapter on 'radical thinking'. Taking the Canadian journalist Naomi Klein as its main focus, the chapter provides a critical overview of her ideas in relation to the 'No Logo' campaign against branding and the power and influence of transnational corporations. It also considers the contribution of the British journalist-writer George Monbiot and the leading spokesperson of the Mexican Zapatista movement, Subcomandante Marcos. The main argument developed through this discussion is that, although much radical thinking finds it difficult not to draw the conclusion that the global capitalist economy should be replaced by another kind of system, few detailed proposals for an alternative to the global market economy have emerged. It thus suggests that radical thinking struggles to produce a different set of prescriptions for action to many reformist thinkers.

Two radical thinkers who are not constrained in this manner, however, are Michael Hardt and Antonio Negri. Their 'revolutionary thinking' about globalization is the subject of chapter 11 which examines at length their contention that the contemporary era of globalization corresponds to a new phase of imperialism where the current period has seen the emergence of a post-national 'empire' without a single nation as its dominant imperial power. Whilst this post-Marxist perspective has been highly influential amongst radical critics of globalization, the chapter draws on a number of detailed critiques to argue that Hardt and Negri's 'globalization-as-Empire' thesis lacks overall credibility as a meta-theoretical position for understanding contemporary global economy and society, as well as the processes that are creating societal interconnectedness.

The twelfth, and penultimate, chapter ends the book's journey through globalization thought with one of the most conceptually difficult aspects to the debate: 'cultural thinking'. It focuses here on perhaps the best-known thinker in this area, the Indian-born academic Arjun Appadurai. Examining Appadurai's arguments in his classic analysis of 'disjuncture and difference' in what he terms the 'global cultural economy', the chapter argues that – despite long-standing contributions to the debate – Appadurai's ideas (and those of cultural thinkers more generally) have only received superficial attention from the main body of the globalization literature. The reason, it suggests, is that culture remains a difficult concept to tackle, and that any consideration of cultural globalization inevitably leads back to difficult fundamental questions about a whole range of key concepts which are widely used by many globalization thinkers. It suggests that the future of globalization thinking may well need to entail a more serious and substantial engagement with theories of cultural interaction in an increasingly interconnected world. Such an argument leads logically to the final chapter which seeks to draw together some conclusions about the current state of thinking about globalization, unresolved issues and the likely direction of future thinking.

2 SYSTEMIC THINKING: IMMANUEL WALLERSTEIN

Introduction

The American social historian Immanuel Wallerstein is perhaps the most appropriate key thinker on globalization to begin this book with. His work is important in that it represents an early and seminal attempt to examine the nature of capitalist integration at the global scale. In this sense, Wallerstein is one of the first major theorists of global interconnectedness and his work has been highly influential across the subsequent literature on globalization. His work is also conceptually ambitious in seeking to understand the emergence of one singular global capitalist system. Wallerstein thus represents a logical first 'key thinker' to engage with, both in terms of his chronological position in the emergence of the globalization debate, and in the breadth and range of his theoretical scope. Of course, his work has been criticized since the late 1970s from a variety of angles (many are common to wider criticisms of Marxist theories). These include a tendency to construct global history in a teleological fashion, the problematic extension of Marxist assumptions about the inevitability of capitalist crisis and revolution and also its rather simplistic division of global territory into three functional geographical areas. In this sense, the chapter will develop an evaluative approach to Wallerstein's work, seeking to demonstrate to the reader how this systemic early precursor to globalization theory has informed subsequent debates. I will also argue that wider theories of globalization like those of Giddens, Castells and Held et al. have by no means escaped the problems or criticisms raised by Wallerstein's early thinking.

Wallerstein was born in New York in 1930 where he subsequently grew up. He attended and then taught sociology at Columbia University, receiving his BA in 1951, followed by an MA and PhD in 1959. During the 1960s, his interests whilst at Columbia focused mainly on African politics and in particular the political struggles around post-war independence. In 1971 he was appointed to a Chair of Sociology at McGill University, staying five years before taking a more senior position at Binghamton University (SUNY) as Distinguished Professor of Sociology. Here he wrote the second two books in his trilogy on the modern world system, and the impact of the ideas in these works across the social sciences enabled him to establish the Centre for the Study of Economies, Historical Systems and Civilization. He remained as Director of the Centre until his retirement in 2005. Wallerstein also held several positions as visiting professor at universities worldwide. This included several periods as the Directeur d'études associé at the École des Hautes Études en Sciences Sociales in Paris. He was also president of the International Sociological Association between 1994 and 1998 and is also an advisory editor for the *Journal of Social Evolution and History*.

It should be clear from this career path that Immanuel Wallerstein is essentially a sociologist. His training, along with his academic positions, has been in departments of sociology. Yet his work successfully straddles multiple social science disciplines, and he himself comments in a later preface to one of his major books that most people regard him as an economic or social historian. In reality, as Wallerstein himself states, his approach is undoubtedly one that is firmly interdisciplinary, straddling many social sciences disciplines (Wallerstein 1974: ix–xi). The significance of this interdisciplinarity to his key role as a forerunner of globalization theory is considerable, as well as the particular 'holistic' tradition in social scientific analysis which Wallerstein works within.

To understand these arguments fully, it is necessary to consider Wallerstein's thought in a series of steps. First of all, I examine the major tenets of Wallerstein's arguably most important theoretical contribution with respect to the globalization debate: his conceptualization of the contemporary era through 'world systems analysis'. My central argument is that his world systems analysis, various criticisms notwithstanding, represents probably the most important precursor to contemporary globalization theories. The following discussion will show how his arguments have in many ways pushed a wide and diverse range of thinkers into engaging with what have become central sub-debates within the globalization literature. The next section thus begins by examining Wallerstein's major theoretical contribution – world systems analysis – and outlines its principal arguments. In the following section, I then go on to consider a number of critical engagements with world systems analysis. I argue that these critiques have been important in shaping Wallerstein's subsequent revisions to his thinking in a manner that has been equally important to the globalization theories that have drawn on his ideas. The fourth section takes up this latter point in assessing the extent to which world systems analysis represents a 'proto-globalization theory', identifying how it links to other key thinkers on globalization but also how it falls short of the arguments developed by full-blown globalization theorists. The final section then considers the legacy of Wallerstein's thinking in contemporary global-ization theories, and how his arguments continue to resonate in ongoing aspects of the debate.

Wallerstein's world systems analysis

The major antecedents of world systems analysis are two distinct schools of earlier twentieth-century historical thought. First, Wallerstein draws on the arguments of a school of French historians, known as the Annales School. This school of thought was linked to the journal *Annales d'histoire économique et sociale*, founded in 1929 by Marc Bloch and Lucien Febvre. The school advocated 'total history' as a synthesizing discipline to counter the separation of enquiry of disci-plines. This was a reaction to the 'excessive detail of early twentieth century history' which emphasized political events over everyday lives of ordinary people (Flint and Taylor 2007). Wallerstein thus begins with a 'holistic' approach in which the actions of key figures such as politicians are just one small part of a wider unfolding history of ordi-nary people. The emphasis in the Annales approach was thus on the economic and social roots of history, captured in the concept of *longue durée* coined by Fernand Braudel.

The second key antecedent to Wallerstein's thought is the Marxist critique of post-war development theories. After the Second World War, modernization theories argued that development in the global South should and could follow the path of the advanced industrial economies of the North as new post-colonial states implemented top-down policies that led to them catching up with the rich North. Notably, Wallerstein's work is closely linked at the outset to that of the Chilean Andre Gunder Frank, who argued that the economic processes of the global economic system would keep the global South in a state of dependent underdevelopment, rather than permitting them to 'catch up' with the advanced industrial economies. Wallerstein shared Frank's view that it was not a matter of waiting for the less developed world to somehow 'develop', but rather a need to change the nature of the world system that prevented them from doing so through a series of structural relations inherent in the world capitalist economy.

Drawing on both of these lines of thought, from the early 1970s Wallerstein produced a series of major works which outline his arguments for his developing world systems approach and about the nature of contemporary world society and economy. In particular, his three books *The Modern World System, Volumes I, II and III* (Wallerstein 1974, 1979, 1989) seek to theorize the development of a singular capitalist world economy from the fifteenth to the nineteenth centuries. The central thesis developed through all three of these books is that during this period a single world economy developed, based on capitalism and an integrated society, which was increasingly planet-wide in its scope. In this respect, a global-scale world system emerged which overtook all other competing economic, social and political systems of organization in human society on earth. The scope of the thesis is clearly 'holistic', both in its approach to academic disciplines and in the object of its analysis: the capitalist world economy. To understand how and why this is the case, we need to consider the wider features of world systems analysis in more depth.

The basis of the epistemological argument for world systems analysis is that social science represents the culmination of attempts to develop general laws for times and places. Wallerstein argues that generalizations need to be specified (i.e., given a context in which they are meaningful), and he does this through the concept of the historical system. They are what he sees as 'societies', and they are systematic because they consist of interlocking parts that constitute a single whole. However, they are also historical because they are entities which are created, develop over a period of time and reach their demise. The underlying thesis of world systems analysis is that many of these systems have existed in the past, but that only one exists today – the modern world system (Flint and Taylor 2007). We will return to this shortly.

For Wallerstein, every social system is unique, but he argues they can be classified into three major types of entity. First, a *mini-system* is an entity that has within it a complete division of labour and a single cultural framework. He argues that such systems no longer exist but were a feature only in very simple agricultural or hunting and gathering societies. Second, in more recent times, there have only existed *world systems* which are defined simply as units with a single division of labour and multiple cultural systems. World systems therefore come in two sub-forms: those with a single political system and those without.

The former is termed a *world empire* and is a system based on a redistributive-tributary mode of production. He suggests that whilst world empires have come with many forms of political system, they all shared the same mode of production based around a large group of agricultural producers who produce a surplus beyond their immediate needs. Examples of such world empires include the pre-modern Roman, Chinese or Egyptian civilizations. He distinguishes these from the nineteenth-century empires such as Great Britain or France that were not world empires but were nation-states with colonial appendages.

In contrast, a *world economy* is an entity based around the capitalist mode of production. Production occurs when it is profitable to do so, and the basic drive of the system is the accumulation of capital and this system-type has no overarching political structure. Markets dominate economic relationships and the system is characterized by competition between producing units. Wallerstein's key argument is that, historically, *world economies* have been extremely fragile and unstable structures leading either towards disintegration or conquest by one group and hence transformation into a world empire. This prevented them from developing into capital-expanding systems. The exception to this, however, is one particular world system. That system is the European world economy which emerged from around 1450 onwards and has survived long enough to take over the whole world based around a capitalist world economy that has become 'global in scope' and has become much more stable.

Within a world systems approach, he goes on then to consider the way in which social change occurs within and between these systemic entities. Broadly speaking, world systems analysis offers four fundamental types of change that have occurred in historical social systems. The first two are essentially shifts in the mode of production. This can occur either as an internal or external process. In the first case, for example, mini-systems have produced world empires at certain historical moments. Similarly, one world empire – feudal Europe – was the predecessor of the modern capitalist world economy. In the second case of change as an external process, transformation occurs as incorporation. As world empires expanded, they conquered and incorporated former mini-systems. Similarly, the expanding capitalist world economy since the fifteenth century has incorporated a whole range of mini-systems and world empires whose populations have become part of the new system.

A third kind of change is discontinuity. This occurs between different entities at roughly the same location where both share the same mode of production. The consequence is that the system breaks down and is replaced by a new one. An example is the sequence of Chinese states in the thousand year-long history of the Chinese Empire. Wallerstein suggests the periods in between these separate world empires are anarchic and exhibit some reversal to mini-systems. The classic example of this would be the 'Dark Ages' in Europe between the collapse of the Roman Empire and the rise of feudal Europe.

Finally, and conversely, a fourth kind of change is a consequence of (dynamic) continuity where Wallerstein argues that, despite the popular notion that cultures are 'timeless', entities are in fact constantly dynamic and changing. He suggests that such changes come in two basic types – linear and cyclical. All world empires, for example, display a cyclical pattern of 'rise and fall' as they expand into adjacent mini-systems but then eventually contract under the burden of bureaucratic and military expansion.

Using this approach to consider nineteenth- and twentieth-century history, Wallerstein's central argument is that one form of world system, based around the modern capitalist economy, has become global in scope. However, this 'scope' does not mean the system is ubiquitously global. Rather, Wallerstein argues that he is interested in charting how this geographical extension to globalness came about and the features that have emerged. He argues that, in essence, the modern world system has three basic elements: a single world market, a multiple state system and a three-tier political structure. This last element relates to the nature of political groupings in modern world society. The argument made by Wallerstein is that the exploitative processes which work in the world economy always tend to produce a three-tier format. This occurs because those at the top of the system will always aim to 'create' a 'middle class' between them and those at the bottom to make confrontation more stable.

World systems analysis also represents a significant evolution of Marxist ideas on development in its arguments concerning the spatial form of the modern capitalist system. Building on Frank's critique of 'development as modernisation', Wallerstein proposes that the modern capitalist world economy divides roughly into a tripartite geographical configuration which reflects the role played by different regions in the systemic processes of capitalism. He is in effect positing a geographical (and Marxian) explanation for how the world economy avoids crisis and revolution. This has had a global geographical dimension insofar as the single capitalist world economy has developed into three structural regions: the core, the periphery and the semi-periphery. The core originally emerged around north-west Europe but in the twentieth century can be understood as broadly equivalent to the First World. The core therefore expropriates surplus value not just from labour but also from peripheral areas of the world economy. A third structural region, the semi-periphery, acts as a political balance. These areas are dominated by neither form of process but social relations involve exploiting peripheral areas whilst at the same time they are themselves exploited by core areas. If there were no semi-periphery, the world economy would be far less politically stable and would not 'run smoothly' (ibid.). In the twentieth century various world systems theorists have viewed Latin America or South Asia as fulfilling semi-peripheral functions that prevent the upper stratum of world society in the core from being challenged by a unified opposition.

In the several decades during which he has developed this perspective, Wallerstein has examined many aspects of the modern world system through his world systems lens. He has variously proposed detailed frameworks, for example, for understanding how power relations play out over time between core, periphery and semi-periphery and how the semi-periphery plays a complex role in maintaining balance in the world capitalist economy. These arguments are supplemented by a substantial social science literature (largely from the 1980s) which adopted and sought to implement a world systems approach for understanding the development of different states and regions. Such work continues to be produced, but it is also fair to state that world systems analysis has to some extent been superseded by more recent theories that place globalization at their epistemological heart. To a large extent, this shift away from world systems analysis towards globalization theory has much to do with the critiques and limits of world systems analysis that have emerged in the literature since Wallerstein first proposed this approach. To understand how these critiques have thus moved the nature of the theoretical debate on, we need now to examine the various critiques of Wallerstein's world systems approach.

Critical engagements with world systems analysis

During the 1980s and 1990s, a number of critiques of world systems analysis emerged which are relevant to understanding the limitations and problems in Wallerstein's approach, as well as his response and the subsequent implications for how globalization theories developed. For it is clear that in the process of developing, refining and defending world systems analysis from its critiques, Wallerstein's thought provides much of the groundwork for what subsequently blossomed into the globalization debate. I want therefore to suggest four major strands of critique – largely focused around world systems analysis as an approach – that are most significant with respect to the above. These critiques have also been instrumental in Wallerstein's own reformulations of his ideas in recent work and remain important for subsequent globalization thinkers who have drawn upon it.

First, world systems analysis received an (unsurprisingly) hostile and highly critical response from right-wing schools of political and economic thought. These can be broadly grouped together under the banner of neoliberal thought which, loosely defined, corresponds to arguments for unfettered markets, the global capitalist economy, as being the best way to achieve economic growth and progressive social and political development. Neoliberal thinkers reject Wallerstein's Marxian conceptions of core and peripheral development outright. From a neoliberal perspective, the operation of free international markets for goods and services will stimulate economic growth in less developed countries by encouraging private capital to invest in production. A free international economy is thus a necessity for economic growth and improved global living standards. It is not free-market capitalism which produces inequalities and maintains underdevelopment in the countries of the global South, but the incomplete development of free markets and the interference of states and other institutions and interest groups which impede the free operation of the market. World systems analysis is thus criticized for its Marxian epistemology which, in the view of the neoliberals, misconceives the nature of relations between nations and economies in the world economic system. Wallerstein and others who make use of dependency theory are attacked for wrongly (in the view of the neoliberals) attributing underdevelopment to the action of capitalist system where its fault lies at the feet of bad government, excessive regulation and corruption in the global South. Neoliberals thus strongly reject the policy implications of world systems thinking that some kind of policy intervention is required if peripheral states are ever to enjoy the level of economic growth and living standards achieved in the global North.

Second, world systems analysis has been widely criticized at the theoretical level for being overly simplistic and reductionist in its understanding of how the world economic system operates and of its relationship with wider socio-cultural contexts. Critics from both within and without Marxian approaches suggest that Wallerstein retains an overdeterministic view of the role of the state in the world economic system and that his analysis lacks a sophisticated engagement with the cultural dimension to theories of state interaction. At the heart of this is perhaps the failure of the world systems approach to overcome the challenge made to Marxist thinking that it reduces explanation to economic relations.

Third, and similarly, the spatial division of the globe into core, semi-periphery and periphery has been criticized for being crude and simplistic. This critique has at least two strands. First, from the outset, various thinkers have questioned whether Wallerstein's tripartite division of the world economy and society was really adequate for understanding the complex position of different nation-states in the world system. Empirical research has sought to assess the validity of simplistically dividing nation states into a tripartite classification. However, a further – and more fundamental – dimension to this critical strand comes from geographical thinkers in particular who have suggested that Wallerstein's spatial epistemology is problematic in conceptualizing the spatial form of the world capitalist economy. Beyond the empirical-based critique of those who question whether certain states belong to core, periphery or semi-periphery runs the deeper criticism that such territorial conceptions misrepresent the nature of the capitalist economy. Thus, global integration produces an uneven topology of 'core' and 'peripheral' spaces that can be much smaller than nation-states or even city regions. For example, a number of theorists have suggested that the key individuals who run the global economy represent a transnational capitalist class or 'social core' who often physically resides very close to those who are highly peripheral to the global capitalist system (Jones 1998). Whilst the extent to which this spatial form of core and peripheral processes is a new development or not remains a moot point, it seems clear that Wallerstein's famous tripartite division by no means captures the full complexity of the world economy's spatial form.

Fourth, and running in part through all the preceding criticisms, is the wider challenge to Wallerstein's thinking posed by philosophical postmodern and post-structuralist critiques. Since the 1980s, postmodern thought within the social sciences has attacked several of the key epistemological assumptions that underpin Wallerstein's work. Much has been written on this topic elsewhere, but three particular issues are of key importance to ongoing debates about globalization theories. First, postmodern critiques argued that grand theorizing in terms of frameworks such as Marxism that claim to produce one total theory of human society are deeply problematic. Postmodern thought questioned the capacity of *any* theoretical framework to adequately provide a universally applicable basis for understanding human society. Wallerstein's world systems analysis, of course, represents one of the most ambitious attempts (even within Marxian approaches) to understanding the nature of human societal development at the planetary scale. As such, it represents an archetypal example of the kind of meta-theoretical framework that postmodern perspectives regard with incredulity (see Lyotard 1984). Second, and relatedly, this links to a postmodern suspicion of the truth claims made by such meta-theoretical narratives. The so-called postmodern 'crisis of representation' questions the capacity of meta-theories to tell the universal truth about the human condition. In relation to world systems analysis, for example, such a perspective would lead to a questioning of whether all world systems displayed similar characteristics across space and time, and whether their development could be explained by common processes. Third, postmodern thinkers also question the very idea that societies and economies can be conceptualized through the concepts of system and process. Drawing on philosophical debates about the nature of scientific knowledge, postmodern critics suggest that epistemologies such as Wallerstein's neo-Marxist approach inappropriately apply ideas of 'systems' to complex societal phenomena that cannot be sufficiently captured by this concept. They would suggest that the concept of the system has been inappropriately borrowed from the natural sciences (physics, biology, etc.) and that societies and economies are not 'systemic' in the way that world systems theory assumes.

This final criticism is of course not exclusively directed at world systems analysis or the work of Wallerstein, and we shall return to it again often in subsequent chapters as it represents one of the key challenges to many theoretical perspectives on globalization. However, for the moment, we need to turn to consider the extent to which Wallerstein's work represents a proto-globalization theory which will be highly pertinent to understanding how subsequent thinkers have also been subject to postmodern critique.

World systems analysis: a proto-globalization theory?

The significance of Wallerstein's work is that it can be considered as the most coherent forerunner of globalization theory. Although

Wallerstein himself only makes use of the word 'globalization' in much later work (Wallerstein 2000), his conceptual framework in many ways represents a clear antecedent to globalization theories that appeared in the later 1980s. Whilst the scope and extent of Wallerstein's historical analysis of world economy and society has many resonances with different parts of the contemporary globalization debate, there are a number of characteristics of world systems analysis which both mark it out as distinctive in pre-empting the globalization debate, and which also continue to permeate the current theoretical understandings of what globalization might be considered to be as a phenomenon.

First, and probably most significant, is the fact that Wallerstein's epistemological perspective rests on the assumption that one world society – as opposed to multiple societies – has emerged during the twentieth century. This runs counter to orthodox conceptions of societies and economies in the modern world as being distributed between different countries and nation-states. Wallerstein rejects this 'multiple society assumption' in favour of what might be termed a 'single society assumption'. The significance of this epistemological shift should not be underestimated. Even at the time that Wallerstein was writing in the 1970s, most social and economic theory conceptualized change as something occurring within national societies. International interactions were recognized but understood in terms of different national economic models, cultures, or state systems coming into contact with each other. Furthermore, the accepted geographical division of the world into First-, Second- and Third-World blocs further emphasized territorially defined divisions between different socio-economic systems. In this respect, world systems analysis makes a bold departure in contending that these apparently discrete national entities (whether economic, political or social) warrant conceptualization as part of the same (albeit imperfectly and unevenly) unified system. Furthermore, Wallerstein has a historical theoretical cut at accounting for the development of this singular system and provides empirical evidence to support his position. In this respect, world systems analysis shares a common epistemological basis to subsequent globalization theories developed by thinkers like Held et al. in a way that earlier socioeconomic analysis does not.

Second, and following on, Wallerstein's work is important in that it represents an early attempt to examine the nature or process by which capitalist integration occurs at the planet-wide scale. Until Wallerstein, the dominant mode of thought among economic theorists treated national economies as relatively separate entities 'contained' (see Agnew 1994) within territorial nation-states. This assumption was based around the strength of control that national governments had over the capitalist free-market economies of the First World. Whilst later globalization theorists have of course documented the reduction in trade barriers, capital flows, FDI, etc. that mark contemporary economic globalization, world systems analysis made the argument from the outset that the fate of different regions and national (free-market) economies across the globe were bound together by sets of common relations within a world capitalist system. Wallerstein's usage of Gunder-Frank notions of dependency with respect to Latin American states most obviously demonstrates this, but in fact the *underlying* theoretical arguments of world systems analysis lay the groundwork for much more far-reaching claims concerning the inter-relatedness of economic activity in different national economies. By seeking to empirically demonstrate the long historical development of global capitalism, Wallerstein's project in WST is therefore intrinsically concerned to identify common processes and interrelationships and thus to provide the conceptual basis for economic activity at the global scale in a way that previous frameworks did not.

Third, Wallerstein arguably also lays the foundation for later globalization theory through the interdisciplinary nature of his thinking. As the introductory chapter discusses, globalization theories by the very nature of the concept draw upon and are entangled in many disciplines – sociology, politics, history, economics, geography, management studies, etc. Wallerstein's contribution is thus important because of his explicit interdisciplinary approach to understanding the development of world economy and society. Certainly at the time he first published *The Modern World System*, this was not a common perspective amongst his peers in history or sociology. Writing in the early 1970s, he states that he does not believe that 'the various recognized social sciences . . . anthropology, economics, geography, political science and sociology – are separate disciplines' (Wallerstein 1974: ix). His goal is to conceptualize them as 'a single subject matter', and in particular to see history and social science in this light. Furthermore, he openly seeks to link this 'historical social science' to politics, arguing for an interdisciplinary (or better 'beyond disciplinary') epistemology which tries to construct abstractions that capture part of a 'global reality'. Such an approach opens up a very different epistemological frame of thinking from much social science at that time and sets the interdisciplinary tone in which thinkers like Giddens, Castells, Held et al. and even Appadurai follow.

Fourth, it can be argued that whilst grounded in a clear neo-Marxian epistemology, Wallerstein's approach (and world systems analysis in particular) has clear common epistemological ground with the 'postmodern view of knowledge' which was beginning to emerge by the 1970s (but which only became widespread in social scientific thought during the later 1980s). This might appear surprising given the centrality of Marxist concepts in his work, but it can be argued that Wallerstein's approach is less vulnerable to the critiques associated with the so-called crisis of Marxism that developed in the 1980s. Marxist analysis was challenged by philosophical arguments from postmodern thinkers who suggested both its grand theoretical perspective and its claims to represent a universal 'truth' of human societal development were unsupportable. During the 1980s, this crisis of Marxism deepened as the collapse of the socialist states of the Second World appeared to reinforce the outmoded and anachronistic nature of Marxist ideas. In this context, key Marxian influences on Wallerstein – notably Gunder Frank's *dependencia* theories – were also viewed as increasingly problematic as a number of countries in the global South achieved rapid rates of industrialization and economic growth.

Yet Wallerstein's arguments avoid many of the supposed worst 'crimes' of totalizing modernist grand theories. His use of Marxian concepts is one which avoids dogmatic or simplistic arguments about universalizing laws. Wallerstein is careful to qualify the extent of his theoretical claims in world systems analysis, arguing that his approach is a model rather than an absolutist theory. Whilst clearly not immune to every criticism developed by postmodern thinkers, it is nevertheless important that Wallerstein's ideas have continued to weather the storm of the crisis of Marxian analysis. This is attributable to his sensitivity to the problems of 'grand theorizing' and attempts by social scientists to develop 'universal laws' from even his earlier works in the 1970s, and to the interdisciplinary and eclecticism of his conceptual influences.

This is significant in the role of Wallerstein's work as a proto-globalization theory. Postmodern thought has challenged the modernist groundings of globalization theories in the classical social theoretical frameworks of Marx, Weber, Durkheim and others. Yet Wallerstein's work provides an earlier example of how such a wide-ranging theoretical perspective as one that theorizes globalization as a planet-wide phenomenon can counter, respond and arguably overcome many of the stronger postmodern challenges to the state of knowledge. After the attacks at meta-theorizing made by postmodern thinkers during the 1980s, world systems analysis in particular provides a clear counter-argument and template for how meta-theoretical frameworks (which globalization theories certainly necessarily are) might still be constructed with sensitivity to the postmodern challenge.

This latter point leads on to a consideration of how Wallerstein has developed his arguments since the inception of the 1990s' globalization debate which is the subject of the next section.

Recent developments in Wallerstein's thought

Wallerstein has argued in recent work that globalization is a misleading concept (Wallerstein 2000, 2005). In his view, 'what is described as globalization has been happening for 500 years', so to warrant a new term for this phenomenon in the 1990s was misguided. In engaging with what he sees as the 'deluge' of discourse about globalization over the last fifteen years, he argues it is a 'gigantic misreading of current reality' (ibid.: 252). He argues in common with several globalization thinkers that these discourses represent a political project which people have also 'imposed on themselves' in the contemporary era. Thus he contends that whilst the world undoubtedly stands on 'a moment of transformation', it is not one of 'an already established, newly globalized world with clear rules' (ibid.: 252). For Wallerstein, in contrast, the current era is one characterized by transition. This transition is not just a change occurring as 'a few backward countries catch up with globalization' but a transition in which the entire capitalist system will be transformed into something else.

He argues that the outcomes of this transition are uncertain, but that the processes labelled as globalization are far from new. Drawing on arguments grounded in Kondratieff and Schumpeter about long waves of innovation and economic growth, Wallerstein posits that the capitalist world economy has entered a crisis phase which characterizes the transition. He suggests that this crisis will be terminal, although it may take fifty years to play out. The question then is what will happen in the coming decades as this crisis of the capitalist world system produces a transition to a new kind of historical system or systems?

In relation to this crisis, Wallerstein has also characterized the emergent anti-globalization (correctly) as the latest incarnation of Marxian counter-movement against the world capitalist system. In relation to this, he argues that neoliberal globalization characterizes a brief historical period between 1970 and 2000 and that what has come after is a faltering of that political project. Globalization of the 1990s 'momentarily' revitalized the developmental optimism of the 1950s, but that a new anarchic and unstable phase has emerged in the twenty-first century.

In these recent contributions, Wallerstein thus continues to offer a thought-provoking contribution to contemporary debates on globalization. His approach remains grounded in neo-Marxian epistemology, and likewise that is where it remains vulnerable to continued criticism. Whilst his world systems approach has been hugely influential, many thinkers find his structural and systemic conception of the global capitalist economy problematic and postmodern critics remain highly sceptical of the structural causal relationships implicit in the world systems approach. Thus, whilst Wallerstein's more recent work has been championed (not surprisingly) by those associated with the anti-globalization movement, his epistemological approach remains one amongst many approaches to theorizing globalization, and not one that has by any means universal acceptance.

'Systemic globalization': the Wallerstein legacy

The legacy of Immanuel Wallerstein's work for contemporary thinking about globalization is undoubtedly substantial. For many, he is in chronological terms the first major thinker to develop a theoretical framework for understanding the historical and present-day emergence of a singular global capitalist economy. At the time he began to write – in the middle of the Cold War – this perspective can also be seen as prescient insofar as the future dominance of free-market capitalism was far from assured or even anticipated. The proposition in the 1970s, therefore, that there is 'one world system' that is 'global' in scope is essentially unprecedented. Much historical and political scientific analysis up to this point had examined the colonial or imperialist periods, but epistemologically the view that the world was comprised of nation-states that essentially administered largely discrete national economies and societies was hegemonic. Much theoretical analysis was concerned with the development of interconnectedness, but at the *inter*national scale. Few thinkers questioned the primacy of the nation-state system, or the assumption that these territorial-political units corresponded to essentially coherent and cohesive national economies and societies over bounded regions of territory. World systems analysis provides the epistemological foundations for doing precisely that.

Wallerstein can also be credited more generally with proposing the first holistic conceptual framework for theorizing the nature of developing global *interconnectedness* in his world systems approach. Of particular importance is the fact that – when compared to other Marxist thinkers of the 1970s and 1980s – Wallerstein is concerned to construct an explicitly *spatial* framework to understand *how* the capitalist world economy has extended its scope. Until the 1990s, this dimension to his work received much less attention than his arguments about dependent development but in fact they also mark out his theoretical arguments as a clear antecedent to current globalization theories. It is these last two factors that probably more than anything else establish his thinking as the clearest theoretical antecedent to the globalization theories that began to appear during the 1990s.

Finally, however, Wallerstein's thinking remains pertinent in terms of the debate it opened up around the nature of theorizing itself. The postmodern shift in social scientific knowledge from the 1980s onwards represents a challenge to the grand ambitions of Wallerstein's world systems approach which is common to many (or arguably all) subsequent attempts to theorize globalization as one phenomenon at the global scale. Globalization is by its very nature an ambitious and totalizing concept. Therefore, regardless or not of whether subsequent globalization thinkers like Held et al. have overcome many of the criticisms levelled at world systems analysis with respect to its crude spatial categorization of the world economy or its notion of dependent development, the challenge made to Wallerstein's world systems approach is equally pertinent or misplaced (depending upon your position) to much thinking about globalization. In that respect, the criticisms outlined in this chapter on Wallerstein's work will continue to permeate much of what follows in the coming chapters as we move to examine further theoretical frameworks that seek to develop an all-encompassing understanding of globalization.

Further reading

Selected key works by Immanuel Wallerstein

Wallerstein, I. (1974) *The Modern World-System, Vol. I: Capitalist Agriculture and the Origins of the European World-Economy in the Sixteenth Century.* New York/London: Academic Press.

Wallerstein, I. (1979) *The Capitalist World-Economy.* Cambridge: Cambridge University Press.

Wallerstein, I. (1980) *The Modern World-System, Vol. II: Mercantilism and the Consolidation of the European World-Economy, 1600–1750*. New York: Academic Press.

Wallerstein, I. (1984) *The Politics of the World-Economy: The States, the Movements and the Civilizations*. Cambridge: Cambridge University Press.

Wallerstein, I. (1989) *The Modern World-System, Vol. III: The Second Great Expansion of the Capitalist World-Economy, 1730–1840s*. San Diego: Academic Press.

Wallerstein, I. (1991) *Unthinking Social Science: The Limits of Nineteenth-Century Paradigms*. Cambridge: Polity.

Wallerstein, I. (2000) Globalization or the Age of Transition? A Long-Term View of the Trajectory of the World System. *International Sociology* 15(2): 251–67.

Wallerstein, I. (2004) *World-Systems Analysis: An Introduction*. Durham, NC: Duke University Press.

Wallerstein, I. (2004) *Alternatives: The US Confronts the World*. Boulder, CO: Paradigm Press.

Wallerstein, I. (2005) After Developmentalism and Globalization, What Next? *Social Forces* 83(3): 1263–78.

Wallerstein, I., Amin, S., Arrighi, G. and Frank, A. (1990) *Transforming the Revolution: Social Movements and the World-System*. New York: Monthly Review Press.

Commentaries and critical engagements

Flint, C. and Taylor, P. (2007) A World System Approach to Political Geography, in *Political Geography: World-Economy, Nation-State and Locality*. Harlow: Pearson, ch. 1.

3 CONCEPTUAL THINKING: ANTHONY GIDDENS

Introduction

Anthony Giddens is one of the most prolific social science thinkers whose work spans social and political thought. His contribution to the globalization debate is substantial, not so much with respect to the quantity of material (although this is not insignificant), but more because of his position as a key conceptual thinker about what globalization is, where it came from and how it might be theorized. Giddens is undoubtedly one of the most important founders of the field of thought that might be loosely termed 'globalization theory', although as we shall see this is not an uncontroversial issue. And his work continues to be heavily drawn upon by proponents and detractors of his theoretical perspective concerning globalization. In this respect, he is a natural next thinker to consider after Wallerstein and has perhaps been most widely cited of any single theorist of globalization. Furthermore, if Wallerstein's work is heavily grounded in the classical political economic thought of Marx, then in Giddens's thought on globalization the influence of the classical sociologists is even more evident. Giddens's ideas are shaped by Marxist theories too, but also importantly by the intellectual inheritance of Max Weber and Emile Durkheim. These are the 'founding fathers' of modern sociology and the fact that he engages and combines the theories of all three perhaps in part accounts for why his work has been so influential.

Giddens was born in 1938 and raised in London, coming from a modest middle-class background insofar as his father worked as a clerk with London Transport and he was the first member of his family to go to university. He got his first degree in Sociology and Psychology from Hull University in 1959, and then took a Master's degree from the London School of Economics. He undertook doctoral research at the University of Cambridge, completing his PhD in 1964. In 1961 he started working at the University of Leicester where he taught social psychology. At Leicester, which played an important role in developing British sociology, he worked with Norbert Elias. In 1969 he was appointed to a position at the University of Cambridge where he later helped create the Social and Political Sciences Committee (SPS), a sub-unit of the Faculty of Economics. Giddens worked for many years at the University of Cambridge, being promoted to full professorship in 1987. During this period he co-founded Polity Press with David Held and John Thompson, which set out to publish social science. From 1997 to 2003 he was director of the London School of Economics and a member of the Advisory Council of the Institute for Public Policy Research. He was also an adviser to Tony Blair during his time as British prime minister, and his arguments for a 'third way' political approach were influential on both Tony Blair and Bill Clinton during the late 1990s. Since 2003, he has continued as a vocal participant in British political debates, supporting the centre-left Labour Party with media appearances and articles. Giddens also remains a regular contributor to the research and activities of the progressive think-tank Policy Network. He was given a life peerage in 2004 as Baron Giddens, of Southgate in the London Borough of Enfield, and sits in the House of Lords for Labour.

Whilst his academic, policy and political thought has been wide-ranging in terms, Giddens's conceptual contributions to thought on globalization are related to and have both shaped and been shaped by his political life and the policy advice he has developed for the UK and other governments. Most notably, his arguments for a 'third way' politics is grounded to a considerable extent in his conceptual theorization of how contemporary modernity and its accompanying processes of globalization impact on people's lives across the planet. Giddens's high-profile status in political and media debates (for example, in giving the 1999 BBC Reith Lectures on globalization) has also in part propelled debates about globalization into the mainstream. Yet not all of his arguments have been well received and his particular diagnoses concerning the nature of modernity and its relationship to globalization have prompted vigorous critique that to some extent parallel criticisms leveled at the third way as a political paradigm. These critical challenges have come from several directions, both from within existing schools of social thought such as international political economy and also from postmodern thinkers.

Whilst many of the criticisms of Giddens's conceptions of modernity, globalization and a progressive politics are interrelated, I will argue in this chapter that most significant in terms of the globalization debate is how critical engagement with his work reveals the fundamental challenges to any meta-theoretical perspective on globalization. A number of critics have argued that Giddens's theorization of globalization is problematic because it is overambitious, overly simplistic or contradictory in its arguments. The extent to which such criticisms are valid or not in relation to Giddens's thinking is crucial to wider debates about the possibility and nature of globalization theories. In this respect the critical response to Giddens's theorization of globalization also bears great relevance to subsequent key thinkers' contributions – notably those from the British social and political school – including David Held and Anthony McGrew. It is for that reason that, despite the considerable volume of his policy writing on the subject, this chapter focuses its attention on Giddens's key theoretical works concerned with globalization and the detailed critiques that have been developed in light of them.

Globalization and modernity

The major contribution Giddens makes to the globalization debate comes in his book *The Consequences of Modernity* (1990), although a number of subsequent books have developed his arguments further. In this key work he lays out the foundations for what many contemporary commentators regard as the conceptual basis for globalization theory and in particular the arguments for why both the concept and a theoretical framework based around it are necessary to understand the nature and development of world society.

Giddens argues that globalization is a phenomenon that cannot be understood outside the context of 'modernity' which is producing it. He argues that the condition of modernity is itself inherently globalizing and that this 'is evident in some of the most basic characteristics of modern institutions, particularly their disembeddedness and reflexivity' (ibid.: 63). Modernity, he contends, is a dynamic and transformative form of social life that emerged in Europe from the seventeenth century onwards and which has subsequently become 'more or less worldwide' in its influence. It is distinguishable from earlier societies primarily by the pace of social change, the scope of that change and the proliferation and development of modern institutions. However, most significant of all is its role in the transformation of time and space, and it is this contention that lies at the centre of Giddens's conceptualization of globalization.

This key characteristic of the transformation of space and time under modernity is that in all pre-modern cultures times were still connected with space (and place) until 'the uniformity of time measurement by mechanical clock was matched by uniformity in the social organisation of time' (ibid.: 18). This produced worldwide standardization of calendars and of time across regions. He contends that this 'emptying of time' was in large part the precondition for the 'emptying of space' and has causal priority over it (ibid.: 8) because 'coordination across time is the basis of the control of space'. He suggests that development of 'empty space' can be understood as the separation of space and place. Place is defined as the 'locale' which is the setting for social relations that are physically together in material terms. Modernity progressively rips space away from this notion of place as relations are fostered between absent (non co-present) others. Place thus becomes *phantasmagoric* insofar as locales are thoroughly penetrated and shaped in terms of social influences that are physically quite distant. These 'distanciated relations' structure the nature of places in the condition of modernity and represent a separation of space from time.

This separation of time from space is one not conceived as a unilinear development and Giddens argues that it has three key facets. First, it is the prime condition of the processes of 'embedding' which is key to his understanding of globalization. Second, it provides the gearing mechanisms for 'that distinctive feature of modern life the rational organisation'. Third, the 'radical historicity' of modernity depends upon modes of 'insertion' into time and space which were unavailable to previous civilizations. History in this sense is the systematic appropriation of the past to facilitate shaping the future.

These three facets produce the extreme dynamism of modernity but it is the first – disembedding – which represents the core process that has and continues to produce globalization. Giddens defines disembedding as 'the "lifting out" of social relations from local contexts of interaction and their restructuring across indefinite spans of time space' (ibid.: 21). He identifies two types of disembedding. First, *symbolic tokens* are 'media of interchange' that can be 'passed around' without regard to the specific character of individuals or groups that handle them at any given juncture. The classic example of this is money which provides 'for the enactment of transactions between agents widely separated in time and space' (ibid.: 24). Second, *expert systems* represent 'systems of technical accomplishment or professional expertise that organize large areas of the material and social environments in which we live today'. He gives the example of driving a car where the driver enters 'settings' that are permeated by expert knowledge which 'involves the design and construction of automobiles, highways, intersections, traffic lights . . .' (ibid.: 28). Both symbolic tokens and expert systems are disembedding mechanisms because they 'remove social relations from immediacies of context'.

Globalization represents, for Giddens, the contemporary deepening and development of the essential dynamism of modernity and its ongoing transformation of space and time. Central to understanding contemporary globalization is the nature of time–space distanciation processes. The central premise of this framework is the need to conceptualize the 'relations between *local involvements* (circumstances of co-presence) and *interaction across distance* (the connections of presence and absence)'. Giddens argues that in what he terms 'the modern era', the level of time–space distanciation is now much higher than at any previous period. Furthermore, the relations between local and distant social forms and events become compoundingly 'stretched'. This is the essence of what globalization 'is' – this stretching process. The result is that contemporary social life is increasingly characterized by modes of these stretched connections as different social contexts or regions become networked across the earth's surface as a whole (ibid.).

Using this perspective, he suggests that globalization can be defined 'as the intensification of worldwide social relations which link distant localities in such a way that local happenings are shaped by events occurring miles away and vice versa' (ibid.: 64). He further contends that the process by which this happens is inherently dialectical. This is because what he calls 'local happenings' may move in an obverse direction from the very distanciated relations that shape them. In *The Consequences of Modernity*, he illustrates this by two examples. The first is the case of urban economic development where global relations may produce prosperity in one city whilst the same processes also lead to economic decline in another. Giddens argues that this is the same process, producing dialectically opposed outcomes. Second, and similarly, the development of globalized social relations serves in some places to diminish some aspects of nationalist feeling whilst simultaneously being causally involved in the intensification of more localized nationalist sentiment.

Giddens criticizes international relations (IR) theory in that, whilst 'not altogether wrong', it focuses problematically on interaction between nation-states and in the unquestioned notion that the world-state system has become progressively more unified. He therefore has praise for Wallerstein for 'successfully breaking away' from the limitations of orthodox sociological thought and its obsession with endogenous models of social change (i.e., from within states). In particular, he credits Wallerstein with shifting the focus onto globalized relationships but argues his perspective remains too narrow by seeing only one dominant institutional nexus (capitalism) as responsible for modern transformations. (ibid.: 69). As discussed in the preceding chapter, the world systems approach is seen to be unable to account for the rise of the nation-state system, nor to illuminate political or military concentrations of power which 'do not align in an exact way with economic differentiations'.

Giddens therefore proposes that the world capitalist economy is one of four dimensions of globalization which he develops from his four-fold classification of modernity. The other three are the nation-state, the world military order and the international division of labour (shown in Figure 3.1).

In relation to the second, the nation-state, Giddens argues that the main centres of power in the world economy are the capitalist states. Whilst the major agents of economic activity – firms – are to some degree 'insulated' from the political realm and can wield immense economic power, he argues their power cannot rival that of states in some key respects. These areas are essentially 'territoriality' and 'control over the means of violence'. He emphasizes that there 'is no area of the earth's surface, with the partial exception of the polar

Figure 3.1   Giddens's dimensions of globalization
Source: A. Giddens (1990), *The Consequences of Modernity*, Polity.

regions, which is not claimed to be under the legitimate sphere of control of one state or another' (ibid.: 71).

The state is therefore bound into the third dimension – that of the military order. Giddens argues that this corresponds to 'the connections between the industrialization of war, the flow of weaponry and techniques of military organization from some parts of the world to others, and the alliances which states build with one another' (ibid.: 74). He suggests these relations exist in the same dialectical 'push–pull' as those between the other dimensions in that the Cold War saw the USA and USSR build an essentially bipolar system of military alliances that was global in scope. The countries involved in these military alliances thus will 'necessarily accept limitations in their opportunities to forge independent military strategies externally' (ibid.: 74). Furthermore, the 'globalizing of military power' is not confined to weaponry and alliances but also concerns war itself. Giddens argues that two world wars attest to the way in which local conflicts become global involvements (although as will be discussed later, this global–local division may be problematic). Thus whilst nuclear weaponry precludes that kind of war between the main powers, a series of orchestrated wars have been instigated in peripheral regions.

The fourth dimension – industrial development – relates to the expansion of the global division of labour and the geography of production. He argues that both firms and states are bound into complex dialectical processes that produce global-scale class relations and which separate workers from the means of production. This 'globalized industrial development' is leading to differentiations between different areas of the world both in terms of the level (or 'order') of job tasks and in regional specialization in terms of types of industry, skills and the production of raw materials. He points to the diffusion of machine technologies as one of the major features of globalized industrialism and argues that it not only affects the sphere of production but also many aspects of day-to-day life (ibid.: 76). Furthermore, this diffusion of industrialism has created 'one world' in a more negative and threatening sense – a world where actual or potential ecological changes of a harmful sort affect everyone on the planet.

Giddens also points to the role of mechanized communications technologies in producing cultural globalization. He sees this as an essential element of the reflexivity of modernity and 'the discontinuities that have torn the modern away from the traditional'. Rather than emphasizing the awareness that globalized media give to people across the planet of events about which they would have otherwise remained ignorant, he suggests that more important is the 'global extension of the institutions of modernity' which would be impossible without the pooling of knowledge known as 'the news'.

However, if globalization is a consequence of modernity, then it impacts on many levels beneath the global capitalist economy and national societies. Under (globalizing) modernity, 'larger and larger numbers of people live in circumstances in which disembedded institutions, linking local practices with globalized social relations, organize major aspects of day-to-day life' (ibid.: 79). This has major implications for the nature of 'trust', 'identity' and their relationship to globalization and modernity.[1] In relation to trust, he argues that the nature of modern institutions is deeply bound into a mechanism of trust in *abstract systems* (the collective term for symbolic tokens and expert systems). As many aspects of modernity become globalized, this means that 'no one can completely opt out of [these] abstract systems' (ibid.: 84) and that trust relations are basic to the extended time–space distanciation associated with modernity. He links this to the argument that in contrast with pre-modern society, our ontological security (defined as the confidence people feel in their self-identity and in the constancy of their surroundings) and in particular its link to place, has been largely destroyed by disembedding and time–space distanciation (ibid: 108). Trust is increasingly disengaged from local contexts.

For individuals, this has five main implications for identity. First, globalization produces for individuals an 'intrinsic relation between the globalizing tendencies of modernity and the localized events in day-to-day life'. Second, individuals have to construct the self as a reflexive project which amounts to finding their identity amid the strategies and options provided by abstract systems. Third, individuals display a drive to self-actualization, founded upon basic trust, which in personalized contexts can only be established by an 'opening out' of the self to others. Fourth, the formation of personal and erotic ties as 'relationships', guided by the mutuality of self-disclosure and, fifth, a concern for self-fulfilment which is part 'a narcissistic defence' against an externally threatening world over which individuals have little control, and part 'a positive appropriation of circumstances in which globalized influences impinge upon everyday life' (ibid.: 123–4). Globalization is thus bound into the transformation of the self and of everyday experience for everyone caught up in the condition of modernity.

The final key dimension to contemporary social life towards which Giddens addresses his theoretical understanding of globalization concerns the nature of risk and danger in the modern world. In this respect, and subsequently developed at length by thinkers such as

Ulrich Beck (see Beck 1992), he argues that the risk profile of modernity is bound into globalized relations. This has at least seven dimensions, but for our purposes here can be summarized around four broader areas. First, Giddens argues that there has been a globalization of risk both in the sense of its intensity (for example, nuclear war) and also in terms of expanding the number of contingent events which affect large numbers of people on the planet (for example, the global division of labour). Second, risk stems from the created environment or socialized nature (which he sees as the 'infusion of knowledge into the material environment'). Third is the development of 'institutionalized risk environments' which again affects the lives of a large number of people on the planet. An example would be global financial markets. Fourth, and finally, are three forms of risk awareness. These comprise the 'awareness of risk as risk' where the knowledge gaps in risks cannot be converted into certainties by religious or magical knowledge as they were in pre-modern society; 'the well-distributed awareness of risk' where collectively faced dangers are known to wide publics; and 'the awareness of the limitations of expertise' where no expert system can be wholly expert. Giddens goes on to explore the implications of these forms of risk at some length but it suffices here to refer to his statement that 'all these forms of risk and danger permeate all aspects of day-to-day life, once more reflecting an extraordinary interpolation of the local and global' (ibid.: 148).

Overall, it should thus be apparent that in these early 1990s' works, Giddens provides a far-reaching, detailed and ambitious theoretical framework for understanding what globalization 'is' as an abstract process, and how it is intimately bound into the experience of modernity. For Giddens, modernity and globalization are inseparable phenomena and one cannot be explained or effectively understood without the other. The scope of his theorization of globalization is thus enormous, amounting to an all-encompassing set of arguments about contemporary global society and economy and how it is developing. His conceptualization of globalization thus goes far beyond that of Wallerstein as it draws on classical sociological theories to provide a theoretical account of how globalization processes impact on individuals, organizations and nation-states that encompasses much more than the economic realm. However, most important of all – as will be seen in this and subsequent chapters – is the theoretical and conceptual framework he offers for understanding what globalization 'is' in terms of a spatio-temporal phenomenon. Giddens's framework provides one of the most important foundations for contemporary globalization theory by providing a set of abstract concepts for understanding the different dimensions to globalization. Such an ambitious and wide-ranging theorization has inevitably been the subject of considerable critical engagement, and we will turn to this shortly. Before this, however, it is important to give further consideration to how Giddens has developed his ideas concerning the implications of globalization.

Giddens, the 'runaway world' and the implications of globalization

Since the early 1990s, Giddens has made a series of wide-ranging arguments about the implications that contemporary globalization processes – understood through the framework outlined above – have for everyone on the planet. This includes specific arguments about the implications for individuals, organizations, nations, firms, government, policy and politics more generally. It is thus important to identify some of the main arguments he makes which in part account for the degree of influence and impact his theoretical claims about globalization have had.

First, and probably most significant, Giddens argues that we are living 'through a major period of historical transformation' (Giddens 1999: 1). He suggests that we feel 'out of control' in a 'runaway world' where many of the influences that were meant to make life feel more predictable such as science and technology have had the opposite effect. Globalization, he argues, is thus 'restructuring the ways in which we live' in 'a very profound manner' (ibid.: 4). As his theoretical conception suggests, since globalization is affecting everyday life as well as economies and states, this runaway world has implications for virtually everyone on the planet. The major implication of contemporary globalization is thus that it is an unavoidable reality.

Second, and following on, Giddens identifies the view that globalization represents both an opportunity and a threat. Traditional societies have already broken down, and traditional values are following. He argues that the implication of globalization is that other traditions, such as religion, are also experiencing major transformation. Religious fundamentalism, he suggests, originates as a reaction to those 'crumbling traditions' and thus needs to be understood on that basis. He sees globalization as promoting 'cosmopolitanism' insofar as in a globalizing world where 'we are regularly in contact with others who think differently, and live differently' (ibid.: 4). This has produced and will continue to produce conflict in the twenty-first century as fundamentalists in the spheres of religion, nationalism and ethnic identity take refuge in 'renewed and purified tradition' as well as violence. Giddens suggests we can 'legitimately hope that the outcome of cosmopolitanism produced by globalisation will be tolerance and democracy', but that globalization also exposes the limits and weaknesses of the institutions that currently promote and maintain democracy.

Third, globalization therefore also means that people need to respond. It is not possible in the contemporary world to stand still, but rather these processes of transformation require a response. Firms need to remain competitive, workers need to re-skill and governments need to address new risks and challenges to security. Giddens's argument is that contemporary globalization produces a heightened need to be proactive and to manage transformations rather than being resigned to the 'runaway world'. In that sense, 'we can never become masters of our own history, but we can and must find ways of bringing the runaway world to heel' (ibid.: 5).

Fourth, and finally, the implication is also the ongoing need to reconstruct institutions to tackle the new challenges posed by globalization. This includes national and international institutions of government but also the family, work, tradition and even nature. His view is that these institutions remain the 'shell' of what they used to represent, but globalization has undermined and transformed the circumstances in which they exist and they are now therefore 'inadequate for the tasks they are called upon to perform' (ibid.: 19). For example, in Giddens's view 'nations today face risks and dangers rather than enemies' which amount to 'massive shifts in their very nature' (ibid.: 18). The powerlessness people feel in the face of globalization is therefore not 'a sign of personal failing' but rather 'reflects the incapacities of our institutions'. It is the degree to which institutions adapt to globalization that will determine how globalization processes play out in the coming decades.

The folly of Giddens's globalization theory?

The influential nature of Giddens's wide-ranging and ambitious theoretical conception of what globalization 'is', where it has come from and how it is bound into the contemporary condition of modernity has inevitably produced considerable critical engagement. It is not possible in this chapter to cover the entirety of every debate that Giddens's work has provoked or contributed to within the globalization literature, but what is more important is to assess the fundamental challenges that have been made to his globalization theories overall. The bulk of the direct critical engagement with Giddens's thought on globalization has largely developed within sociology and international political economy (IPE), operating within a modernist paradigm, and for that reason these critiques will be examined here. However, the final section will also consider the wider but indirect critique that emerges from postmodern social science.

The most sustained and influential critique of Giddens's conception of contemporary globalization centres on Justin Rosenberg's contribution. Rosenberg works within IPE and, in *The Follies of Globalization Theory* (2000), he sets out a detailed critique of Giddens's theorization of globalization as outlined in *The Consequences of Modernity* and subsequent works. These critiques go to the heart of the epistemological framework of Giddens's thought on globalization.

Rosenberg sets out to dismantle Giddens's foundations of globalization theory around five critical strands, which to some extent follow on from each other in a logical sequence. First, and most significant, Rosenberg argues that Giddens's theorization of globalization rests on the cornerstone idea of 'a spatio-temporal problematic for social theory' and that his wider globalization theory ultimately relies on this (ibid.: 90). Rosenberg's primary challenges is that this is fundamentally incoherent and that there is no epistemological or theoretical basis for arguing that modernity requires a new spatio-temporal understanding of social relations. The consequence is that the concept of globalization has no theoretical or epistemological coherence around which the mighty edifice of Giddens's globalization theory can be constructed.

The central problem, Rosenberg argues, is the overall reliance on time–space distanciation as a transformative characteristic of social relations in the modern era. He suggests that in Giddens's theoretical framework 'it *looks* like time–space distanciation is explaining globalization – either in the sense that globalization is a product of time–space distanciation (viewed as a tendential property of modernity)', or in the sense that 'globalisation is quintessentially a spatial phenomenon which the spatialized categories of time–space distanciation (viewed as a problematic) uniquely enable us to analyse' (ibid.: 119). Rosenberg argues it is hardly surprising that this definition has proved so influential since 'if either of these implicit claims could be made to stick, then the term "globalization" would indeed become more than just a descriptive geographical category.' Globalization would in fact become a 'master category' that 'uniquely captures both the expansive dynamic of modernity and the transformations in the very social texture of space itself' (ibid.: 119). Time–space distanciation is then the crucial link which grounds the concept of globalization in a broader account of the social world (ibid.: 120).

Unfortunately, Rosenberg argues, time–space distanciation fails to provide this link and it also fails to 'explain' globalization. The reason boils down to the fact that Giddens's argument relies on the implicit assumption that spatio-temporal definitions of social phenomena are the key to explaining 'the historical character of modernity' (ibid.: 120). Rosenberg suggests that no one, including Giddens, has yet been able to establish this and that furthermore, in Giddens's own analysis 'many of the spatio-temporal phenomena turn out again and again to be derivative of other institutional features of modernity which are not defined in these terms'. In short, time–space distanciation does not provide an explanation for globalization. It too is simply a description.

This leads Rosenberg to argue that Giddens's globalization theory is based on a misguided 'reification of space' and a spatializing of social theory which inevitably sees time–space compression at unprecedented levels in modernity. He thus contests Giddens fundamental claim – the idea that 'modernity is inherently globalising'. Instead he argues that Giddens's circular definition of globalization has 'detached the concept from any deeper explanation than that contained in its own definition' (ibid.: 121). The problem is that through 'expanding the reach of the spatial categories by colonizing the deeper levels of substantive and abstract theory', time–space distanciation prevents the re-entry of non-spatio-temporal concepts. This has the effect of making 'globalization' appear to rest securely on underlying social theory because there can be no social theory that is non-spatio-temporal.

The second target of Rosenberg's critique follows on from this first point and concerns Giddens's arguments about abstract systems and globalization. As discussed earlier, abstract systems, expert systems and symbolic tokens 'are the great disembedding mechanisms of modernity'. Abstract systems 'lift out' social relations from local con-texts of interaction and produce their restructuring 'across indefinite spans of space-time' (ibid.: 122). Because trust in this world is more vital and more problematic than ever before, modern life involves a peculiar recombination of co-presence and absence by which 'disem-bedded relations are re-embedded in local contexts' (ibid.: 123). The problem, argues Rosenberg, is that abstract systems loom very large in the explanation of globalization, but their causal properties are not addressed. Viewed through time–space distanciation, their most significant attribute becomes their disembeddedness which in effect evacuates them of 'social content.' In short, there is no explanation. This is again description posing as explanation.

Third, Giddens's arguments concerning the transformation of intimacy are questioned. Rosenberg argues that Giddens's propositions about the decline of kinship in modernity rests on the capacity of abstract systems to 'explicitly overcome the dependency on personal ties'. He argues that 'unless that capacity can be shown itself to derive from the spatio-temporal attributes of abstract systems', then it adds nothing new to the concerns of institutional transformation that concerns classical sociology. He suggests that this is indeed the case, and therefore that whilst 'there may indeed be direct connections between the transformation of intimacy and the globalizing tendencies of modernity', these connections 'are not the most significant ones for explaining either of these phenomena' (ibid.). Again the implication is that there is nothing within Giddens's globalization theory that warrants a new (globalization) theory which cannot be provided by existing epistemologies within social theory.

Fourth, and similarly, he questions Giddens's spatio-temporal arguments in relation to risk and ontological security in modernity. In essence, Rosenberg's main point in this respect is that Giddens fails to demonstrate that 'changes in the spatio-temporal conditions of ontological security' are the most causally significant feature of 'high modernity' (ibid.: 146). Rather, Rosenberg suggests, Giddens in fact cites rather more familiar 'causes' for the growth of risk in modernity which include militarization, industrialism and the rise of bureaucracies. He thus questions whether it is the globalizing of these phenomena that is the most important cause of greater risk and insecurity in the contemporary era.

Fifth, and finally, Rosenberg completes his critique with the argument that the dialectics of time and space around which Giddens bases his framework do not in fact amount to a dialectic. He argues that whilst Giddens distinguishes four dialectics of space and time – displacement and re-embedding, intimacy and impersonality, expertise and re-appropriation, and privatism and engagement (Giddens 1990: 140–1) – only the first two have any possible space–time component (and the second only weakly). Moreover, with regard to the first, he suggests that the processes of embedding and re-embedding cannot be successfully differentiated in dialectical terms. They both appear to refer to 'the (re)insertion of social relations into any socio-temporal matrix, however extensive' (ibid.: 151) which appears to contradict the earlier importance of locality to the definition of embedding.

The above summary can only be cursory, and Rosenberg goes into considerable detail in elaborating these critiques. However, the main features of his critique should now be evident. His major challenge to Giddens is that the project of developing any globalization theory – based around globalization as a singular phenomenon or process – is flawed because it 'cannot escape the contradictions that must attend . . . at every stage' (ibid.: 90). In all respects, Giddens's framework is problematic. This is undoubtedly a powerful and important challenge which resonates beyond Giddens's theoretical framework. Many theorists have based their conception of globalization on time–space distanciation but Rosenberg argues that this assumption fails to provide viable epistemological foundations. Whether or not every minutiae of Rosenberg's critique is justified remains a moot point, but the major elements of his scepticism as to whether Giddens really does supply the basis for a 'new' social theoretical framework based around the concept of globalization is important and one which ramifies across the academic globalization literature.

Conclusion: Giddens and the debate about globalization theory

Engaging with the thinking of Anthony Giddens about globalization is – to some considerable extent – an engagement with the very idea of globalization theory. Giddens's work represents one of the major foundational blocks of the globalization debate and it permeates the views of many of the thinkers whose ideas will be examined in the coming chapters. Even those who seek to problematize Giddens's theoretical framework often retain much in common in terms of his epistemological basis insofar as they seek to identify the nature of globalization as a singular common process or phenomenon that permeates contemporary social life. The key proposition in Giddens's work is thus to argue that 'modernity is inherently globalising' and to further define it as a spatio-temporal process that can be identified in every major aspect of contemporary social life. Such a proposition probably represents the single most ambitious claim for the concept made by any thinker, and has provided the basis for developing a range of different globalization theories, including the influential framework proposed by David Held and his co-authors which we will consider shortly. It is almost impossible to envisage any critical discussion of the wider features of the debate about globalization which does not involve addressing Giddens's work.

Yet what is also clear is that Giddens's foundations for both the concept of globalization and his theoretical framework for understanding it as a feature of the contemporary world are far from uncontested. On the contrary, the critical arguments of many within sociology, politics and international relations theory which Rosenberg draws together in his critique indicate that globalization may be built on precarious epistemological and theoretical foundations. The most enduring aspects of the critiques can perhaps be reduced to three central claims. The first is that globalization is a 'description' masquerading as an 'explanation', and as such can offer no insight into the causes of change in today's interconnected world society. The second is that there is nothing intrinsically different about contemporary social life that the conceptual language and theoretical frameworks of existing classical social theories cannot explain as well as globalization theory, and therefore there is no real need to develop a new kind of theorization based around this new concept. Third is that even if the first two criticisms are misguided, globalization – defined as a spatio-temporal process – cannot be satisfactorily defined as a 'pure' phenomenon that is prevalent and relevant to all the different aspects of contemporary societal transformation that Giddens claims it is. The ultimate challenge is that not every aspect of modernity is globalizing and, even when it appears to be, there is no singular process at work 'causing' this spatial and temporal reconfiguration in a consistent manner. If various aspects of contemporary spatio-temporal reconfiguration are contradictory (as Rosenberg argues), then the concept of globalization cannot adequately capture what in reality corresponds to multiple and sometimes opposing forms of transformation.

This last strand is probably the most potentially damaging to Giddens's arguments about globalization. It questions the very existence of such a thing as 'globalization', rather opening up the possibility that Giddens presents a theoretical framework concerning the transformation of time and space in the contemporary era that runs the risk of being monocausal and is overly simplistic. Such a scepticism also resonates with a wider school of thought within postmodern social science that doubts the capacity of meta-theory to be able to tell convincing stories of the social world. Just as with Wallerstein's world systems approach, postmodern thinkers point to the complexity and multiplicity of social relations and the organizations and institutions which they produce. Postmodern thought thus remains at odds with

Giddens's epistemology – an epistemology that shares a modernist and 'structuralist' lineage with Wallerstein and classical social theories. Giddens has of course written extensively on the philosophy of social science, most notably in his work on historical materialism and structuration theory – which are beyond the scope of this chapter (although references are indicated in the Further Reading below), and counter-arguments to the postmodern critique are present in his work. However, the issue in this respect remains unresolved insofar as whether or not such a phenomenon as 'globalization' does warrant demarcation as a concept and this process lies at the heart of ongoing theoretical debate. Nevertheless, for many globalization scholars Giddens's work provides an important template and foundation for constructing further globalization theories. In that sense, we will revisit this debate about the viability of globalization theory at several points in the coming chapters as we examine how others have sought to develop meta-theoretical perspectives on globalization and responded to similar critiques as those levelled at Giddens.

Further reading

Works by Anthony Giddens on globalization

Beck, U., Giddens, A. and Lash, S. (1994) *Reflexive Modernization: Politics, Tradition and Aesthetics in the Modern Social Order*. Cambridge: Polity.

Giddens, A. (1990) *The Consequences of Modernity*. Cambridge: Polity.

Giddens, A. (1991) *Modernity and Self-Identity: Self and Society in the Late Modern Age*. Cambridge: Polity.

Giddens, A. (1992) *The Transformation of Intimacy: Sexuality, Love and Eroticism in Modern Societies*. Cambridge: Polity.

Giddens, A. (1999) *Runaway World: How Globalization is Reshaping our Lives*. London: Profile Books.

Giddens, A. (2007) *Europe in the Global Age*. Cambridge: Polity.

Hutton, W. and Giddens, A. (eds) (2000) *On the Edge: Living with Global Capitalism*. London: Vintage.

Commentaries and critical engagements

Beck, U. (1992) *Risk Society: Towards a New Modernity*. London: Sage.

Bryant, C. and Jary, D. (eds) (1996) *Anthony Giddens: Critical Assessments*. London: Routledge.

Bryant, C. and Jary, D. (2001) *The Contemporary Giddens: Social Theory in a Globalizing Age*. Basingstoke: Palgrave Macmillan.

Robertson, R. (1995) Glocalization: Time–Space and Homogeneity–Heterogeneity, in M. Featherstone, S. Lash, and R. Robertson (eds), *Global Modernities*. London: Sage, ch. 2.

Rosenberg, J. (2000) *The Follies of Globalisation Theory*. London: Verso.

Tucker, K. (1998) *Anthony Giddens and Modern Social Theory*. London: Sage.

4 SOCIOLOGICAL THINKING: MANUEL CASTELLS

Introduction

The sociologist Manuel Castells is widely known for his ideas about the 'network society' and the 'information society', both broadly associated with the impact of information and communications technologies on all aspects of contemporary economy and society. In this respect, it is not immediately evident why we should consider him as the next key thinker on globalization. Yet whilst he may have written few books that explicitly use the word 'globalization' in their titles, almost all of his work over the last fifteen years has been concerned with the issue in one way or another. Furthermore, his thinking also shares much common heritage with Wallerstein and Giddens in its development of classical social theory and Marxism. It is for this reason that it makes sense to consider next his hugely influential – if at times indirect – contribution to the globalization debate.

In this chapter, we will examine how both his concepts of the network society and informationalism are permeated by arguments concerning globalization. The 'network society', put simply, refers to Castells's far-reaching contention that contemporary society is characterized by 'key social structures and activities that are organized around electronically processed information networks' (Castells 2000a). This is a far more ambitious claim than the modest propositions he makes around the rise of informationalism in recent times that equates to the growing dominance of 'a specific form of social organization in which information generation, processing and transmission become the fundamental sources of productivity and power' (Castells

2000a: 21). Yet an engagement with both concepts is essential in order to understand how Castells situates his thinking about globalization in a wider thesis concerning the transformation of contemporary society and economy in relation to technology, organizations, identity and politics. In particular, the first of these – technology – is central. For Castells, changing information and communications technologies present a unifying thread that provides the link between so many of the globalizing processes that are occurring in the contemporary world. The volume of his writing on this topic is enormous – typified in his epic trilogy of books on *The Information Age* (Castells 2000a, 2000b, 2003 – and, as with Giddens, it is a challenge to condense all of his often complex arguments within a single chapter. Therefore, the following discussion represents an engagement with the most influential aspects of his thought rather than an exhaustive analysis of every implication of his work for the debate.

Castells was born in Hellin, Spain, in 1942. As a child he lived all over Spain including Madrid, Cartagena, Valencia and Barcelona where he completed his secondary education. In 1958, he then went to study law and economics at the University of Barcelona. However, as a student, he became an activist against Franco's dictatorship and was forced to flee to Paris in 1962. In France, he won a political refugee fellowship at the Sorbonne's Faculty of Law and Economics and completed his undergraduate studies in 1964. His doctoral research involved a statistical analysis of location strategies of industrial firms in the Paris region, and he received his PhD in Sociology from the University of Paris in 1967. Upon completing his doctorate, he immediately took up an academic post at the same university, teaching methodology of social research, and researching on urban sociology. In 1970 he transferred within the university École des Hautes Études en Sciences Sociales and in 1972 published his first book, *La Question urbaine*. This was very successful and was translated into ten languages, establishing his international social science reputation. Castells was also during this period one of the intellectual founders of what came to be known as the New Urban Sociology.

In 1979, and with a growing international reputation, he was appointed Professor of Sociology and Professor of City and Regional Planning at the University of California, Berkeley. He still holds this post, although he has also been professor and director of the Institute for Sociology of New Technologies, Universidad Autonoma de Madrid, Research Professor at the Consejo Superior de Investigaciones Cientificas in Barcelona, and a visiting professor at fifteen universities in Europe, the United States, Canada, Asia, and Latin America. In

1998 he was awarded the Robert and Helen Lynd Award from the American Sociological Association for his lifelong contribution in the field of community and urban sociology. Over his career, Castells has published 20 books, and over 100 articles in academic journals, as well as co-authored or edited 15 additional books. Among his various distinctions and awards, he was appointed to the European Academy in 1994 and was a member of the European Commission's High Level Expert Group on the Information Society between 1995 and 1997. He has been an adviser on globalization and the information society to many national governments, UN agencies and programmes and non-governmental organizations (NGOs). He currently lives in Berkeley in California.

The development of his thinking about what we now call globalization predates the recent debate in many ways. As with Wallerstein and Giddens, Castells has long been interested in the transformation of society in the context of modernity and the developing world economy. The inevitable focus of much of this chapter will be the ideas expounded in the *Information Age* trilogy, but his earlier works on urban form and processes undoubtedly build an important foundation for ideas that have subsequently been adopted and adapted as the concept of globalization has come to the fore in recent decades. And in this debate, his contribution is nothing short of epic in terms of the volume of empirically grounded argument and the scope of societal transformations his work addresses. His thinking on globalization is clearly ambitious to the extent that critics have argued – as with thinkers we have already considered – that his theoretical framework represents an overly simplistic meta-narrative about the contemporary world and how societal interconnectedness is developing. Yet unlike Wallerstein or even Giddens, Castells does not claim in his work to present a final or all-encompassing globalization theory that is grounded in one process, systemic development or purifiable phenomenon. In that respect Castells is a more difficult target for those who argue against the feasibility of a globalization theory because his use of both the concept and his theoretical accounts of globalization as a process are more diverse and context-specific. Much of his work is more focused in its theoretical arguments about what might be understood as specific 'dimensions' to globalization.

However, that is not to suggest that Castells does not make general theoretical arguments about globalization. On the contrary, his thought is well known for proposing a string of new concepts including, for example, terms such as the *space of flows*, *the network society* and *informationalism* which have attracted wide usage across the social science literature. In this respect, my critical engagement with Castells's thinking about globalization revolves around whether his multiple theoretical interventions on issues such as information technology, the transformation of cities and regions or new forms of political organization form a coherent framework through which to understand globalization. The contention developed in this chapter is that this is at the very least questionable. Whilst his theoretical approach is undoubtedly important and stimulating in the globalization debate, we will see that Castells's enormous range of work is sometimes in contradiction with itself or in need of further theoretical development. In many ways, therefore, I will argue that Castells's conception of globalization opens up as many issues as it sheds light on. Furthermore, as with Giddens, given the clear influence of Castells's work on Held et al.'s ideas about a transformationalist approach to understanding globalization, engaging with his work in depth forms an important basis for the analysis in the next chapter.

The following discussion seeks to develop these arguments by drawing out the key propositions Castells has to make about globalization. Even more than with other thinkers, in the case of Manuel Castells, this must be a highly selective exercise, given the sheer volume of his writing relevant to the subject. I have therefore divided the discussion around the key elements of his thinking, rather than presenting any kind of chronology which would be a gargantuan task. The next section thus begins by examining Castells's conception of time and space, and how these form the basis for his understanding of what globalization 'is'. The third section then moves on to consider Castells's landmark contribution to the debate in *The Rise of the Network Society* (2000a) with a specific focus on his arguments about *global informational capitalism* and how it shapes wider globalization. In contrast to this economic dimension to his work, the fourth section addresses his social and political thinking about globalization as largely outlined in the second volume of The Information Age trilogy. The key contributions here concern Castells's view of the evolving nature of global politics and the nation-state. I then seek to draw all of this analysis together in the fifth section which examines the major critiques that have been developed in relation to Castells's thinking about globalization. This is far from exhaustive but it does provide the basis for developing a series of concluding arguments in the final section as to how Castells's ideas relate to the wider debate and which aspects of this theorization remain unresolved or problematic.

Castells's conception of space and time

Whilst Castells is probably best known for his thinking on global informational capitalism which we will come to shortly, his conception of globalization is underwritten by a series of philosophical and epistemological arguments about the nature of space. In his earlier work as an urban theorist, Castells proposes a series of arguments concerning space which he developed in relation to cities. This is most notable in his arguments in *The Informational City* (1991) where he argued that 'whilst organizations are located in places, and their components are place-dependent, the organizational logic is placeless, being fundamentally dependent on the space of flows that characterizes information networks' (ibid.). Applied to the evolution of cities and regions in the first instance, this conception provides a framework for understanding the transformation of the urban landscape. However, more generally, this is a core argument behind Castells's view of the transformation of space (Stalder 2006). To understand its scope and how it forms the basis for his arguments concerning globalization, we need to examine three strands of these arguments which are particularly important.

First, there is Castells's conception of space and time. As Stalder (2006) succinctly puts it, Castells conception of space is grounded in a philosophical strand of thinking derived from Gottfried Leibniz (1646–1716). Leibniz argued against the (Newtonian) idea that space exists per se, instead contending that space can only be said to exist when it has been created 'in between things'. Space is thus 'a social product' (ibid.: 143), and social relations are inherently spatial insofar as 'people . . . cannot but live and act in space, and the spaces they create reflect and shape social life in its totality' (ibid.: 141).[2] The implication of this position for Castells is that any transformation in the nature of space is the outcome of changing social relations. And of course globalization corresponds to such a range of contemporary transformations. Importantly, and furthermore, space also 'brings together practices that are simultaneous in time' (ibid.: 144). For much of history, the only locations where such 'time-sharing practices' could occur were 'physically contiguous' local places. Globalization however has changed this by producing a new type of space – one where social actors can 'share time' across physically distant places, akin to time–space distanciation.

Second, and closely related, is this concept of the *space of flows*. Castells shares Giddens's view that time–space distanciation is one of the major features of modernity. However, he argues there is an historical limit to the process and that time and space cannot 'disappear'. Rather, the negative process of time–space compression (less space, less time) eventually produces a qualitatively new condition which represents a new type of space–time. The concept of the 'space of flows' seeks to capture this new condition that corresponds to 'a new material basis for time-sharing' where 'the dominant social processes are reorganized and managed through flows' (ibid.: 146). It represents a purposeful, repetitive, programmable sequence of exchange and interaction between physically disjointed positions held by social actors (Castells 2000a). The space of flows does not therefore replace geographical space, but rather by selectively connecting places to one another it changes their functional logic and social dynamics (Stalder 2006). The important point is that this represents a 'new era' which in essence corresponds to what is novel about contemporary globalization, with the underlying implication that up until a point around the mid-1980s, social practices which relied on physical places for time-sharing were dominant over those built around time-sharing over distance. The effect of the growth in the latter (due in large part to the information technology revolution) has been to change the 'social distance' between physical places. We might thus argue therefore that Castells has a certain 'cut' on the processes driving Giddens's time–space distanciation. For Castells, it is the emergence of the 'space of flows' that equates to the establishment of a globalized social world with a new, non-linear spatial logic.

As a central, organizing concept in his globalization thinking, it is important to emphasize the materiality inherent in the space of flows. Castells differentiates three dimensions in this respect. The first is the 'circuit of electronic exchanges' which are the global communication and technological infrastructures that enable real-time interaction across the globe. This includes not just digital technologies but also high-speed transportation facilitating the mobility of people and goods. The second dimension is the way in which the space of flows produces 'a distributed network with clusters around nodes and hubs'. In these nodes, multiple services are provided and consumed which create the critical mass for a 'self-sustaining ecology capable of continually reproducing the material basis for the space of flows' (ibid.: 148). Global cities are the most obvious examples of these nodes, but he also points to other places where academic and industrial knowledge are concentrated which he calls 'milieux of innovation'. The third and final dimension concerns how network nodes represent places 'where people meet and elites constitute themselves'. In territorial terms, price differences separate elites from other social groups, manifest in the elite office and residential districts of global cities. Gated communities are the most visible expression of this dimension to the space of flows.

Third, and following on from the space of flows, is the difficult concept of *timeless time*. Castells closely follows Leibniz in conceptualizing time as synonymous with 'sequence'. In other words, 'time' equates to the sequence in which events happen and 'the historically determined way of how this sequence is ordered constitutes the social character of time'. Furthermore, this social character of time is always 'the result of a specific mix of multiple temporalities', although 'one tends to be dominant' (Castells 2003: 465). For example, in the Middle Ages time was cyclical in that it followed the rhythms of nature which dominated human culture. In contrast, in the modern era, with the development of clocks, linear time becomes dominant, making possible concepts of punctuality or saving and wasting time, and clearly demarcating present, past and future (ibid.: 464).

Castells argues that both cyclical and linear temporalities establish relatively predictable linear sequences but that the development of informationalism has disturbed this predictability. The reason is that informationalism reorganizes events into instances without meaningful sequence, leading to what Castells (rather confusingly) calls 'timeless time' (ibid.: 494). The consequence of this transformation (and what is novel), is that 'there is no longer a dominant temporality, neither traditional nor biological time, nor modern clock time' (ibid.: 494). Instead, the contemporary era is increasingly characterized by an experience of time as a chaotic sequence of events, and society as a whole has lost its ability to establish a reliable pattern of sequences in relation to which individual and collective actors can organize themselves. For example, in the contemporary era events may be recorded to be retrieved and acted upon at a later date (Stalder 2006). For Castells, this shift towards timeless time is being driven by 'the twin revolutions in microelectronics and genetic engineering' which are leading to a new temporality that is characterized neither by natural rhythms nor by a unifying linear abstract time (ibid.). Timeless time thus amounts to something more than Giddens's conception of time–space distanciation, or David Harvey's *time–space compression* (see Harvey 1989) because time cannot only be selectively stretched and compressed, but is also experienced disjunctively without any sequential pattern. Timeless time then is an annihilation of time in social life, akin to the annihilation of space that is endemic in the contemporary (information) age.

Globalization and informational capitalism

For Castells, globalization is essentially the processual manifestation of the transformation of time and space outlined above, with all its multiple implications throughout society and the economy. Prior to the 1990s, these ideas about time and space are evident themes in what certainly amounts to proto-globalization thinking concerning cities and regions. *The Informational City*, for example, develops at length the arguments that contemporary cities have become the material basis or 'staging posts' for the incessant flow of information, goods and people and that cities are increasingly characterized by places and activities that constitute nodes in the space of flows. However, whilst such arguments have important similarities with Sassen's thinking about 'global cities' which we will turn to in chapter 6, they do not explicitly engage in the conceptual terminology of globalization. It is therefore only with the publication of *The Rise of the Network Society* (2000a) that Castells develops a more explicit generalized set of arguments about globalization itself.

The Rise of the Network Society (2000a) – the first of the 'information age' trilogy – concerns itself primarily with the economic sphere and its important contribution to the globalization debate revolves around the central contention that 'the informational economy is global' (ibid.: 101). Drawing on Wallerstein, Castells differentiates between what he suggests is a historically new reality of a global economy, as opposed to the earlier world economy. For Castells, the difference between the two is that a global economy is 'an economy whose core components have the institutional, organizational and technological capacity to work as a unit in real time, or chosen time, on a planetary scale' (ibid.: 101). The key issue is that whilst capitalism is characterized by relentless expansion, always trying 'to overcome the limits of time and space', it is only in the late twentieth century that the world economy has been able to become 'truly global'. Castells thus suggests that contemporary capitalist globalization does not mean that 'everything in the global economy is global'. On the contrary, he points to the fact that most production, employment and firms are – and will remain – local. Nevertheless, he argues 'we can assert that there is a global economy because economies around the world depend on the performance of a globalized core' which includes 'financial markets, international trade, transnational production and to some extent science, technology and labor' (ibid.: 101).

These arguments have much in common with the (subsequent) thinking of Held et al. or Dicken, but where Castells's ideas differ overall is that he sees the key basis for this global capacity as new information and communications technologies which have been assisted by deregulation and liberalization policies. More specifically, he highlights at least eight major arguments about the nature of this globalized informational economy.

The first argument is that the growth in international trade is a less important feature of contemporary globalization than that of financial integration and the internationalization of FDI and production. Castells contends that the fact that capital markets have become globally interdependent is no small matter in a capitalist economy. Since global financial flows have increased dramatically in their volume, velocity, complexity and connectedness, monetary polices have become interdependent. He suggests the outcome of this process is 'the increasing concentration of value and of value making in the financial sphere' conceived as 'a global network of capital flows managed by networks of information systems and their ancillary services'. Thus, the globalization of financial markets 'is the backbone of the new global economy' (ibid.: 106).

Second, contrary to much of the globalization debate's concern with patterns of trade, Castells contends that more significant than the growth in trade per se is 'the deeper transformation in the structure of trade'. The most important aspect of goods and services in terms of added value, he argues, is increasingly their 'knowledge component'. This is producing a new international division of labour between the 'knowledge-rich' economies of the global North and the knowledge-poor ones of the global South. This maintains the 'trade dominance of the countries of the global North, especially in high-value trade, through the technological deepening and trade in services' (ibid.: 110). So whilst trade is producing the integration of 'newly industrialising economies', this integration is extremely uneven and introduces 'a fundamental cleavage between countries and regions' (ibid.: 110).

Third, he suggests that the apparent contradictory tension between trade liberalization and the development of regional trading blocs in the global economy (which characterized much of the 1990s debate about globalization) in fact belies a more complex transformation in interregional trade which *does not* amount to greater regionalization. Castells suggests that to consider entities like the EU as trading blocs is inadequate because the EU is increasingly akin to a single economy in the way that the US is, and that despite institutional agreements like

NAFTA and MERCOSUR, 'the process of regionalisation in the global economy has largely dissolved in favour of a multi-layered, multi-networked structure of trade patterns' which cannot be understood by using countries as units of analysis (ibid.: 114). He thus argues that the debate over the regionalization of the global economy denotes a more important issue than apparent regionalization: 'the role of governments and international institutions in the process of globalization' (ibid.: 116). Castells argues that networks of firms trading in the global market are 'only part of the story' because the actions of public institutions in fostering and shaping free trade as well as supporting the interests of firms is equally important. The patterns of interaction between government strategies and trade competition cannot be understood through any simplistic narrative of regionalization or trading blocs.

Fourth, Castells suggests the 1990s saw an accelerated process of internationalization of production, distribution and management of goods and services. He argues this process has three elements: the growth of foreign direct investment (FDI), the decisive role of multinational corporations as producers and the formation of international production networks. All three are linked by the role of MNCs in the global economy. Castells argues that these firms are 'increasingly decentralized internal networks, organized in semi-autonomous units, according to markets, processes and products' (ibid.: 96). He suggests each unit links to other semi-autonomous units of other MNCs in the form of 'ad hoc strategic alliances' which represent networks. These are 'networks of production networks' which constitutes a global web of production (after Robert Reich). Thus Castells argues against the concept of the global corporation in any simplistic sense because in fact firms are bound into complex cross-border production networks. The implications, he suggests, is that 'the new international division of labor is increasingly intra-firm or, more precisely, intra-networks of firms' (ibid.: 108).

Fifth, Castells contends that in the contemporary global economy, productivity and competitiveness derive from 'informational production'. Knowledge generation and technological capacity are key tools for competition between firms and ultimately countries. The implication is that the geography of science and technology should have 'a major impact on the sites and networks of the global economy' (ibid.) and that there is a stock of science and technology in a few countries. However, he also argues there is an increasingly diffuse flow of technological know-how, albeit in a highly selective pattern, which is concentrated in decentralized, multidirectional production networks. This pattern of technology generation contributes decisively to globalization because it closely mirrors the structure and dynamics of transnational production networks (ibid.). Overall the unevenness of science and technology 'de-localizes the logic of informational production from its country basis, and shifts it to multilocational, global networks' (ibid.).

Sixth, he argues that, although 'labor is the decisive factor of production in the informational economy,' the process of globalization that affects it is 'complicated'. Castells's proposition is that there is a globalization of 'specialty labor' (by which he means not only highly skilled labour) that is 'in exceptionally high demand around the world' and thus will not 'follow the usual rules in terms of immigration laws' (ibid.). He argues this is high-level professional labour including top business managers, financial analysts, consultants, scientists, etc. as well as a less obvious group including artists, performers, sports stars and professional criminals. Essentially, global labour is anyone with the capacity to generate exceptional value. On the other hand, the global market for low-skilled labour is still heavily restricted by national barriers. Hence, 'the bulk of labor is local.' Only an elite specialized force can be understood as 'truly globalized'.

Seventh, for Castells the global economy is characterized by a fundamental asymmetry between countries with respect to 'the level of integration, competitive potential and share of the benefits from economic growth' (ibid.). He sees this segmentation as being characterized by a 'double movement'. On the one hand, 'valuable segments of territories and people' become 'linked in the global networks of value making and wealth appropriation'. On the other, 'everything and everyone' that does not have value according to 'what is valued in the networks or ceases to have value' becomes 'switched off the networks and ultimately discarded' (ibid.).

Eighth, and finally, Castells argues that this global informational economy 'in the precise sense', as he defines it, has only come into existence in the last twenty years (i.e., since around 1975) (ibid.). It is, he contends, largely a result of 'the restructuring of firms and financial markets in the wake of the 1970s' crisis' (ibid.). It thus expanded by using new information and communications technologies (rather than being driven by it), and was 'made possible, and by and large induced' by 'deliberate government policies'. Thus, the global economy 'was not created by markets, but by the interaction between markets and governments and international financial institutions acting on behalf of markets' (ibid.). This does not mean, however, that because it was 'politically inducted', it can easily be undone. The reason is that 'the global economy is now a network of interconnected segments of economies' which play a decisive role in the economy of each country. Given that the network now exists, any node that 'disconnects' is simply 'bypassed', rather than undermining the whole. What is more, the cost of disconnection is huge so 'the process of [this] globalization is set, and it accelerates over time' (ibid.).

Global politics and the fate of nations

The emergence of a global informational economy represents the most significant of Castells's three elements of the wider transformation captured in the idea of the 'network society'. If 'global informational capitalism' deals with the economic sphere, then it is also bound into two further spheres: experience and power. It is not possible here to review in depth all of Castells arguments in relation to these spheres of social life, but given that the emergence of the network society is intrinsic to contemporary globalization, two key interrelated strands of thought are most important.

First, in the realm of experience, Castells argues that societal change generally occurs through collective agency and for this reason social movements should be an important explanatory focus of theory. These movements are always purposive in that they self-consciously seek to achieve goals in changing societal structures. His thinking on social movements is rooted in his urban Marxian ideas from the 1970s, where he saw them as emancipatory forces which addressed 'real issues' such as social inequality and injustice. In considering the impact of globalization, he was therefore initially pessimistic about the capacity of social movements to achieve change as there is 'a mismatch between the globalization of the economy and the local character of movements'. However, in *The Rise of the Network Society* he argues that social movements have themselves globalized and ceased to be emancipatory, rather becoming transformative forces for change of any kind. Globalization has increased their potential effectiveness but they have simultaneously become rooted in identity rather than in places or localities. Contemporary social movements are thus seen as raising questions of who we are and how we should lead our lives. This enables them to extend their influence and operations globally. Quite clearly new forms of ICT – notably the internet, e-mail and other media – have been a central facilitator to this globalization process.

The second, and related, strand of Castells's thought which no account of his globalization thinking can ignore concerns the nature of global politics in general, and the future of nation-states in particular. This falls within the third element of Castells conception of the network society – power. Castells sees power in terms of the classical Weberian conception as the relationship between human subjects which imposes the will of some subjects on others (Castells 2003). Most of his analysis of power focuses on the (Westphalian) nation-state, which in common with many globalization theorists he sees as being challenged in a globalized world. Like many other thinkers, he rejects as fallacy the notion that globalization produces 'the end of the nation-state'. Rather, Castells argument is that the nation-state is losing power but not influence (ibid.). As Stalder (2006) observes, Castells does not clearly define 'influence' but it appears to be a weaker form of power. The globalizing world is one where states are not sovereign, and have power without being able to act alone. States are no longer able to manage their affairs, internal or external, on their own. He focuses on four specific arenas where sovereignty has been lost: domestic economic policy, international policy-making, the military and the media. The erosion of state power thus includes almost every aspect of economy and society, ranging from the loss of production to transnational firms to the problems of environmental degradation, migration or the global criminal economy. States do form new linkages, becoming 'network states', and do still exercise influence over the fate of their citizenry. However, in the contemporary era of globalization they are better understood more as strategic actors than sovereign entities.

There are several arguments Castells makes in support of this, but two are especially important. First, politics itself has changed. This crisis of the state in the contemporary era is attributed by Castells to the rise of what he argues is the transformation of party politics to 'informational politics'. The global media is at the centre of this transformation, as the key facilitator of global flows that mean politics is 'fundamentally framed, in its substance, organization, process and leadership, by the inherent logic of the media system' (Castells 2000b). Second, the concept of the 'network state' aims to capture how states and their capacity for agency are in essence becoming networked. States can only create policies as part of a new power-sharing constellation of actors in the contemporary world. They remain important, but power in the contemporary globalized world has become diffused through a range of different intersecting networks.

While the first of these two arguments concerning the crisis of nation-states is in keeping with much of the globalization literature and is perhaps uncontroversial, the second is more novel but is potentially far more problematic. It is thus to such critical issues around Castells thinking on globalization that we now turn.

Limits to the globalized network society?

It should be clear by now that Castells's work has had a major impact on theories of globalization. Few thinkers have written at such length, on such a range of topics, and with such ambitious scope to their ideas. Inevitably, therefore, his conceptualization of globalization has produced debate and critical reaction. I can only address a few of those debates in general terms, but in this section I have sought to identify what might be considered to be the most important and generalized lines of critical engagement.

First, and undoubtedly crucial, are the theoretical arguments he makes about the nature of space and time, and their relationship to societal change. In essence, Castells's epistemology rests on three concepts in this respect: the space of flows, timeless time and the network. The concept of the network forms the metaphorical means of understanding the implications of the transformations captured by the other two concepts. All of Castells's further conceptual propositions (the network society, the network enterprise, the network state, informational capitalism) rest upon these foundational concepts. A key point of critical engagement, therefore, is that in both the space of flows and timeless time, there is the overarching argument that a new sense (and practice) of time and space is challenging, if not already replacing, existing conceptualizations of modernity.

Such an argument has its limitations. At the forefront is the ever-present issue of precedence. It could be argued that Castells's contention that these transformations of space and time have occurred almost entirely since the 1970s is highly problematic. Related is the equally familiar issue of pervasiveness. *The Information Age* trilogy in particular develops what amounts to a meta-theoretical position, using empirical case studies to demonstrate the relevance of the space of flows to almost every dimension of society. I would argue that this is, at various points, more and less convincing. Whilst Castells's new conception of space–time does add significantly to understandings of globalization, it is sometimes doubtful as to whether the transformations associated with the space of flows are pertinent to every aspect of social life. For example, the concept of the space of flows appears to have much greater traction in considering the development of global financial markets and global cities than it does in mainstream politics within

nation-states. Some have argued that his arguments are thus too generalized and rely on specific case studies from which he extrapolates
wider arguments that in fact have limited applicability. Nevertheless,
as Stalder (2006) suggests, it seems likely that Castells's concepts of
the space of flows and timeless time are likely to be among his most
enduring contributions and they continue to carry wide currency in
the globalization literature.

Second, and related, the metaphor of the network – so pervasive in
Castells's work – has been argued to be problematic. There are different versions of this criticism, but they share a common concern that
social relations (indeed any human relations, whether economic, political cultural and so on) are not well captured by the network metaphor.
The concept of the network implies more of a division between the
nodes and flows than many theorists suggest is desirable. A post-
structuralist-informed critic might argue that relationality needs, at the
very least, to be introduced into Castells's conception of the network
firm, organization or social movement. This would provide scope to
theorize the differential importance of different types of linkages and
relations, as well as an understanding of how every actor (conceived
as a node) in a social network is not equally empowered to act nor is
significant.

Third, the concept of informational capitalism is not unproblematic. Not least is the lack of precision in Castells's work as to the nature
of information itself, and how it constitutes a product. However,
Stalder (2006) argues this is a minor issue. He suggests that the major
limitations to informational capitalism centre on Castells's arguments
about where control resides in the global economy. First, he argues
that Castells's theory implicitly claims the global informational
economy – both at the level of financial markets and at the level of
networked production – is essentially *beyond* anyone's control. Castells
sees the global markets as 'chaotic systems' whose properties are emergent rather than designed. This is not uncontroversial. Individuals, in
this world, are effectively dominated by 'faceless capitalist markets'
which are a source of action but in a sociological sense coherent
'actors' because they are an outcome of multiple heterogeneous rationales. However, second, and perhaps even more problematic, is
Castells's concomitant argument that there is no global capitalist class
that can really be said to *control* the global economy. Stalder argues
his theoretical logic here is not supported by detailed empirical explanation, and other theorists such as Leslie Sklair offer quite a different
argument about the existence and power held by the emerging *transnational capitalist class* (Sklair 2001). Stalder further claims a fair

amount of empirical evidence exists to suggest a global business class (in terms of a Weberian definition of class) does exhibit shared values and elements of collective action, and in this respect it seems Castells's thinking on this issue may need further development.

Fourth, and following on, is the issue of how power is more generally conceptualized in Castells's thinking. A number of thinkers have been critical of his definition of power in Weberian terms as domination. Much contemporary social scientific theorization argues that power needs to be understood as much more than domination (Allen 2003) and, in this respect, Castells has little to say on the issue. This links back to the earlier problem identified with the metaphor of the network insofar as there seems to be insufficient attention in Castells's work to how power exists in the network society and the network enterprise. Again, Castells does not extensively address how power relations vary between different nodes in networks, and this clearly must represent an important issue in understanding both how networks develop, and how they affect global-scale societal interconnectedness.

Fifth, and finally, Castells's concept of globalization (manifest in the network society, enterprise and informational capitalism) might be argued to be technology-centric – or at least too reliant on the role of ICT at the expense of other factors. His emphasis on the role of ICT in promoting informationalism in contemporary global society has been questioned by commentators who argue that other processes play a key role in producing the changes associated with globalization. Whilst ICT is undoubtedly important, Castells's work remains open to the challenge that it prioritizes the role of technology over other transformations (for example, changes to the system of international political governance).

Conclusion: information and networks as globalization?

There is much more of Castells's work which links both directly and indirectly to the 'globalization debate' that could have been considered in this chapter. As I suggested at the start, the sheer breadth of his contribution to theoretical and empirical analyses of contemporary societal change means his work is hard to ignore in any intervention in the debate. Inevitably, this critical engagement has therefore been selective and unable to cover every strand of thinking that Castells has contributed to. However, in mapping the major arguments concerned with space and time, the network society, informational capitalism and the development of contemporary global politics, the unifying threads of his thought on globalization should be clear. For Castells, it is undoubtedly technological change and the information revolution that is at the centre of the transformations of space and time associated with globalization. Informational capitalism is inevitably a globalizing system, and the emergence of globalized networks (whether they be enterprises or political movements) is a phenomenon made possible, shaped and facilitated by new information and communication technologies. His underlying theoretical arguments concerning time and space are themselves grounded in an empirical base of research concerned with technological change. It is the ICT revolution that has facilitated the contemporary phase of globalization, and for Castells it has permeated all aspects of society and the economy.

Yet it is important to reiterate that, whilst his thought clearly does have wide-ranging scope and is ambitious in seeking to explain societal change in general, the concept of globalization is not its main object. Castells does not seek to explain transformations to global society and economy with a generalized conception of 'globalization', but sees it as a consequence of a range of more specific factors that are leading to globalization processes. In that respect, Castells's thinking on globalization is also a more slippery target when it comes to the criticisms levelled at Wallerstein or Giddens in terms of a totalizing or 'grand' theory of globalization. Castells uses the term 'globalization' extensively, and both his conceptual and empirical analyses engage with a range of sub-debates amongst globalization theorists, but he tends to avoid wedding his arguments to theories of globalization per se, and in that sense he is less vulnerable to a postmodern critique.

To conclude, therefore, it is likely that Castells's work will continue to play a central role in future thinking about globalization. Stalder (2006) argues that, from a theoretical perspective, the most enduring of his concepts will be the 'space of flows' and 'timeless time' (although perhaps by another name). It is hard to disagree, and the space of flows in particular has been an important conceptual feature of his work now for several decades and has been widely disseminated in academic thought and beyond. Nevertheless, as discussed in the previous section, Castells's theoretical conception of space and time, his concept of the network and of informational capitalism is not without its critics. Perhaps most significant, however, is the overarching scope and ambition of Castells's project. Despite the fact he avoids laying a meta-theoretical framework for understanding globalization, Castells still offers what amounts to a meta-theory (albeit of a different and more empirically grounded kind) based around informationalism and the ICT revolution. Contemporary globalization is a secondary concept, itself largely explained by the information revolution. The real question is whether technological change – manifest primarily as the information revolution – does provide a sufficient or comprehensive explanation for the nature of global interconnectedness. As we turn to the thought of Held and McGrew, along with their associated 'revised transformationalist' approach to globalization, it can be argued that Castells's work does not fully succeed in making this argument convincingly.

Further reading

The scope of Castells's contribution to the globalization debate is enormous, and therefore it is difficult to isolate specific extracts from his writing. Any further reading should however start with *The Information Age* trilogy.

Works by Manuel Castells

Castells, M. (1977) *The Urban Question. A Marxist Approach*, trans. Alan Sheridan. London: Edward Arnold. (Original publication in French, 1972).

Castells, M. (1977) *City, Class and Power*. London: St. Martin's Press.

Castells, M. (1983) *The City and the Grassroots: A Cross-Cultural Theory of Urban Social Movements*. Berkeley: University of California Press.

Castells, M. (1991) *The Informational City: Information Technology, Economic Restructuring, and the Urban Regional Process*. Oxford: Blackwell.

Castells, M. (2000a) *The Rise of the Network Society: The Information Age: Economy, Society and Culture, Vol. I*, 2nd edn. Oxford: Blackwell.

Castells, M. (2000b) *The End of the Millennium: The Information Age: Economy, Society and Culture, Vol. III*, 2nd edn. Oxford: Blackwell.

Castells, M. (2001) *The Internet Galaxy: Reflections on the Internet, Business and Society*. Oxford: Oxford University Press.

Castells, M. (2003) *The Power of Identity: The Information Age: Economy, Society and Culture, Vol. II*, 2nd edn. Oxford: Blackwell.

Castells, M. and Himanen, P. (2002) *The Information Society and the Welfare State: The Finnish Model*. Oxford: Oxford University Press.

Commentaries and critical engagements

Stalder, F. (2006) *Manuel Castells*. Cambridge: Polity.

5 TRANSFORMATIONAL THINKING: DAVID HELD AND ANTHONY MCGREW

Introduction

In turning now to the issue of 'transformational thinking', I consider as the central figures in this chapter two political scientists who have written extensively on globalization together – David Held and Anthony McGrew. The suggestion that Held and McGrew represent 'transformational thinkers' is based on their influential attempt to develop a generic theoretical approach to understanding globalization which draws heavily on a certain conception of globalization as 'a differentiated phenomenon' associated with a range of 'transformations' in all aspects of social life. This perspective builds upon but significantly develops the ideas of what they see as a distinct (if broad) 'transformationalist school' of thinking about globalization (which includes Giddens and Castells). Held and McGrew's key significance is thus arguably to have made a more sustained contribution than anyone else to the possibility of developing generalized globalization theory. Even those who might disagree with this view would find it difficult to argue that their conceptual framework – most notably in the development of the 'revised transformationalist' view of globalization – has not been a widely cited and highly influential contribution to the globalization debate. So much so that in some segments of the social science literature, their revised transformationalist framework has become de facto conceptualization of what globalization is understood to be – although I will argue in this chapter that this is not unproblematic.

Held and McGrew also represent a logical next pair of thinkers to consider in terms of the development of the overarching arguments through this book. In part the reason is chronological insofar as their first major work (with two other authors) intervened at what can be seen as a key moment in the development of globalization thought towards the end of the 1990s. The development of the revised transformationalist approach represented a significant shift in both the terms of the globalization debate, and the concepts in circulation. It also managed to create the theoretical space for understanding how globalization related to more than just the economic sphere. However, it is also appropriate to move to Held and McGrew's arguments about the nature of globalization at this point because their revised transformationalist framework represents perhaps the most ambitious attempt to develop a unifying theoretical framework for conceptualizing globalization. Their thinking forms the basis for what I will argue is a more 'modest' meta-theoretical approach to globalization that is more sensitive (implicitly more than explicitly) to some of the criticisms of grand theory made by postmodern and other 'post-' critics of the later 1980s and the 1990s. It thus remains, in terms of both influence and scope, an enduring generalized conceptual framework that is not so vulnerable to the more direct criticism of meta-theoreticians such as Wallerstein or, to a lesser extent, Giddens. Likewise, the extent to which they are successful in developing a generalized theory of globalization typifies what is probably the most significant epistemological issue for any globalization theorist.

Both David Held and Anthony McGrew are political scientists, and have thus approached the globalization debate from this disciplinary perspective. Held was born in Britain in 1951 and spent most of his childhood there. His education, however, also involved spells in France, Germany and the United States. His academic career has been primarily British-based, although he has held numerous Visiting Appointments in the United States, Australia, Canada, Spain and elsewhere. He is currently the Graham Wallas Professor of Political Science and Co-Director of the Centre for Global Governance at the London School of Economics. Anthony McGrew is also British by birth and was educated in the UK. He began his career at the Open University in the early 1980s and was appointed Professor of International Relations at Southampton University in 1999. He too has also held a string of Visiting Appointments outside the UK, including spells in Japan, Ireland and Australia. While both authors wrote together at earlier stages in their careers, it is with the publication of *Global Transformations* with their co-authors David Goldblatt and

Jonathan Perraton in 1999 that their thinking on globalization has become widely circulated.

The next step in this chapter is therefore to critically examine in depth the arguments that Held et al. make for a revised transformationalist approach to understanding globalization. In so doing, I argue that Held and McGrew present one of the most successful generalized explanatory frameworks of globalization which was important in the conceptual debate in escaping the narrow and polarized terms it occupied during the 1990s. The third section moves on to consider how Held in particular has subsequently developed their revised transformationalist understanding of globalization into a series of politically engaged arguments about more and less desirable future forms of globalization. The fourth section then examines how Held and McGrew engage with the anti-globalization debate, and the ongoing controversy of globalization as both an idea and as a political project. The chapter ends with an analysis of both the strengths and weaknesses of Held and McGrew's transformationalist position, arguing that they have progressively moved to respond and adapt this approach to various lines of critiques. However, it also suggests that their position retains a political science bias, and does not quite achieve the universal applicability that it sets out to.

The nature of the globalization debate

In *Global Transformations* (1999), Held and McGrew with their co-authors set out to offer what James Rosenau described as 'the definitive work' on globalization. The book's scope is ambitious, aiming to tackle every aspect of globalization which they divide into eight groupings summarized as: the state and territorial politics; military globalization; trade and markets; finance; corporations and production; migration; culture; and the environment. All eight of these heavily empirical and historically grounded analyses are set in the context of a critical commentary on the globalization debate up to the end of the 1990s which is laid out in the first chapter. Most importantly, this chapter also sets out a conceptual framework for understanding what globalization as a phenomenon might be understood to 'be' in abstract terms. However, important as the empirical body of *Global Transformations* is, it is quite simply impossible to summarize even half of the more specific arguments that Held et al. develop in these eight chapters. Furthermore, these chapters all rely substantially on their theoretical claims from the framework developed in the preliminary theoretical chapter. Thus, the key significance and impact of Held et al.'s thinking rests heavily on their critical appraisal of the globalization debate and of the transformationalist conceptual framework that emerges. It is therefore these two strands of thought that need to be the focus here.

Let us consider first Held et al.'s major arguments in relation to the evolution of the globalization debate up to the end of the 1990s. They begin by defining globalization at the outset as 'the widening, deepening and speeding up of worldwide interconnectedness in all aspects of contemporary social life, from the cultural to the criminal, the financial to the spiritual' (ibid.: 2). In presenting this definition, their position is already differentiated from the vast majority of writing on globalization at the time in two ways – first, insofar as that there is any attempt to define the concept at all, and secondly, in that globalization is taken to refer to anything other than the 'economic sphere'. The definition offered thus marks out the ambitious and wide-ranging conception Held et al. are arguing that the concept warrants.

The next step is to divide the globalization debate into what they argue are the three distinct 'schools' of thought discussed in the introductory chapter to this book. First are the 'hyperglobalizers' whose position is at root characterized by the view that contemporary globalization defines a new era in which everyone on the planet is increasingly subject to the disciplines of the global marketplace. This school of thought is typified in the work of commentators such as Kenichi Ohmae who argue that the nation-state has become 'an unnatural, even impossible business unit' in the contemporary world (see Ohmae 1995). The hyperglobalist position thus sees globalization as having hollowed out both the state and citizenship at the level of global market forces and at the level of regional blocs like the EU, as well as having circumscribed the range of choices of states. States have thus become merely conveyor belts between citizens and market forces. They argue there is divergence within the hyperglobalist perspective between neoliberals who 'welcome the triumph of individual autonomy' and 'the radicals or neo-Marxists' for whom contemporary globalization is akin to the triumph of an oppressive capitalism (ibid.: 4). Despite this divergence, the hyperglobalists warrant a common label on the basis of their view that an integrating global economy is imposing a neoliberal discipline on all governments.

The second, and contrasting, school identified by Held et al. is that of the sceptics. They see the key premise of this school of thought as being that contemporary globalization is not historically unprecedented, and that evidence suggests economic activity is undergoing a significant regionalization as the world economy revolves around three major financial and regional trading blocs – Europe, Asia-Pacific and North America (ibid.: 5). Held et al. suggest that rather than 'globalization', which to the sceptics necessarily implies a perfectly integrated worldwide economy, the historical evidence at best confirms heightened levels of internationalization (ibid.: 5). Much of this argument draws heavily on the work of Hirst and Thompson, whose ideas will be the subject of the next chapter, although Held et al. group their arguments with a wider (primarily) political science literature. They argue that the sceptical position considers the hyperglobalist thesis to be fundamentally flawed as well as politically naive. This naivety is manifest in particular as a misunderstanding of the importance of institutions and sceptics see governments not as the passive victims of globalization but rather as its primary architects. Overall, Held et al. characterize the sceptical position as one which seeks to 'expose the myths which sustain the globalization thesis' (ibid.: 7).

The third school of thought in the globalization literature is the transformationalist perspective. This is implicitly argued to be a more sophisticated conceptual framework for understanding globalization that differs substantially from either of the preceding schools of thought in the 1990s' globalization debate. This school of thought includes a range of thinkers who conceive of globalization as a central driving force behind the rapid social, political and economic changes that are currently reshaping modern societies and also the world order (ibid.: 7). Central amongst these transformationalist thinkers are Giddens, Castells and also Jan Art Scholte (Scholte 2004), although it is from Giddens that the 'transformational' characteristic of globalization as a 'process' is derived. Held et al. suggest that the transformationalist position centres on Giddens's argument that globalization needs to be conceived 'as a powerful transformative force' which is responsible for a 'massive shake-out of societies, economies, institutions of governance and world order' (Giddens 1996). They argue this 'shake-out' is uncertain, since globalization is an 'essentially contingent historical process replete with contradictions' (after Mann 1997). They also point to the fact that in comparison to the hyperglobalists and the sceptics, the transformationalists make no claim about the future trajectory of globalization, nor do they seek 'to evaluate the present in relation to some single, fixed "ideal type" globalized world' (ibid.: 7). Furthermore, at the core of this perspective is 'a belief that contemporary globalization is reconstituting or re-engineering the power, functions and authority of national governments' (ibid.: 8). Globalization is thus, in this school of thought, associated with a

transformation or 'unbundling' of the relationship between sovereignty, territoriality and state power (ibid.: 8), whereby the power of
national governments is not necessarily diminished by globalization
but is rather being reconstituted and reorganized in response to the
growing complexity of processes of governance in a world which is
more interconnected (ibid.: 9).

I do not want to go into greater depth in this book into the nuances
that Held et al. associate with each of the these three schools of thought
in the 1990s' globalization debate. More important to the task here is
to consider how Held, McGrew and their co-authors draw on these
three schools of thought to develop what they term an 'analytical
framework' for rethinking globalization and which to a large extent
represents a 'revised transformationalist position'. It is clear from their
analysis that they see most use in this third school, and construct it as
in some ways a 'middle ground position' insofar as it rejects the more
extreme claims from both the hyperglobalist and sceptical camps.
Essentially, with respect to the former, Held et al. share the transformationalist rejection of the view that globalization is essentially 'economic', that it represents the 'end of the nation-state' or that some
kind of perfectly integrated globalized world is possible. Equally,
however, they also reject several elements of the sceptical argument
that there is no qualitative difference between the kind of societal
interconnectedness that has developed in the last few decades and that
of earlier periods.

In developing their analytical framework for conceptualizing globalization, Held et al. (1999) suggest that the globalization debate up
to the end of the 1990s revolved around five principal sources of contention. First is the conceptualization of globalization, which in the
1990s debate was 'prefigured by both sceptics and hyperglobalizers' as
'a singular condition or an end-state'. They argue that even on its own
terms, this approach is flawed since there is no a priori reason to
assume global markets need to be 'perfectly competitive' any more
than national markets have ever been (ibid.: 11). Furthermore, this
'ideal type' approach is unacceptably teleological insofar as the present
is (and apparently should be) interpreted as the stepping stone in some
linear progression towards a given future end-state although there is
no logical or empirical reason to assume that globalization has one
fixed end condition. It is also unacceptably empiricist in that the statistical evidence of global trends is taken by itself to confirm, qualify
or reject the globalization thesis. Held et al. further argue globalization
needs to be conceived in differentiated terms, rather than as a singular
process. And it cannot in their view be confined to the economic realm.

Second, Held et al. argue that much of the globalization literature tends to cluster around two distinct explanations of the causation behind contemporary globalization. These divide between those that identify a single or primary imperative, such as capitalism or technological change, and those that explain globalization as 'the product of a combination of factors, including technological change and market forces, ideology and political decisions' (ibid.: 12). They characterize this as a distinction between monocausal and multidimensional explanation which 'conflates globalization with expansionist capitalism'. In contrast they argue that 'any convincing analysis of contemporary globalization has to offer a coherent view of causation', and in so doing engage with the wider debate highlighted by Giddens, Appadurai and others concerning the relationship between globalization and modernity more generally. At the centre of this issue is whether or not globalization should be understood as a phenomenon that equates to something more than the expanding reach of western power and influence (ibid.: 12).

The third source of contention is periodization. Held et al.'s argument is that any attempt to describe the shape of contemporary globalization necessarily relies on some form of historical narrative, and that how this narrative is developed will have significant implications for the conclusions drawn about 'what is new' in relation to contemporary globalization. They contest the idea that globalization is primarily a phenomenon of the modern age and argue there is a need to look beyond the modern era in any attempt to offer an explanation of the novel features of contemporary globalization (ibid.: 13).

Fourth, they argue that much of the globalization literature has a rather deterministic conception of globalization as an 'iron cage' which imposes a global financial discipline on governments, severely constraining 'the capacity for progressive politics and undermining the social bargain on which the post-Second World War welfare state rested' (ibid.: 13). They suggest such a view is misplaced, pointing to a literature that casts doubt on the idea that globalization 'immobilizes' national governments. Their view is thus that contemporary globalization needs to be understood as having differential impacts in a manner that appreciates how its social and political impact is mediated by domestic institutional structures and state strategies and also a country's location in the global pecking order (ibid.: 13).

Fifth and finally, Held et al. argue that each of the three schools of thought on globalization has a particular conception of the trajectories of social change. They argue that the hyperglobalists tend to represent globalization as a secular process of global integration which elides globalization with a linear process of human progress. This in part accounts for the sceptics' preoccupation with evaluating globalization in relation to prior historical epochs. Held et al. appear to favour the transformationalist view which has little time for either of these conceptions, favouring a view of history as a process punctuated by dramatic upheavals or discontinuities. This view stresses the contingent nature of history and how change arises out of the confluence of particular historical conditions and social forces.

The outcome of Held, McGrew and their co-author's evaluation of the globalization debate is to argue that none of these existing frameworks provides a sufficient conceptual framework for understanding what globalization 'is'. Whilst they clearly have most sympathy for the transformationalist position, Held et al. (1999) propose rethinking globalization and constructing 'an analytical framework which moves the globalization debate beyond the present intellectual limits' (ibid.: 14). This analytical framework has had widespread currency over the last decade and it is to its specific arguments for conceptualizing the nature and form of globalization to which we now must turn.

A (revised) transformationalist view of globalization

In defining globalization as 'the widening, deepening and speeding up of global interconnectedness', Held et al. admit such a concept offers too general and vague an understanding of what this phenomenon is. In seeking therefore to specify in much greater detail the precise nature and form of globalization, they propose an analytical framework that has three main epistemological components.

The first of these epistemological components is a fourfold conceptual framework for understanding the concept of globalization. First, and foremost, they argue that globalization implies a *stretching* of social, political and economic activities across frontiers 'such that events, decisions and activities in one region of the world can come to have significance for individuals and communities in distant regions of the globe' (ibid.: 15). This is in essence Giddens's notion of transregional interconnectedness encapsulating the widening reach of networks of social activity and power, and the possibility of action at a distance (ibid.: 15). It also has some parallels with Friedman's later popular conception of the 'flat' world. Second, Held et al. suggest there is a detectable *intensification* or growing magnitude of interconnectedness, patterns of interaction and flows. This means that globalization is not random but that connections across frontiers are regularized. Third, they argue that this growing extensity and intensity is accompanied by a *speeding up* of global-scale interactions and processes as the development of global transport and communications increases the potential velocity of ideas, goods, information, capital and people. Fourth, and finally, all three – extensity, intensity and velocity – are associated with a deepening enmeshment of the local and global such that the *impact* of distant events is magnified, while 'even the most local developments may come to have enormous global consequences' (ibid.: 15). Held et al. argue that any satisfactory definition of globalization needs to capture each of these elements and that, equally, a satisfactory account of globalization must also examine each element thoroughly (ibid.: 16).

In light of this framework, Held et al. propose a more precise definition of globalization as: 'a process (or set of processes) which embodies a transformation in the spatial organization of social relations and transactions – assessed in terms of their extensity, intensity, velocity and impact – generating transcontinental or interregional flows and networks of activity, interaction and the exercise of power' (ibid.: 16). They use the concepts of flow and network here much as Castells does, referring to the former as 'the movement of physical artefacts, people, symbols, tokens and information across space and time' and the latter as 'regularized or patterned interactions between independent agents, nodes of activity or sites of power' (ibid.: 16).

Held et al.'s key argument is that this framework overcomes a number of the limitations of existing approaches for theorizing globalization. In particular, it helps address the failure 'to differentiate globalization from more spatially delimited processes' – namely, 'localization, nationalization, regionalization and internationalization'. Thus, they argue that globalization can be distinguished from more restricted social developments. Localization can be taken in their conceptualization to refer to the consolidation of flows and networks 'within a specific locale', nationalization as the process whereby social relations and transactions are developed 'within the framework of fixed territorial borders', regionalization as a clustering of transactions, flows, networks and interactions 'between functional or geographical groupings of states or societies' and internationalization as referring to patterns of interaction and interconnectedness 'between two or more nation-states irrespective of their geographical location' (ibid.: 16). The key point is that there is no a priori reason to assume that any of these processes 'exist in an oppositional or contradictory relationship to globalization'.

The second epistemological component to Held et al.'s analytical framework is concerned with the novelty (or otherwise) of contemporary globalization. They argue that in order to distinguish 'the novel features of globalization' in any epoch requires some kind of analytical framework for organizing such comparative historical enquiry (ibid.: 17). They thus propose the concept of 'historical forms of globalization' as the basis for comparing different forms of globalization over time. The concept is defined as 'the spatio-temporal and organizational attributes of global interconnectedness in discrete historical epochs' (ibid.: 17). Using their fourfold framework, they suggest it is possible to analyse historical patterns of globalization in both quantitative and qualitative terms. The strength of this approach is argued to be that it avoids the tendency to presume that either globalization is something fundamentally new or that there is nothing novel about contemporary levels of global economic and social interconnectedness because they appear to resemble those of previous periods (ibid.: 17). In order to account for different historical forms of globalization, they develop three further conceptual tools for analysing the differences between epochs.

The first of these conceptual tools concerns the issue of impact. Held et al. acknowledge that within their approach, impact – as one of their four concepts for understanding globalization – is particularly difficult to operationalize. Consequently, they distinguish between what they argue are 'four analytically distinct types of impact' (ibid.: 18) on states and communities which can have direct or indirect bearing on them. First is *decisional impact*, which refers to 'the degree to which the relative costs and benefits of policy choices confronting governments, corporations, collectivities and households are influenced by global forces and conditions.' This enables the theorist to understand how globalization 'influences the preferences and choices of decision-makers'. Second, *institutional impacts* highlight 'the ways in which organizational and collective agendas reflect the effective choices or range of choices available as a result of globalization'. This form of impact thus captures the degree to which 'certain choices may never even be considered as options at all' (ibid.: 18). Third, *distributional impacts* refer to 'the ways in which globalization shapes the configuration of social forces (groups, classes, collectivities) within societies and across them'. Held et al. point to the fact that some groups may be more vulnerable to globalization than others. Fourth, and finally, *structural impacts* capture the way globalization 'conditions patterns of domestic, social, economic and political organizational and behaviour' (ibid.: 18). That is to suggest that globalization (as a process) may be 'inscribed within institutions and the everyday functioning of societies'.

In conjunction with these different forms of impact, they argue that a second tool is necessary to conceptualize the nature of a given historical form of globalization. This concerns the organizational profile of a 'globalization epoch' and again they propose four different conceptions of organizational profile. First, the *infrastructures* which facilitate global flows, networks and relations need to be mapped in a given period of globalization. These may be physical, regulative/legal or symbolic, but in practice often are constituted through some combination of all these types of facility. They offer the example of the financial system as an illustrative example. A key point about infrastructures is that they 'may facilitate or constrain the extensity and intensity of global connectedness in any one domain' because they 'mediate flows and connectivity'. The consequence is that they influence the overall level of interaction capacity in every sector and thus the potential magnitude of global interconnectedness (ibid.: 19). Such a conception is perhaps rather more informative than Castells's somewhat vaguer formulation on the interaction between technology, infrastructure and networks. Second, and related, Held et al. suggest infrastructural conditions facilitate *institutionalization* of global networks, flows and relations (ibid.: 19). Institutionalization refers to the 'regularization of patterns of interaction' and 'their reproduction across time and space'. They argue that to think in terms of patterns of global trade, for instance, involves acknowledging the ways in which global networks become regularized and embedded in the practices and operations of agencies.

Third, infrastructures and institutionalization also lead to the need to understand *power* in a given historical period of globalization. They define power as 'the capacity of social agents, agencies and institutions to maintain or transform their circumstances, social or physical', and as 'concerning the resources which underpin this capacity and the forces that shape and influence its exercise' (ibid.: 20). Power is conceived as 'relational' in this conception – in contrast to Castells but line with Giddens and others (Allen 2003), and cannot be conceived simply 'in terms of what agents or agencies do or do not do' (ibid.: 20). The reason is that Held et al. retain a structural view of power (Lukes 1974), understanding it as a phenomenon 'shaped by and in turn shaping the socially structured and culturally patterned behaviour of groups and the practices of organizations' (ibid.). Globalization thus transforms 'the organizational, distribution and exercise of power', and globalization in different epochs 'may be associated with distinctive patterns of global stratification' which require attention. Stratification is argued to have both a social and spatial dimension, defined in Falks's (1990) terms as hierarchy and unevenness respectively. Hierarchy refers 'to asymmetries in the control, access to and enmeshment in global networks and infrastructures' whereas unevenness denotes 'the asymmetrical effects of processes on the life chances and well-being of peoples, classes, ethnic groups and the sexes' (ibid.: 20). Held et al. contend these categories provide a mechanism for identifying the distinctive relations of global domination and control in different historical periods (of globalization). Fourth, they propose that the differences between different epochs of globalization exhibit important differences in the 'dominant modes of interaction'. These include imperial or coercive, cooperative, competitive, conflictual types of interactions which can be differentiated from the primary instruments of power such as military or economic instruments.

The third of the epistemological components to Held et al.'s analytical framework for understanding globalization is concerned with 'determining the shape of contemporary globalization'. By 'shape' they propose a typology for understanding different forms of globalization which is derived by mapping global flows, networks and relations onto 'their fundamental spatio-temporal dimensions' (extensity, intensity, velocity and impact). They suggest that this provides the 'groundwork' for moving the globalization debate beyond the economistic ideal type and 'one world' of the sceptics and the hyperglobalizers.

As Figure 5.1 illustrates, four potential 'shapes' to globalization are of especial interest because they 'represent the outer limits' of the exercise where a high degree of extensity is combined with the most extreme values for intensity, velocity and impact (ibid.: 21). Figure 5.1 shows what Held et al. see as four discrete 'logical types of globalization which reflect very different patterns of interregional flows, networks and interactions' (ibid.: 21).

Type 1 globalization represents a world 'in which the extensive reach of global networks is matched by their high intensity, velocity and impact across all domains of social life'. They term this *thick globalization* and its nearest historical occurrence was arguably the late nineteenth century. Type 2 refers to 'global networks which combine high extensity with high intensity and velocity but low impact'. This is termed *diffuse globalization* because its impacts are 'highly mediated and regulated' (ibid.: 22). This type of globalization has no historical equivalents. Type 3 is characterized by 'high extensity of global

Determining the Shape of Globalization

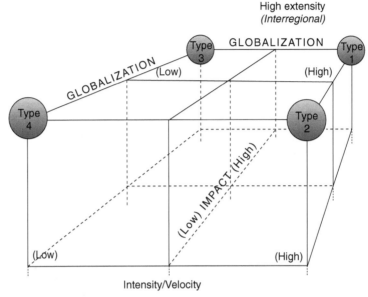

Type 1 = thick globalization
    (*high extensity, high intensity, high velocity, high impact*)

Type 2 = diffused globalization
    (*high extensity, high intensity, high velocity, low impact*)

Type 3 = expansive globalization
    (*high extensity, low intensity, low velocity, high impact*)

Type 4 = thin globalization
    (*high extensity, low intensity, low velocity, low impact*)

Figure 5.1   Held et al.'s typology of globalization
Source: Figure 1.4 from Held et al. (1999), *Global Transformations*, Polity.

interconnectedness combined with low intensity and velocity but high impact'. Termed *expansive globalization*, Held et al. suggest this form of globalization existed in the early modern period of western imperial expansion. Finally, Type 4 is termed *thin globalization* and is characterized by high extensity but low intensity, velocity and impact. They argue this is equivalent to the early silk and luxury trade circuits connecting Europe with China and the East.

The suggestion is that there are many other configurations for conceiving of different forms to globalization but overall globalization is not 'a singular condition or linear process'. The task of the empirically informed body of *Global Transformations* is thus to see how globalization as a differentiated phenomenon involves 'different domains of activity and interaction' with different patterns of relations and activities. A key argument is that it is simply not possible for 'a general account of globalization to be read off' or to 'predict from one domain what might occur in another' (ibid.: 25). Such is the problem they see as common to much of the globalization debate which has been weakened by contributions which take, for instance, changes in the world economy and the interstate system to be typical of wider changes occurring in other domains of human activity.

Such an argument is undoubtedly pertinent and insightful. However, the extent to which Held, McGrew and their co-authors succeed in developing a 'general theory of globalization' which yet remains sensitive to the 'differentiated nature of the phenomenon' is more problematic. The remainder of *Global Transformations* – which cannot be discussed here – makes a bold attempt to do this in applying their theoretical framework to every dimension of social life from warfare to environmental politics with an almost encyclopaedic empirical approach. Yet throughout this analysis – which any reader of this chapter is certainly advised to engage with – there remains the underlining issue of the degree to which Held et al.'s meta-theory of globalization is applicable in such universal terms. However, before I consider this issue and other limitations and potential problems with their 'revised' transformationalist conceptualization of globalization, we need first to examine how Held and McGrew have developed some of their arguments about both the concept of globalization and the nature of the debate since the late 1990s.

Debating the 'dangers' and 'demise' of globalization

Held and McGrew have together developed the arguments proposed in *Global Transformations* in a substantial array of books and articles. Many of these are edited collections which include, at various times, joint-authored interventions in the ongoing globalization debate of the last decade. It is impossible here to examine all of these contributions, but it is important to discuss some of the key arguments. At the forefront of this is their joint authored book *Globalization/Anti-Globalization* (which appeared in a substantially revised second edition in 2007). In this book, Held and McGrew (2007) develop and partially reformulate their analysis of the ongoing nature of the globalization debate.

I want to identify three key arguments of particular significance. First, in seeking to address the globalization debate in the aftermath of 9/11, Held and McGrew (2007) argue that an emerging literature proclaiming 'the demise of globalization' has characterized a 'post-globalist' turn which 'connects with the popular belief that the catastrophic events of 9/11 proved an historical watershed in global politics' (ibid.: 1). They argue that the sceptical viewpoint has shifted to a view that world politics after 9/11 'appears to have returned to normality, as geopolitics, violence and imperialism' reasserted themselves with a vengeance (ibid.: 1). Sceptics have thus argued that the last decade has seen a slowing of globalization, corresponding to 'the erosion of the liberal global order which underwrote the intensification of globalization' (ibid.: 6). The implication is that globalization 'is in jeopardy' and is 'no longer, if it ever was, a useful description of the current world order, nor does it provide a cogent explanation of the social forces shaping it' (ibid.: 6).

Conversely, Held and McGrew argue that the hyperglobalist position of the 1990s has subsided in this school of thought into a globalist position that regards 'the war on terror and the war in Iraq' as 'evidence of an enduring and pervasive clash of civilizations'. Globalists do not agree that there has been a 'demise of globalization' but rather that current trends suggest globalization is more resilient or socially embedded than sceptics believed or desired (ibid.: 8). This is based on the argument that there is little evidence to suggest that the 'domestic and transnational social forces on which the advance of economic globalization is contingent have lost their ardour for it' (ibid.: 8). The 'slowdown of globalization' is thus seen as largely cyclical, and there remain 'a number of deep drivers which are likely to be operable for the foreseeable future' (ibid.: 9). Overall, Held and McGrew argue that in the last decade the globalist/sceptical schools within the globalization debate have persisted but reconfigured their positions in light of world political events.

Second, they argue that the globalization debate itself over the last decade has become ever more riddled with controversy and divergent responses from both academic and political commentators. They see the academic and political controversies around globalization as inter-related, 'connecting how the contemporary world order is best understood and explained' to the issue of 'what values and ethical principles should inform its future development' (ibid.: 2). They argue that four questions posed by these controversies are most critical: first, whether globalization is being eclipsed by a resurgent geopolitics or militarization; second, whether 'empire' and 'globalization' are complementary or contradictory explanations; third, whether globalization is at risk or can be tamed; and fourth, what alternative global worlds are imaginable and possible? The latter three of these questions will in particular occupy us in later chapters as we turn to the ideas of Michael Hardt and Antonio Negri on 'empire', as well as both radical and reformist globalization thinkers including Naomi Klein and Joseph Stiglitz.

Third, Held and McGrew argue that controversies about globalization are shaped by two principal axes of disagreement. First is 'the contested intellectual hegemony of the concept' in the social sciences which equates to its 'descriptive, analytical and theoretical purchase'. Second is the issue of 'values and normative attachments' which amounts to whether 'on ethical grounds globalization as a political project or ideal is to be defended, transformed, resisted or rejected' (ibid.: 5). They argue that in combination these two controversies represent a 'conceptual space' for what distinguishes 'the plurality of voices in the debate'. Their mapping of this space is shown in Figure 5.2.

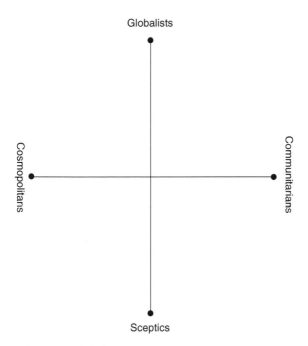

Figure 5.2 The great globalization controversy
Source: Figure 1.1, Held and McGrew (2007), *Globalization/Anti-Globalization*, Polity.

Conclusion: the limits to the transformationalist analytical approach

Much of this chapter has necessarily been concerned to review the main arguments of David Held and Anthony McGrew's (as well as their co-authors) detailed conceptual theorization of the nature of globalization. Their thought undoubtedly represents one of the (if not the) most comprehensive attempts to develop a meta-theoretical framework for conceptualizing what globalization 'is', how it might be understood historically and to provide an overall commentary on the nature of the globalization debate. Yet in this final section, I want to argue that there remain significant limitations with the revised trans-formationalist approach developed by Held, McGrew and their co-authors. These lines of critical engagement are particularly important in the wider context of the globalization debate because certain segments of the now vast literature appear to unquestioningly accept the Held et al. framework as the near definitive approach for defining and theorizing globalization. Not wishing to diminish the utility and significance of their contribution, I would argue this is dangerous as several potential problems with their framework are far from satisfactorily resolved.

First, and perhaps most significant, in developing and (in many ways) furthering the transformationalist approach, Held and McGrew remain vulnerable to criticisms concerning the capacity of *any* 'grand' theoretical framework to universally and adequately capture every possible aspect of global interconnectedness. It is certainly true that they are sensitive to the difficulty in developing a universally applicable conceptualization of globalization that can be applied to every conceivable dimension of social life. This is clearly present in their point that globalization is a 'differentiated' phenomenon, that it is 'contingent' and cannot be reduced to one process. Yet in the end, their revised transformationalist approach relies on the assumption that understanding the diversity of growing societal interconnectedness as a singular phenomenon is conceptually and/or even politically useful. In one sense there is no wrong or right answer to this issue because it is clearly possible to do so, and their approach provides a near-exhaustive empirical attempt at so doing. However, the sheer ambitiousness of their concept of globalization so broadly conceived certainly can be questioned. Is understanding every societal transformation in the contemporary world necessary, and does it *add* to understanding or in fact detract by oversimplifying social reality? This is quite clearly where Held and McGrew's approach remains at odds with a number of the thinkers they terms as 'sceptics'.

Second, their fourfold framework might be limited by the skewed degree of complexity encapsulated in the four concepts (intensity, extensity, velocity and impact). These sub-concepts at first sight appear equally weighted but the difficulty with specifying the fourth – impact – is clearly evident in their later analysis. It could be argued that impact is an inappropriate fourth concept here, insofar as it is qualitatively different and more complex than the other three. This is evident in the way in which impact receives special treatment, and has to be further specified through a range of additional concepts. One of the difficulties, therefore, in their universal theoretical framework for understanding globalization is that this concept of 'impact' is much 'bigger' than intensity, extensity or velocity, all of which derive in one way or another from concepts of time–space distanciation (cf. Giddens) or compression (cf. Castells). This conceptual unevenness in their primary epistemological tools for conceptualizing globalization calls into question whether or not this fourfold framework is entirely adequate for conceptualizing what globalization 'is' in all contexts.

Third, in characterizing the globalization debate, it can be argued that Held et al. oversimplify both the terms of the existing debate (even during the 1990s), and also the sophistication of a number of key thinkers within specific schools of thought. Held et al. do of course acknowledge the diversity of positions within the globalist and sceptical schools, but this polarized view of the globalization literature is questionable. Many commentators within both 'camps' differ substantially in their arguments about the nature of globalization and, when examined closely, there are plenty of thinkers attributed to one or other of these schools of thought who in fact occupy conceptual positions associated with both. We will examine this problem in greater depth when we turn to the sceptical thinking of Hirst and Thompson in the next chapter. However, here it is sufficient to highlight the point that Held and McGrew's characterization of the debate runs the risk of oversimplifying extremely nuanced arguments about the form of global interconnectedness into a crude 'for' and 'against' binary.

Overall, in concluding this chapter, it is fair to state that despite such potential limitations, David Held and Anthony McGrew have made a substantial and highly influential contribution to thinking about globalization. The theoretical framework laid out in *Global Transformations* has been widely adopted and, even where critics disagree, it is hard to engage in any conceptual debate about the nature of globalization without taking heed of their contribution. If the key potential limitation with their approach is the extent to which a general theory of globalization is possible, then we know from previous thinkers considered thus far in this book that they are not alone in facing this challenge. Yet I would end by reiterating that, whilst their revised transformationalist perspective may overcome some of the problems of other meta-theorists of globalization, it still has limits and should not be regarded as a panacea.

Further reading

Works by David Held and Anthony McGrew

Held, D. (2002) Cosmopolitanism: Ideas, Realities and Deficits, in *Governing Globalization: Power, Authority and Global Governance*. Cambridge: Polity, ch. 15.

Held, D. (2003) From Executive to Cosmopolitan Multilateralism, in D. Held and M. Koenig-Archibuigi (eds), *Taming Globalization: Frontiers of Governance*. Cambridge: Polity, ch. 6.

Held, D. (2005) Globalization: The Dangers and the Answers, in D. Held et al. (2005) *Debating Globalization*. Cambridge: Polity, ch. 1.

Held, D. and McGrew, A. (2007) *Globalization/Anti-Globalization: Beyond the Great Divide*. Cambridge: Polity.

Held, D., McGrew, A., Goldblatt, D., and Perraton, J. (1999) *Global Transformations: Politics, Economics and Culture*. Cambridge: Polity.

McGrew, A. (2002) Between Two Worlds: Europe in a Globalizing Era. *Government and Opposition* 37(3), 343–58.

McGrew, A. (2008) *Politics Beyond Borders: The Principles of Global Politics*. Cambridge: Polity.

Edited collections by David Held and Anthony McGrew

Held, D. and McGrew, A. (eds) (2002) *Governing Globalization: Power, Authority and Global Governance*. Cambridge: Polity.

Held, D. and McGrew, A. (eds) (2003) *The Global Transformations Reader: An Introduction to the Globalization Debate*. Cambridge: Polity.

Held, D. and McGrew, A. (eds) (2007) *Globalization Theory: Approaches and Controversies*. Cambridge: Polity.

McGrew, A. and Poku, N. (2006) *Globalization, Development and Human Security*. Cambridge: Polity.

6 SCEPTICAL THINKING: PAUL HIRST AND GRAHAME THOMPSON

Introduction

So far in this book, I have charted a path through 'thought' on globalization that follows some kind of broad chronology. Wallerstein's work was a natural place to begin, representing a clear antecedent in Marxian analysis from the 1970s and 1980s to the contemporary globalization debate. Likewise, Giddens and Castells both predate and influence the work of Held and McGrew discussed in the previous chapter. However, at this juncture it becomes necessary to move away – or at least take a pause – from this chronological narrative. The reason lies in the 'state of the art' aspect to Held and McGrew's thinking, and in their attempt to provide a commentary on the emerging schools of thought about globalization in the 1990s. As the last chapter argued, their characterization of three distinct schools of thought has become widely accepted in the academic literature on globalization and to a large extent has set the terms of engagement for subsequent thinkers. Yet the last chapter also suggested that it is problematic (and probably unwise) to regard either their account of the debate, or their own theoretical revised transformationalist approach, as the 'last word' on the globalization debate. Held and McGrew's later interventions are not insensitive to this, and certainly seek to revise and realign their characterization of the discussion, but ultimately they continue to characterise three schools of thought and this classification persists in more recent commentaries as discussed in the introduction to this book (see Bisley 2007).

In this chapter, I want to therefore to step back from the chronological approach by problematizing this accepted characterization of the globalization debate in greater depth. I suggested that one of the problems with Held et al.'s characterization of the debate is that not all of those clumped together as '(hyper)globalists' or 'sceptics' were happy to accept the label, and that there remained considerable diversity of opinion between many of the key thinkers in each school. It is to the ideas of two such key thinkers in the 'sceptical school' that this chapter now turns: Paul Hirst and Grahame Thompson. Their ideas are considered together on the basis primarily of their important co-authored book *Globalization in Question* although both thinkers have made contributions to the globalization debate individually as well. Their arguments concerning contemporary globalization are certainly 'sceptical', although they represent only one strand of the loose confederation of ideas in the so-called sceptical school. Yet this 'strand' is arguably the most significant one insofar as their ideas largely represent the most well known of a body of thinkers adopting an international political economy approach who take the generalized claims of the 1990s globalization debate to task through detailed empirical analysis of the global economy. It is for this latter reason that we will spend a chapter engaging with their line of critique in some depth.

Both Paul Hirst and Grahame Thompson are British political scientists. Paul Hirst was born in 1946, just after the end of the Second World War. He spent most his childhood in Britain, although with spells in Germany, moving around a lot because of his father's job in the RAF. Finishing his schooling in Plymouth, he went to Leicester University, joining what was at that time a path-breaking sociology department led by scholars including the Belgian Elia Neustadt and the German refugee Norbert Elias. Whilst also involved in radical student politics, he gained a first-class degree and then moved to Sussex University in 1968 to study for a Master's degree. In 1969, at the unusually early age of 23, he was appointed to a lectureship in sociology at Birkbeck College, University of London where he remained for the rest of his academic career. He became reader in social theory in 1978, and professor in 1985 – a post he held until he died prematurely at the age of 57 in 2003. Like Hirst, Grahame Thompson also grew up in Britain. He originally took a degree in Economics and after his PhD was appointed to the Economics department at the Open University in the UK. However, in 2000 he moved to the Government and Politics department in the same institution. He has spent most of his academic career at the Open University where he is now professor of political economy, but he has also been a Visiting Professor at institutions outside the UK including a recent period at the Copenhagen Business School in Denmark.

Hirst and Thompson's work on globalization is important primarily because it was one of the first major critiques of the (hyper)globalist and business school-oriented rhetoric of the early 1990s globalization debate. Their backgrounds in political science and economics contrast sharply with the management handbook language of early 1990s' globalization commentaries such as Kenichi Ohmae, and apply a much more empirical form of analysis than the broader theoretical themes found in the work of Wallerstein, Giddens or even Castells (to a lesser extent). In this chapter, I argue that this important intervention has played a key role in tempering hyperbolic arguments about globalization and led the debate of the last decade to become much more careful about generalized claims and how globalization might be best defined. However, I also suggest that Hirst and Thompson's most enduring impact on thought concerning globalization has been to introduce a degree of empirical rigour into what was a heavily abstract and at times rhetorical set of ideas. In contrast to Held et al.'s characterization of Hirst and Thompson's work as at the heart of the sceptical school of thought, therefore, I argue that their thought is far more nuanced in its response to the generalized umbrella concept of globalization, and is not diminished in its insight by definitional debates around the extent to which a singular concept of globalization is meaningful.

In order to elaborate these arguments, the first step in this chapter is therefore to critically examine in depth the key features of Hirst and Thompson's contribution in *Globalization in Question*. The next section therefore assesses the principal components of their challenge to what they call *strong* versions of the economic globalization thesis and in particular how Hirst and Thompson construct their argument that globalization is a 'necessary myth' for the contemporary global economy to function effectively. I then go on in the third section to evaluate their contention that the world economy is in fact (still) 'international' rather than global, and hence that arguments concerning globalization have been substantially overstated. The fourth section addresses their interventions in other parts of the globalization debate, especially in relation to the questions raised about governance, new forms of sovereignty and the implications of 'globalization' for the developing world. I end the chapter by evaluating the validity of their sceptical critique, arguing that whilst much of their empirically based intervention has been a welcome and powerful contribution, their scepticism does not succeed in undermining the wider concept of globalization in the way some of the literature suggests.

Globalization as a necessary 'myth'

In the preface to the second edition of their key text *Globalization in Question*, Hirst and Thompson (1999) reiterate that 'the basic focus of the book remains the same' inasmuch as it seeks to 'challenge the concept of globalization that has been dominant in public economic discourse' (ibid.: xii). Whilst the second edition to the book is significantly revised from the first, much of this revision concerns the updating of empirical data and the addition of further empirical chapters engaging with the cases of North–South trade and the welfare state. The goal of their critique is in essence to debunk the idea of 'a rapid and recent intensification of international trade and investment such that distinct national economies have dissolved into a global economy determined by world market forces' (ibid.: xii). Hirst and Thompson's target – sometimes misrepresented in the wider globalization literature – is not therefore to 'disprove' this 'globalist' position (in the language of Held et al.), but to question the explanatory utility of the concept as a tool for understanding the state and developmental trajectory of the world economy altogether. They 'are not merely sceptical about globalization, but advocate an alternative view of the international economy and its governance' (ibid.: xiii). This is important, because on close reading this does not quite fit the characterization by Held et al. of Hirst and Thompson's position as the archetypal sceptical stance. In outlining the key tenets of their scepticism towards globalization, I also want to argue that Held et al. have to some extent misrepresented (or at least been insensitive) to both the subtlety and epistemological dimensions to their critique.

These arguments will be developed shortly, but first it is necessary to explore their overall position. In *Globalization in Question*, the proposition that globalization is a 'myth' is based around five major arguments. First, Hirst and Thompson contend 'the present highly internationalized economy is not unprecedented' (ibid.: 2). Rather, it is one of 'a number of distinct conjunctures or states of the international economy that have existed since an economy based on modern industrial technology became generalized from around 1860' (ibid.). A key component to this argument, based on their empirical analysis, is that 'to some extent the current international economy is *less* open and integrated than the regime that prevailed from 1870 to 1914' (ibid.).

Second, they argue that 'genuinely transnational companies appear to be relatively rare'. Instead they argue that 'most companies are based nationally and trade multinationally on the strength of major national location of assets, production and sales' and there is 'no major tendency towards the growth of truly international companies'. Third, Hirst and Thompson turn their attention to capital mobility in the international economy, arguing that 'it is not producing a massive shift of investment and employment from the advanced to the developing economies' (ibid.). Their empirical analysis indicates that foreign direct investment (FDI) is highly concentrated among advanced industrial economies. In short, the developing world 'remains marginal in both investment and trade', notwithstanding a few newly industrializing countries (NICs).

Fourth, they point to the fact that the world economy is far from being genuinely global insofar as trade, investment and financial flows are all concentrated in the triad of Europe, Japan and North America whose dominance appears set to continue (ibid.). Fifth, and finally, they further argue that these three major economic power regions have 'the capacity, especially of the coordinate policy, to exert powerful governance pressures over financial markets and other economic tendencies' (ibid.). The consequence is that global markets are 'by no means beyond regulation and control' even if 'the current scope and objectives of economic governance are limited by divergent interests' (ibid.: 3).

On the basis of these arguments, Hirst and Thompson make a series of further contentions about the nature of the globalization debate and the literature on the topic. The first is that, whilst their concern is with the economic dimension to the debate, they believe that 'without the notion of a truly globalized economy many of the other consequences adduced in the domains of culture and politics would either cease to be sustainable or become less threatening' (ibid.: 3). The second is that, although the globalization literature (by the end of the 1990s) was vast, 'the great bulk of the literature that considered the international economy was based on untenable assumptions' (ibid.: 3). The third major contention is therefore that there needs to be a distinction between trends towards internationalization and the strong version of the globalization thesis, and that 'globalization' should not be used to refer to both (ibid.: 4). In advocating an analysis based around an historically grounded understanding of internationalization, they seek to counter the way in which the concept of globalization 'subsumes and subordinates national-level process' (ibid.).

Overall, therefore, it is not too great a simplification to suggest that for Hirst and Thompson the crux of the 'globalization problem' centres on the proposition that there has been a structural shift to a new, truly 'global' economic system. They argue that the concept of globalization can only be assessed if 'there is a relatively clear and rigorous model of what a global economy would be like', as well as 'how it represents a new phase in the international economy and an entirely changed environment for national economic actors' (ibid.: 7). In order to arrive at this, they develop 'two basic contrasting ideal types of international economy, one that is fully globalized' and what they term 'an open international economy that is still characterized by relatively distinct national economies and in which many outcomes . . . are still determined by processes occurring at the national level' (ibid.: 7). It is these two models that need to be considered next.

The 'international economy' rather than globalization

Hirst and Thompson's scepticism towards globalization is founded in the contrast between the two ideal-type models. The first model is that of 'the international economy'. This is a world economy 'in which the principle entities are national economies' and where 'trade and investment produce growing interconnection between these still national economies' (ibid.: 8). This process involves the 'increasing integration of more and more nations and economic actors into world market relationships'. Trade relations reflect national specializations in this model, but over time become progressively replaced by 'the centrality of investment relations between nations which increasingly act as the organizing principle of the system' (ibid.). An important feature, however, is that the nature of interdependence between nations remains of the 'strategic kind, meaning that there remains a relative separation of the domestic and international frameworks for policy-making' (ibid.). In this model 'international events do not necessarily or directly penetrate or permeate the domestic economy, but are refracted through national political processes'.

Furthermore, and crucially, the international and domestic levels remain relatively separate as spheres of governance or they work 'automatically' with adjustments being a consequence of 'unorganized' or 'spontaneous market forces' (ibid.: 8). The classic case of 'automatic adjustment' they cite is the Gold Standard period that existed from the mid-nineteenth century to 1914 under the Pax Britannica. During this period, adjustment took place through 'overt domestic policy interventions' whereby national governments 'through domestic expenditure-reducing policies' influenced their current accounts' positions, and through interest rate policy influenced their capital account. In citing this classic case, however, Hirst and Thompson do not seek to make a historical analogy with the present because 'such an international economic system is unlikely to reproduce itself now' (ibid.: 9). The key point is that this pre-1914 system was 'genuinely international, tied by long-distance communications and industrialized means of transport' (ibid.: 9).

The second (contrasting) ideal type is the *globalized economy* which is 'a global system of national economies subsumed and rearticulated into the system by international processes and transactions' (ibid.: 10). Whereas in an international economy there is 'a wide and increasing range of international economic transactions', in the global economy the economic system becomes autonomized and socially disembedded, as markets and production become 'truly global' (ibid.: 10). Domestic policies routinely must reflect 'international determinants of their sphere of operations' and 'systemic interdependence grows over time in such a way as the national level is permeated and transformed by the international' (ibid.). Economic actors thus become systematically interdependent and any regulatory efforts must cope with this issue.

Hirst and Thompson suggest this ideal type has several consequences. The first is that 'governance is fundamentally problematic'. Socially decontextualized markets are difficult to regulate, and policy integration by regulators hard to achieve. This is likely to mean that the populations of even the successful states and regions would be 'at the mercy of autonomized and uncontrollable market forces' (ibid.). A second major consequence is 'the transformation of multinational companies (MNCs) into transnational companies (TNCs)'. These TNCs would 'be genuine footloose capital, without specific national identification and with an internationalized management'. They would further 'at least potentially [be] willing to locate and relocate almost anywhere in the globe to obtain either the most secure or highest returns' (ibid.: 11). The TNC, unlike the MNC, 'could no longer be controlled or even constrained by the policies of particular national states', and would represent 'the main manifestation of a truly globalized economy' (ibid.: 11).

Third, globalization would lead to 'the further decline in the political influence and economic bargaining power of organized labour' (ibid.: 12). The result would be that 'globalized markets and TNCs would tend to be mirrored by an open world market in labour'. Whilst 'companies requiring highly skilled and productive labour might well continue to locate in the advanced countries', 'the trend towards the global mobility of capital and relative national fixity of labour would favour those advanced countries with the most tractable labour forces and lowest social overheads' (ibid.). The likelihood would be that 'the tendency of globalization would be to favour management at the expense of even strongly organized labour'. Fourth, and finally, they suggest an 'inevitable consequence of globalization is the growth in fundamental multipolarity in the international political system' (ibid.: 13). By this, they mean that 'hitherto hegemonic national power would no longer be able to impose its own distinct regulatory objectives in either its own territories or elsewhere' (ibid.). This would mean that the 'distinct disciplinary powers of states would decline, even though the bulk of their citizens . . . remained nationally bound'. In such a world, national military power becomes less effective and increasingly tied to non-economic issues such as nationality and religion.

So far so good, but clearly the axiomatic issue in this analysis is the purpose of constructing these two contrasting models. Their argument is straightforward in answer to this: to try 'to clarify exactly what *would* [my emphasis] be involved in making the strong claim that we are either firmly within a globalizing economy', or even that 'the present era is one of strongly globalizing tendencies' (ibid.: 13). Such a position is, as we know, criticized by Held et al. for misrepresenting the nature of globalization as an 'end state' – the truly global world. The global model does indeed present a detailed ideal type of such an end state, but a closer reading suggests that their argument cannot be so easily dismissed. The reason is that Hirst and Thompson are not suggesting that the global economy is 'actually existing', but rather proposing an ideal type which can be used as a benchmark to assess globality. Furthermore, and crucially, in assessing the contemporary world economy against these two models, they suggest that a diagnosis is difficult. Using a historical approach, they apply their two ideal-type models to assess actual trends within the international economy in order 'to distinguish its particular and novel features' (ibid.: 15). The opposition of the two models provides conceptual clarity but also opens up the possibility that it 'conceals the possibly messy combination of the two in reality'. However, the argument Hirst and Thompson make is that 'a process of hybridization is not taking place' (ibid.: 16). They argue that their evidence is consistent with 'a continuing international economy' and much less so with 'a rapidly globalizing hybrid system' (ibid.). The opposite of 'a globalized economy' is therefore not 'a nationally inward-looking one', but rather an open world market based on trading nations 'and regulated to a greater or lesser degree by both the public policies of nation-states and supranational agencies' (ibid.: 16). Their historical analysis indicates 'such an economy has existed in some form since the 1870s' and that it has also 'continued to re-emerge despite major setbacks, the most serious being the crisis of the 1930s' (ibid.). The key point is that 'it should not be confused with a global economy' (ibid.).

To understand the basis for this position, we now need to consider the empirical dimensions to Hirst and Thompson's contribution.

An international or global economy?

The basis to the argument that the contemporary world continues to be one that is better characterized as international rather than global has a series of empirical strands to it that Hirst and Thompson outline in various chapters of *Globalization in Question*. It is clearly not possible to do this analysis justice in a short summary, but for the purposes of my argument in this chapter I want to highlight four major dimensions to the empirical grounding of their conceptual argument that globalization is (at best) a limited phenomenon.

Trade and 'openness'

The first concerns Hirst and Thompson's analysis of the development of international trade and the openness of the world economy. Hirst and Thompson use a historical and empirically based analysis to argue against both the novelty and pervasiveness of transnational firms, as well as to question the appropriateness of the prefix 'transnational' itself. They point out that 'the history of the internationalization of business is a long one in no way confined to the period since the 1960s' (ibid.: 19). Tracing the development of international companies back to the sixteenth century (as Held et al. 1999 also do), they point out that 'manufacturing multinationals' have existed since at least the mid-nineteenth century (ibid.: 20) and that there existed highly developed international production in the period prior to the First World War. In relation to trade, a similar point is made – that world foreign trade expanded rapidly in the period between 1870 and 1913.

Second, Hirst and Thompson point out that, while there has been a period of increased international labour migration since the end of the Second World War, the nature of contemporary global labour market migration remains a long way from the ideal globalized model and is, in many cases, not without historical precedent. They point out that, whilst 'it is generally agreed that migration is (or has become) a global phenomenon', this contention of globality is based on the fact that 'since the mid-1970s in particular, many more countries have been affected by migration', a growing diversity in migrant origins and that 'migrants are of a wider range of socioeconomic status' (ibid.: 23). Thus, there have been 'phases of massive international migration over many centuries' and there seems 'nothing unprecedented about movements in the post-Second World War period' (ibid.: 30). Furthermore, migration between 1815 and 1914 was much more open than the contemporary period (ibid.: 30). The era of globalization has not produced the rise of a new and unregulated internationalized market for labour. Rather, in the post-Second World War period, 'global trends' favoured the controlled movements of temporary workers with only the highly skilled able to move more freely. Their contention therefore is that 'a world market for labour just does not exist in the same way as it does for goods and services' (ibid.: 29), that 'most labour markets continue to be nationally regulated and only marginally accessible to outsiders' and that 'even a rapid and sustained expansion of the world economy is unlikely to significantly reduce the barriers to the movement of labour' (ibid.: 29). This is further reinforced by the fact that 'in as much as there is a global international migration for employment, it is concentrated in the Gulf States, North America and Western Europe'.

Third, they argue that the openness of the international economic system was also greater in terms of trade and capital flows in the Gold Standard period than it was even by the 1990s. Using the ratio of traded merchandise to GDP as a measure, they point out that 'ratios were consistently higher in 1913 than they were in 1973' and that even in 1995, Japan, the Netherlands and the UK were still 'less open than they were in 1913' (ibid.: 27). The US was the only country more open than it was in 1913. Furthermore, whilst there is an identifiable growth in trade openness after the Second World War, 'the evidence also suggests greater openness to capital flows in the pre-First World War period compared to more recent years' (ibid.: 27). Whilst they acknowledge important differences in the nature of both trade and capital flows between the present and earlier historical periods, their analysis severely questions any simplistic view of a progressive opening up of trade and financial in the world economy over the last century.

Overall, Hirst and Thompson's conclusion is that 'the level of integration, interdependence, openness . . . or national economies in the present era is not unprecedented' (ibid.: 60). In particular, advanced economies had greater autonomy under the Gold Standard than they did in the 1990s. Furthermore, they argue that the existing governance mechanisms for the international economy have been in place over almost 'the entire twentieth century' and that although national autonomy has varied in the last century, 'complete national economic autonomy' has never existed and is an 'impossibility' (ibid.: 61).

MNCs and international business

In turning their attention to the issue of firms and the role of foreign direct investment (FDI) in the world economy, Hirst and Thompson develop a series of conclusions from their empirical analysis which call into question both the globality of the activities of MNCs and of the firms themselves as productive entities. Firstly, they argue that the evidence shows that any 'internationalization of production and trading activity remains extremely unequally distributed' and is dominated by the 'Triad countries' apart from 'a few rapidly expanding less developed countries' (ibid.: 94–5). The consequence is that 'the vast proportion of the world's population is heavily disadvantaged, and almost ignored by these developments'.

Second, 'the extent of the internationalization of business activity is often exaggerated in both popular and academic accounts' (ibid.: 95). Their analysis found that around two thirds 'of MNC value-added continues to be produced in home territory' (ibid.: 95) and thus the degree to which firms have become transnational has been exaggerated. Whilst they again acknowledge 'some internationalization', in many ways 'national systems [of production and innovation] are being reinforced and strengthened by the internationalization of business' because 'firms are locking themselves into the advantages offered by particular locational production configurations' (ibid.: 95) and that these are 'enhancing their ability to compete'.

Third, they argue that their analysis of MNCs and international business leads to two 'governance consequences'. One is that if 'national systems of production, business and technology still remain relatively firmly embedded', then there still exists 'scope for the management of these in the interests of the stability and productivity of the national economy' (ibid.: 95). The other is that 'if MNCs remain tethered to their home economies', whether these are specified nationally or regionally, then 'the opportunity arises for national or sub-national regional bodies to more effectively monitor, regulate and govern them than if they were genuinely footloose capital' (ibid.: 96).

The overall argument in relation to MNCs is therefore that 'the extent of internationalization and its potential detrimental consequences for the regulation of MNC activity and for national economies is severely exaggerated' (ibid.). Hirst and Thompson's late 1990s' position is that 'international businesses are still largely confined to their home territory' and they remain 'nationally embedded' – although we will see when we turn to the work of Dicken in the next chapter that such a conclusion appears problematic a decade later.

Economic governance

In relation to the question of economic governance in the international economy, Hirst and Thompson argue that there exist five interdependent levels at which governance can operate and that at each of these levels there are possibilities for 'the enhancement of the scope of governance and the development of more effective regulatory mechanisms' (ibid.: 191).

The first level is governance 'through agreement between major political entities, particularly the G3 (Europe, Japan and North America) to stabilize exchange rates, to coordinate fiscal and monetary policies and to cooperate in limiting speculative short-term transactions' (ibid.: 191). In terms of how the world economy is currently governed, Hirst and Thompson point to the fact that, despite the enthusiasm by globalization commentators for NICs, 'the major nation-states of the advanced countries and increasingly the emerging trading blocs are the dominant players' (ibid.: 194). They therefore see the probability in the twenty-first century being that 'cooperation will be of a minimalist nature – cooperation to manage periodic international crises – or that it will be cooperation by default as policies in the stronger economies dictate those in the weaker ones' (ibid.: 194). They suggest also that the international economy has become 'integrated to the degree that an outright return to protectionism between the major trading blocs, whilst still a possibility, remains unlikely' (ibid.: 195). Their argument therefore is that what they term 'a minimal modified-multilateral international governance structure' will prevail 'for the immediate future' (ibid.: 201). It will be a modification of the previous regime when the US was hegemonic, but will be dominated still by the three main trading blocs. They think this system will be sufficient to 'ensure the continued openness of the international economic system' even if that system is moving further away from the traditional post-war full liberal multilateralism. It is also certain that the world economy will remain 'centred on its main existing players'.

Second, there is the level of 'a substantial number of states creating international regulatory agencies for some specific dimension of economic activity' (ibid.: 191). Hirst and Thompson offer the role of the WTO and its job of policing the GATT settlement as an example here, but this level applies equally in their analysis to how financial markets are currently governed. In the case of the former, they refer to the extensive literature outlining the 'highly tuned nature of the regulatory system in place' (ibid.: 209) but point to the uncertain developing role in the twenty-first century of 'tensions between multilateralism, bilateralism and minilateralism'[3] and the 'proliferation of international standard setting activity' (ibid.: 211–14). In relation to the latter, however, they argue that three distinct areas of regulation have developed: the general relationship between coordinating and regulating the monetary, fiscal and exchange rate relations between the G3; international payment mechanisms; and 'the supervision of those organizations conducting banking and financial market business' (ibid.: 202–6). They suggest that these represent 'not totally unregulated markets but an elaborate system for the detailed management of international financial transactions' (ibid.: 207). Their view is that 'national governments have not remained totally powerless in the face of an overwhelming "globalization" of international finance,' but rather have 'joined together in various ways to organize the supervision of the new situation' (ibid.). This supervision remains limited, however, and 'there are no grounds for complacency'. Furthermore, they suggest that measures to 'cool the casino', such as the Tobin tax, face considerable technical challenges and are unlikely to be implemented in the near future. For Hirst and Thompson, the issues around further financial regulation in the international economy are not technical but political insofar as they require 'political will on the part of leaders of major nations' (ibid.: 209).

The third level of governance is 'the governance of large economic areas by trade and investment blocs such as the EU or NAFTA' which are large enough to pursue social or environmental objectives in a way that 'a medium-sized nation-state may not be able to do independently' (ibid.: 191). Such blocs are argued to be 'big enough markets in themselves to stand against global pressures if they choose' (ibid.: 192). In discussing the case of the EU, they argue that it is 'still at the point where a great deal of institutional work needs to be done to ensure that its effective economic integration is irreversible' (ibid.: 254). They see its 'primitive, as a single market, integration as irreversible' but suggest the 'same does not hold for the extended economic governance of this single economic space' (ibid.). Furthermore, they argue that the EU 'is very unlikely to evolve into a continent-wide single unified state'. More likely is its development into 'a form of confederal arrangement' where its capacities continue to derive from treaties between member states and from processes of decision-making in which those states have a major part to play (ibid.: 255). In short, nation-states will remain important in any future EU.

Fourth, there is scope for governance at the national level when policies 'balance cooperation and competition between firms and the major social interests' which produce 'quasi-voluntary economic coordination and assistance in providing key inputs such as R & D, the regulation of industrial finance, international marketing etc'. The effect is to enhance economic performance and promote industries located in the national territory (ibid.: 192). The broad trajectory of their argument in this respect is that it is hard to see how what they term 'less solidaristic and more market-oriented nations' can benefit in the current changed conditions of the international economy. By 'solidaristic', they mean those states that to some extent seek to manage their economies for societal welfare as well as economic outcomes. Hirst and Thompson's argument is that the reason is it is 'difficult to see how the future of complex social systems, investment in manufacturing, training etc. can be left in the hands of firms that compete' (ibid.: 225). Those economies that engage in 'non-economic governance' are thus likely to be at an advantage.

Fifth and finally, they argue that governance through regional level policies can 'provide collective services to industrial districts, augmenting their international competitiveness' and also giving some degree of insulation from 'external shocks' (ibid.: 192). The argument here is similar to that forwarded in relation to the role of the state in fostering competitiveness. They suggest that with the re-emergence of industrial districts and regions in the international economy, many of the factors that lead to the success of these regional economic systems are to do with national and sub-national governance (ibid.: 226–7).

Globalization and the nation-state

A fourth issue – and one closely related to wider issues of governance – is that of the impact of so-called globalization on the nation-state.

Hirst and Thompson make a significant intervention in the debate about the erosion of national sovereignty in the contemporary period. They argue that, whilst in the 1990s globalization debate it became 'fashionable to assert that the era of the nation-state is over' and that 'national-level governance is ineffective in the face of globalized economic and social processes' (ibid.: 261), this is in fact a new political rhetoric of 'an anti-political liberalism' (ibid.: 262). Their view is that 'set free from politics, the new globalized economy allows companies and markets to allocate the factors of production to their greatest advantage, and without the distortion of state intervention' (ibid.). In this guise, globalization 'realises the ideals of the mid-nineteenth century free trade liberals' and that for both Left and Right commentators, globalization represents a 'mutual celebration of the end of the Keynesian era' (ibid.).

For Hirst and Thompson as for others, these arguments about the demise of nation-states are overblown and their critique focuses on four dimensions. Firstly, whilst acknowledging that the 'weakening of the nation-state' position has some force, they suggest that in the contemporary world, rather than demise, there is a changing 'role for the nation-state'. State sovereignty in the contemporary world is less dominated by war, and states 'are no longer conceivable as autonomous actors' (ibid.: 265). And whilst cultural integration may have eroded state 'control over ideas', it remains the 'controller of its borders and then movement of people across them' (ibid.: 267). Second, whilst the era of exclusively state-centred politics may have passed, states remain important as 'one level in a complex system of overlapping and often competing agencies of governance' (ibid.: 269). Rather than being superseded by new governing powers, the state is central 'to a process of suturing' whereby the policies of states in distributing power upwards to the international level and downwards to subnational agencies are the ties that hold the system of governance together (ibid.: 270).

A third dimension to Hirst and Thompson's argument concerning nation-states and their relationship to 'globalization' is the idea that nation-states have a new form of sovereignty where they can act as 'loci from which governance can be proposed, legitimated and monitored' (ibid.: 275). States remain sovereign, 'not in the sense they are all-powerful within their territories' but 'because they police the borders . . . and are representative of the citizens within those borders' (ibid.: 275). For the world economy to work as an international system, this role is crucial. It is a paradox insofar as internationalization 're-instates the need for the nation-state'. Fourth and finally, they argue that the nation-state will persist because 'it is the primary source of binding rules – law – within a given territory' (ibid.: 277). This is an essential prerequisite for regulation through international law because 'international law cannot function without national states'. Supranational bodies cannot fill this role, and in that sense 'the state as the source and respecter of binding rules remains central to an internationalized economy and society' (ibid.: 280).

Conclusion: the limits to scepticism

Most of this chapter has been concerned to outline in some depth the contribution of Hirst and Thompson in *Globalization in Question*. This is not an attempt to downplay the reception of and critical engagements with their work, but rather a luxury afforded by the previous chapter which in many ways pre-empts this discussion in considering how Held, McGrew and their co-authors respond to the 'sceptical school'. However, in drawing some critical conclusions about Hirst and Thompson's thinking, there is a need to critically re-engage both with this characterization of their position and also the critique of their ideas developed in the revised transformationalist approach. In outlining the key critical responses to their work, I want to also argue in the final section that Hirst and Thompson's thought has been partially misrepresented (or at least 'glossed over') in the literature.

At least three major aspects of the response to Hirst and Thompson's work emerge. First, and perhaps most important, in taking the reception of their work overall, it is not unreasonable to suggest that their analysis and thought has had a very substantial impact on the globalization debate. *Globalization in Question* in particular has been heavily cited as a key intervention which can be arguably summarized around two factors. On the one hand it represents a detailed and sustained *empirically based* engagement with the principal claims of globalization theories in the 1990s. As the debate expanded through the 1990s, a growing body of criticism from many commentators concerned the lack of detailed empirical analysis upon which to ground the proliferating and often radical claims about globalization on all sides of the debate. Hirst and Thompson's work represents one of the major responses to this. On the other, their argument corresponds to one of the most detailed critiques of the idea that highly developed global integration which is significantly different to earlier periods emerged in the late twentieth century. Their scepticism runs deeper than many others who Held et al. have subsequently grouped within the so-called sceptical school.

This leads to a second aspect of the critical response to their work that specifically concerns their most fundamental conceptual and theoretical arguments: that the late twentieth century did not bear witness to the emergence of a new phenomenon in the form of a truly global economy and wider processes of globalization, but what emerged was rather an 'inter-national' economy and new forms of more limited integration and inter-linkages between (some) nation-states. The Held et al. response to this position is of course that Hirst and Thompson overstate continuity with a past international economic system, and underplay the development of new forms of global-scale interconnectedness and process. In particular, Held et al.'s (1999) argument that there is a need 'to address the failure of existing approaches to differentiate globalization from more spatially delimited processes . . .' – 'localization', 'nationalization', 'regionalization and 'internationalization' (ibid.: 16) – has clear resonance as a response to Hirst and Thompson's arguments. Held et al.'s aim, of course, is not to dismiss Hirst and Thompson's empirical analysis which they regard as a valuable counter to the hyperglobalists. Rather Hirst and Thompson's thinking is regarded as a partial intervention that does not undermine the concept of globalization as comprehensively as it appears to intend and which can feed into the revised transformationalist position they develop.

This view of Hirst and Thompson's contribution appears to have been widely accepted. However, I want to argue that their analysis adopts a more sophisticated stance than a simple 'sceptical' label does justice to. In the preface to the second edition, they outline an epistemological position that had much wider resonance with critiques of globalization theory as a meta-theoretical framework. In particular, they are concerned that 'the main conception of globalization . . . treats global processes and the local responses to them as part of a long-run tendency toward the dissolution of local and national societies' (ibid.: xiii). Such a point highlights the problematic teleological tendencies of globalization that even the theoretical approach of revised transformationalists like Held et al. does not wholly escape. Furthermore, Hirst and Thompson's analysis cannot be neatly dismissed as failing to deal with spatially delimited processes. Rather, their arguments concerning the complex multi-scalar nature of international integration call into question the epistemological distinctiveness of 'globalization' from 'nationalization' or 'regionalization' in conceptual terms. Their analysis is more sophisticated and sensitive to the complexities of these spatial relations than critiques appear to give them credit for.

Finally, and following on, the third issue is arguably the most enduring and significant legacy of their arguments. This is the implication that their arguments have for the concept of globalization itself and for globalization theories in general. Although Hirst and Thompson do not engage directly in the more abstract theoretical debates that have concerned globalization theorists (and concerns Held et al.), the ramifications of their empirical 'de-bunking' of the novelty and depth of contemporary economic and societal interconnectedness is that the usefulness and validity of both the concept and of globalization theory is questioned. The implicit conclusion that can be drawn from their empirical analysis is that there is no empirical justification to support globalization as a new concept or globalization theory as a new framework for understanding the contemporary world.

This is a key issue which Held et al. gloss over in their categorization of Hirst and Thompson as 'sceptics'. Hirst and Thompson's critique is based on more than a premise that globalization is akin to 'a perfectly integrated worldwide economy' (Held et al. 1999: 5), or that levels of economic integration fall short of this ideal type (ibid.: 5). Rather, although not explicit in their work, Hirst and Thompson's analysis continues to provide an empirical critique of the very validity of developing globalization theory. And whilst aspects of their argument are overstated, or have been overtaken by developments in the last decade (as I will argue in relation to their view of MNCs in the next chapter), many components of their detailed exposition of the continued importance of national-level institutions and organization cast doubt on Held et al.'s revised transformationalist meta-theoretical approach to globalization as much as they did on the hyperglobalist rhetoric of the early 1990s. Sadly, since Paul Hirst's untimely death in 2003, further updates of *Globalization in Question* have not been written. However, it remains likely that critical engagement with the wider globalization debate will continue to find traction in their argument that 'it is crucial to keep arguments of different kinds and levels separate unless they can be linked by a real general theory' (Hirst and Thompson 1999: xiv). Much contemporary globalization theory has yet to prove it can successfully respond to this point.

Further reading

Works by Paul Hirst and Grahame Thompson

Hirst, P. (1997) *From Statism to Pluralism*. London: UCL Press.
Hirst, P. (2001) *War and Power in the 21st Century*. Cambridge: Polity.
Hirst, P. (2005) *Space and Power: Politics, War and Architecture*. Cambridge: Polity.

Hirst, P. and Thompson, G. (1999) *Globalization in Question* (2nd edn). Cambridge: Polity.

Commentaries and critical engagements

Held, D. and McGrew, A. (eds) (2003) *The Global Transformations Reader: An Introduction to the Globalization Debate*. Cambridge: Polity.
Held, D. and McGrew, A. (eds) (2007) *Globalization Theory: Approaches and Controversies*. Cambridge: Polity.

7 SPATIAL THINKING: PETER DICKEN AND SASKIA SASSEN

Introduction

Having argued that Hirst and Thompson's work has been too easily glossed over and categorized as simple 'scepticism' towards globalization by some of the globalization literature, it is appropriate now to turn to several thinkers whose ideas and work do represent a more significant challenge to their well-founded empirical critique of the 1990s' globalization literature. I have grouped these thinkers under the title of 'spatial thinking' because one of the major lines of engagement they bring to the globalization debate is that contemporary global interconnectedness creates the need to reconfigure concepts of space and the spatiality of socio-economic relations. It is perhaps odd that this seemingly obvious contention made a fairly late appearance in the mainstream 1990s' debate, although several key 'spatial thinkers' were contributing extensively to early globalization theories by the late 1980s. This chapter focuses on two 'spatial' thinkers whose ideas have been developed within the disciplinary approaches of geography, planning and urban studies: Peter Dicken and Saskia Sassen. They represent an important but contrasting combination in terms of the empirical object of their theorizing. Peter Dicken's work has long been concerned with the nature of the emerging world economy and the changing organization of productive activity in particular. Since the early 1980s his empirical research has focused on firms, production networks and industrial sectors, examining how the key units of production in the world economy have evolved. Saskia Sassen, in contrast, has for the last couple of decades been concerned with the development of cities and of the international urban system in the context of growing interconnectedness. She coined the idea of the 'global city' in the early 1990s and has subsequently reformulated her arguments considerably around the wider role of cities in the contemporary world. Both thinkers' work represents highly significant empirical interventions in the globalization debate, although they have not always directed their arguments at the 'mainstream' of the debate that has largely revolved around political science.

In disciplinary terms, Peter Dicken's background is that of human geography and within that the subdisciplinary field of 'economic geography'. Dicken is a British academic who has spent most of his academic career at the University of Manchester, where he is now emeritus professor of economic geography in the School of Environment and Development, and from where he has published and revised successive editions of his key book, *Global Shift*. Over his career he has held visiting academic appointments at universities and research institutes in Australia, Canada, China, Hong Kong, Mexico, Singapore, Sweden and the United States. He is an Academician of the Social Sciences and holds an honorary doctorate from the University of Uppsala, Sweden. Saskia Sassen's disciplinary background, in contrast, is that of urban planning. She completed her PhD at the University of Notre Dame in 1974 and worked in several academic departments. It is, however, the publication of the first edition of *The Global City* in 1991 while she was professor of urban planning at Columbia University, New York, that established her significance as a globalization thinker. During the 1990s, Sassen held dual academic positions on both sides of the Atlantic, taking up the Ralph Lewis Chair in Sociology at the University of Chicago, and also as Centennial Visiting Professor at the London School of Economics. She has a significant profile as a policy adviser as a Member of the National Academy of Sciences Panel on Urban Data Sets, a Member of the Council of Foreign Relations, and Chair of the Information Technology, International Cooperation and Global Security Committee of the SSRC. She has written for leading newspapers around the world, including the *Guardian* (UK), the *New York Times, Le Monde Diplomatique*, the *International Herald Tribune, Newsweek International, Vanguardia, Clarin* and the *Financial Times*.

Taken together, Dicken's and Sassen's work represents both a key diversification and also, to some extent, a new dimension to the globalization debate. Much of the early discussion of globalization focused on international politics, the nation-state and a 'God's eye' view of multinational and transnational firms that was more concerned with the wider implications of the development of such firms than the specific nature of that development. In the case of the latter, the importance of Dicken's work (and the body of research that it heads up) cannot be overemphasized. Dicken's combination of meticulous empirical analysis of firms and sectors, combined with an altogether different and spatially aware form of theorizing, casts the evolving nature of global economic activity in a very different light to the hyperbolic generalization of the 'hyperglobalists' criticized by Held et al. Likewise, Sassen's primary empirical concern for the transformation of cities, labour markets and the movement of people – along with the impacts of such transformations on the built environment – has fuelled a substantial literature and academic debate in itself about the consequence of global integration at different scales on the material world and on people's lives. During the 1990s, such concerns were notably absent from the mainstream of the globalization debate but in fact clearly represent an important aspect of wider theorizations of globalization in their own right. It is notable, for example, that in Held et al.'s key text, *Global Transformations*, there is no discussion of the global city debate at all.

However, there is a further significance to the thought of Dicken and Sassen (taken collectively) that I want to develop at this stage in our theoretical journey. My argument is that both Dicken and Sassen provide an important (and still largely unexplored) contribution to epistemological questions about what we might understand globalization to 'be'. Specifically, the thinkers we have considered thus far have in various ways asserted the epistemological primacy of the changing nature or experience of time and space as being a centrally defining feature of globalization, but do not take a consideration of new forms of spatiality in the contemporary world as their focus. Thinkers like Giddens and Held et al. of course identify time–space distanciation as a central 'process' behind globalization, but there is only limited attention to how this relates to the real (i.e. material) world of people, places and things. In different but related way, I want to suggest that both Dicken's and Sassen's work provides a rich set of insights into what the reconfigured spatialities that are developing in the contemporary era of globalization consist of. Furthermore, in so doing, I argue that their contributions reveal crucial absences in the epistemological foundations of several meta-theoretical frameworks for understanding globalization. They also open up a central set of questions about what the concept 'globalization' should be understood to mean, and what kinds of globalization theories are desirable.

Dicken's questioning of 'gobalization'

Dicken's contribution to thinking on globalization is undoubtedly centred on his major work *Global Shift: Mapping the Changing Contours of the World Economy* (2007). This book is now in its fifth edition and was originally written around an undergraduate textbook in the early 1980s. However, the book is both much more than a textbook and much more than 'one' book. On the former issue, *Global Shift* contains a vast amount of informed, critical and original thinking rather than simply summarizing the academic literature as a traditional textbook might do. In relation to the latter, Peter Dicken has spent most of the last three decades revising, extending and rewriting it and thus it is perhaps better understood as the culmination of a career-long project. When it was first published, the concept 'globalization' was unknown to all but a very few management theorists, yet his concern for the internationalization of production in the first edition represents a clear antecedent and foundation to later debates about economic globalization. However, through successive editions from the 1990s, *Global Shift* has been substantially rewritten and extended to reflect both the developing direction of debate about the evolution of a globalized economy and also the rapidly changing empirical reality of global economic interconnectedness of the last twenty-five years. It is important to understand this long history to Dicken's work on globalization in order to assess the context of his current thinking on globalization in conceptual terms.

In the fifth edition of *Global Shift*, he outlines his main arguments in relation to the concept of globalization. Dicken regards the term as 'one of the most used, but also one of the most misused . . . and most confused words around today' (ibid.: 3). He argues that the current explosion of interest reflects 'the pervasive feeling that something fundamental is happening to the world' and that lots of 'big issues are somehow interconnected under the broad umbrella term "globalization"' (ibid.: 3). He is, however, critical of any idea that the concept represents 'a single causal mechanism' that can explain all of these issues, and that in fact this 'catch-all term [is] used by many to bundle together virtually all the "goods" and "bads" facing contemporary societies' (ibid.: 4). In *Global Shift*, he also agrees with the Held et al. characterization of the globalization debate around hyperglobalist and sceptical schools of thought but develops his own framework which rejects the strong globalization thesis of the hyperglobalists. Dicken's focus is on the economy and the argument that, 'whilst there are undoubtedly globalizing forces at work, we do not have a fully globalized world economy' (ibid.: 8). However, this does not mean he subscribes to the internationalist view developed by Hirst and Thompson, arguing in effect that contemporary global economic interconnectedness is more complex than perhaps they suggest.

Globalization as spatial processes

Globalization for Dicken is 'not a single unified phenomenon, but a syndrome of processes and activities' (ibid.: 8) (and see Mittelman 2000). These processes must be understood as *spatial*, and globalizing processes are both reflected in, as well as being influenced by, multiple geographies, rather than a single global geography. It is a phenomenon under which 'the local and global intermesh, running into one another in all manner of ways' (after Thrift 1990). Such a conception draws on the sociologist Bob Jessop's conception of the phenomenon as 'a supercomplex series of multicentric, multi-scalar, multitemporal, multiform and multicausal processes' (see Jessop 2002). This 'supercomplex' understanding of the concept represents an important departure from much of the political science-dominated mainstream of the 1990s' globalization debate.

Dicken identifies four scalar processes in his approach: *localizing* processes that are geographically concentrated activities with varying degrees of function integration; *internationalizing* processes which correspond to the simple geographical spread of economic activities across national borders with low levels of functional integration; *globalizing* processes that are characterized by both extensive geographical spread and also a high degree of functional integration; and finally *regionalizing* processes which essentially correspond to the operation of globalizing processes at a more geographically limited (but supranational) scale (ibid.: 8).

Dicken's understanding of how these different forms of globalization process are manifest is primarily economic. He argues that 'even allowing for the hype of much of the globalization debate, there is no doubt we are witnessing the emergence of a new geo-economy that is qualitatively different from the past' (ibid.: 8). His contention is that in order to understand what is going on there is a need to adopt an approach 'that is firmly *grounded* in the uneven geographical reality of globalizing structures, processes and outcomes' and not one which is submerged in the hype and excessive or inflated language that characterizes much of the globalization debate (ibid.: 8). Dicken thus

argues that globalization needs to be understood as a complex phenomenon and proposes the framework shown in Figure 7.1 as an entry
point.

The aim of this diagrammatic representation of his conceptual
framework is 'to provide both a structural perspective on globalization

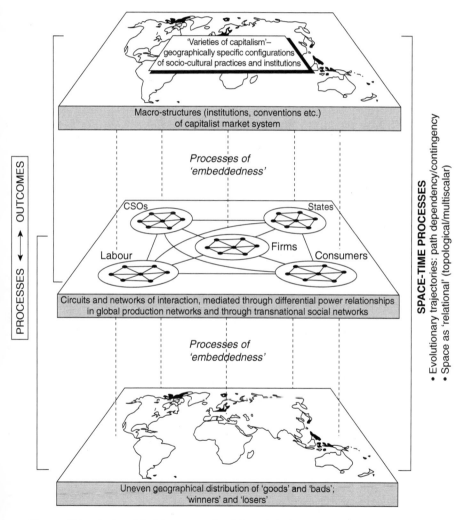

Figure 7.1   A simplified framework of the global economy
Source: Figure 1.3 from Peter Dicken (2007), *Global Shift: Mapping the
Changing Contours of the World Economy*, 5th edn, Sage.

processes and outcomes and also a sense of how key "actors" behave' (ibid.: 9). A key emphasis is on 'the complex ways in which they are interconnected and governed through highly uneven power relationships' (ibid.: 9). Dicken acknowledges that this diagram is of course a gross oversimplification and an *idealized* representation of something 'infinitely more complex' but argues that such simplification is necessary as the 'highly interconnected system' shown can be 'cut' at many different points.

However, a key distinction also exists between Dicken's conception of a process in this context and the conception of a process used by thinkers we have encountered thus far. In contrast to the rather 'structuralist' conception of process we encountered in the thinking of Wallerstein, Giddens, Held and McGrew, Dicken argues that these (economic) globalization processes (he identifies production, distribution and consumption as specific forms) need to be conceived 'in terms of connections of activities, linked through *flows* of both material and non-material phenomena (like services) into circuits and networks' (ibid.: 10). To some extent this emphasis on circuits and flows echoes Castells, but Dicken develops his interpretation of these concepts further. He proposes that circuits and networks constitute what he terms *relational structures* and processes in which *power relationships* between key actors, such as firms, states, individuals and social groups, are uneven (ibid.: 10). This relational approach to networks pushes the ideas of Castells in new directions, especially insofar as it is informed by post-structuralist epistemological arguments. Dicken argues that networks must not be understood as stable but rather 'as always in a state of flux' and 'always in a process of becoming' (ibid.: 11). This means they should be seen as dynamic, and do not exist in isolation, but are 'embedded in the broader macrostructures of the global economy' as well as being 'grounded in the prevailing geographical structures of the real world' (ibid.: 11). He terms this framework 'a situated network approach' (ibid.).

The macrostructures he refers to are 'the institutions, conventions and rules of the capitalist market system' which he argues are not natural givens but rather need to be understood as socially constructed – in their present form predominantly as neoliberal political ideology. The key point is that 'such institutions and conventions continue to be manifested in *specific configurations* in specific places' (notably within national states but 'not only at that scale') and are territorially embedded in such a way as to produce different varieties of capitalism. Within this 'geographically differentiated macrostructural framework', he further contends that it is primarily 'the actions of interaction, and especially the interactions between' the five actor-centred networks shown in Figure 7.1 'that shape the changing geographical configurations of the global economy at different spatial scales' (ibid.: 11). He argues in this respect that, despite various segments of the globalization literature suggesting we should not 'privilege' one set of actors over others, there can be little doubt that some actors *are* more significant than others and he conceives the entire system as 'one of asymmetric power relations'. For Dicken, given his focus on the global economy, particular emphasis needs to be placed on transnational corporations (TNCs) and states. It is to this relationship, and to those between other actors, we now need to turn.

TNCs, states, production circuits and production networks

Dicken argues that two variables are the most significant in determining the relative power between actors. The first is 'control over key assets such as capital, technology, knowledge, labour skills, natural resources and consumer markets'. The second is 'the spatial and territorial range and flexibility of each actor' (ibid.: 12). He argues that the two are not unconnected because the ability to control access to a specific asset is a major bargaining strength and assets are often localized which means actors that can access them across geographical space have a distinct advantage over those that cannot. A further layer is added to this conception shown in Figure 7.1 – namely that each of the major actors is involved in cooperation and collaboration on the one hand, *as well as* conflict and competition on the other (ibid.: 12). His point is that such paradoxical behaviour is a warning against assuming that the relationship between certain actors is always of one kind. The examples he offers are those of the relationship between TNCs, between TNCs and states or TNCs and labour. In this regard, TNCs in the same industry are often in fierce competition 'but also enmeshed in a complex web of collaborative relationships'. Likewise, states compete 'in cut-throat fashion' with other states to entice internationally mobile investment from TNCs, but at the same time increasingly engage in preferential trade agreements (ibid.: 12).

In Dicken's analysis, in theorizing the global economy around the triad of production, distribution and consumption, the starting point is production. Contrary to the analytical starting point of sceptics like Hirst and Thompson, Dicken is doubtful about the utility of conceptualizing contemporary economic activity on the basis of nationally aggregated statistics. His view is that such analysis 'is less and less useful in the light of the changes occurring in the organization of economic activity' (ibid.: 13). He argues national boundaries 'no longer contain production processes in the way they once did', and that production can be better conceptualized around two different spatial concepts.

The first is the production circuit (as opposed to the more linear production chain). Production in the global economy, he argues, is 'circular' insofar as the major stages of the production process consist of feedback loops connecting consumption with the processes of production and distribution (ibid.: 14). Figure 7.2 shows a hypothetical production circuit.

At the core of the production circuit are four basic operations but Dicken emphasizes that the processes are two-way and that 'each of the individual elements in the production circuit depend upon many other kinds of inputs' (ibid.: 15). In particular, services are crucial in the contemporary economy because they 'provide linkages between the segments of production', as well as 'geographical and transactional connections' and they '*integrate* and *coordinate* the atomized and globalized production process' (Rabach and Kim 1994, cited in Dicken 2007: 15). Financial systems 'are also important' in lubricating production circuits. Such an argument provides an important link to the argument of Sassen to whom we will come presently.

The second of Dicken's spatial concepts is the production network. His argument is that, in essence, 'individual production circuits are themselves enmeshed in production networks of inter- and intra-firm relationships' (ibid.: 15). These networks 'are, in reality, extremely complex structures with intricate links – horizontal, vertical, diagonal – forming multidimensional, multilayered lattices of economic activity' (ibid.: 15). They vary considerably, both within and between different industries, but three general dimensions to them are especially important. First, their *governance* in terms of how they are coordinated and regulated is undertaken in the contemporary global economy primarily by firms of all sizes. However, Dicken argues that 'transnational firms' – defined in broad terms as firms that have 'the power to coordinate and control operations in more than one country' even if they do not own them – play a key role in coordinating production networks. Second, Dicken proposes that 'every production network has a spatiality', understood as 'the particular geographical configuration and extent of its component elements and the links between them' (ibid.: 17). At the most basic level, production can be organized along a spectrum from that which is geographically concentrated to that which

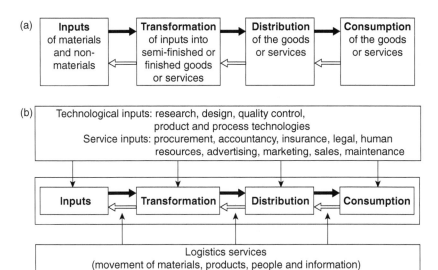

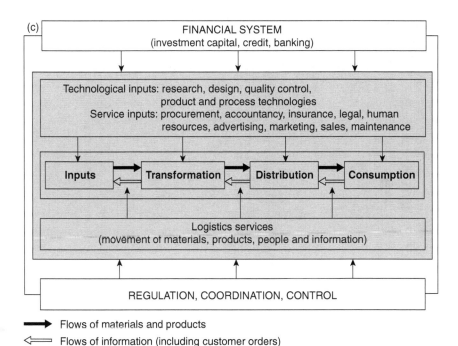

Flows of materials and products
Flows of information (including customer orders)

Figure 7.2 Basic components of a production circuit
Source: Figure 1.4 from Peter Dicken (2007), *Global Shift: Mapping the Changing Contours of the World Economy*, 5th edn, Sage.

is geographically dispersed. In the contemporary global economy, he suggests, 'we are witnessing the emergence of *global production networks* (GPNs) whose spatiality in scalar terms is far more complex than can be captured around simplistic concepts of the local, regional, national or global' (ibid.)

Territorial embeddedness, consumption and clusters

Having set out his conception of the complex spatiality of production in the contemporary global economy, Dicken goes on to argue that, contrary to the notion within the globalization debate that 'anything can be located anywhere' in an era of hypermobile capital and footloose firms, production in fact remains *territorially embedded*. Production networks 'don't just float freely in a spaceless/placeless world' and, although 'transportation and communications technologies have . . . been revolutionized, both geographical distance and, especially, place are fundamental' (ibid.: 18). His contention is that 'every component in a production network – every firm, every economic function' – is, quite literally, 'grounded' in specific locations (ibid.: 18). This grounding 'is both physical' (in the form of the built environment) and also 'less tangible' (in the form of localized social relationships and in distinctive institutions and cultural practices). The result is that 'the precise nature and articulation of firm-centred production networks are deeply influenced by the concrete socio-political, institutional and cultural contexts within which they are embedded, produced and reproduced' (ibid.) (see also Hess 2004; Jones 2008).

Such a position shares common ground with that articulated by both Held and McGrew and also Hirst and Thompson inasmuch as Dicken emphasizes the continued importance of the national state as 'the most important bounded territorial form in which production networks are embedded', and that 'all the elements in a production network are regulated within some kind of political structure', including supranational institutions like the IMF, WTO, EU and NAFTA (ibid.: 18). However, Dicken explicitly takes issues with what he suggests are the overly strong views of deterritorialization, disembeddedness and the space of flows. Citing Castells's arguments in respect of the latter in particular, he contends that 'seductive as such ideas are, they are highly misleading' (ibid.: 18). For Dicken, the contemporary world is *both* a 'space of places' and 'a space of flows'.

A further important issue here is the breadth of Dicken's conception of 'production'. Not only is production territorially embedded, but is also intimately shaped by the concomitant process of consumption. Dicken argues that both production circuits and production networks 'are driven, ultimately, by the necessity, the willingness and the ability of customers to acquire and consume the products themselves, and to continue doing so' (ibid.: 19). This for Dicken is a major absence in much of the existing literature that 'rarely figures in the script'. He points to at least three important characteristics of the consumption process. First, there is the important distinction between the consumption of producer goods or services (purchased by firms within a production circuit for further transformation) and consumer goods or services (final demand goods). Second, consumption is very much more than the economic process of demand. It is greatly influenced by income but is also 'a complex set of *social and cultural* processes, in which all kinds of personal motivations are involved' (ibid.: 19). Third, because consumption is influenced by symbolic, positional and other qualities that shape the desire to buy particular products, it can and is manipulated. How far is open to question in Dicken's view, but he suggests there is certainly evidence that some production networks are *buyer-driven* (rather than producer-driven). The consequence of this understanding of consumption is that in order to effectively understand the contemporary global economy 'we must see the entire circuit of production, distribution and consumption' as a *dynamically interconnected whole* with power, according to circumstance, lying at different positions within the circuit and different circuits having different configurations of power.

A final key element of Dicken's theorization of the globalized economy that needs mentioning is that of *geographical concentration*. The key concept here is 'the cluster'. Dicken takes issue with the hyperglobalist argument that 'increasing geographical dispersal at a global scale is now the norm' (ibid.: 21). Rather he suggests that 'geographical concentrations of economic activity not only still exist' but also represent 'the normal state of affairs'. Whilst he acknowledges that 'we may find tendencies of *both* concentration *and* dispersal', there remains 'a very strong propensity for economic activities to agglomerate into *localized geographical clusters*' (see also Krugman 1998; Porter 1990, 2000).

Dicken proposes two principal forms of cluster: *generalized* and *specialized*. Generalized clusters 'simply reflect the fact that human activities tend to agglomerate to form urban areas' (ibid.: 21). These clusters generate 'the basis for sharing the costs of a whole range of services' where, for example, a large city encourages 'the emergence and growth of a variety of infrastructural, economic, social and cultural facilities that cannot be provided when customers are geographically dispersed' (ibid.: 21). In contrast, *specialized clusters* reflect 'the tendency for firms in the same or closely related industries to locate in the same places to form what are sometimes termed "industrial districts"' (ibid.: 22). The bases of these clusters 'arise from the geographical proximity of firms performing different – but *linked* – functions in particular production networks'.

He argues that both forms of cluster generate two types of interdependency. The first are *traded interdependencies* which 'are direct transactions between firms in the cluster' (ibid.: 22). Spatial proximity is 'a means of reducing transaction costs either by reducing transportation costs or by reducing some of the uncertainties of customer–supplier relationships' (ibid.: 22). The second are *untraded interdependencies* which are less tangible benefits that range from 'the development of an appropriate pool of labour, to particular kinds of institutions . . . to broader socio-cultural phenomena' (ibid.: 22). Of particular importance is how clustering facilitates three important processes in economic activity: face-to-face contact; social and cultural interaction; and enhancement of knowledge and innovation (ibid.). Dicken argues that whilst 'the reasons for the origins of specific geographical clusters are highly contingent', once established, 'a cluster tends to grow through a process of *cumulative, self-reinforcing development*' – that is to say that the process is *path dependent* (ibid.: 23).

The concept of cluster or agglomeration forms a second set of *geographical networks* to complement the *organizational networks* in the form of production circuits and networks. His argument is that such an approach 'helps us to appreciate the interconnectedness of economic activities across different geographical scales and within and across territorially bounded spaces' (ibid.: 23). Thus, this represents a theoretical attempt to understand how 'the production of any commodity, whether it is a manufactured product or a service, involves an intricate articulation of individual activities and transactions across space and time' (ibid.: 23). His geo-economic approach provides a framework through which to theorize the complexity of this process both at the international scale in terms of the changing geography of production, and within specific industries. Indeed much of the substantial body of *Global Shift* which I have not discussed here grounds these arguments in extensive and detailed empirical analysis. However, rather than consider this empirical analysis here, we need now turn to

Saskia Sassen whose work adds important insights into two of the key issues identified by Dicken: the nature and exercise of power in the global economy, and the nature and role of agglomeration and geographical unevenness in the developing interconnectedness of economic activity.

Sassen and a network of global cities

The concept of the 'global city' has had an enormous impact on contemporary thinking about globalization, although to some extent this discussion has run in parallel rather than in unison with the mainstream of the globalization debate. This is in several senses an unfortunate development because the so-called 'global cities debate' has much to add to understandings of how globalization plays out in the real (or certainly the material) world.

Sassen's 'global city' thesis was first proposed in 1991 in the first edition of the book by the same name. Her argument has subsequently evolved and been revised but we should begin by considering the original framework. In essence, the key argument she made was that by the early 1990s 'the combination of spatial dispersal and global integration has created a new strategic role for major cities' (Sassen 1991: 3). These cities, she suggested, have come to 'function in four new ways': first, as 'highly concentrated command points in the organization of the world economy'; second, as 'key locations for finance and for specialized service firms, which have replaced manufacturing as the leading economic sectors'; third, as 'sites of production, including the production of innovations, in these leading industries'; and fourth, as 'markets for the products and innovations produced' (ibid.: 3–4). Sassen's argument is these changes have had 'a massive impact upon both international economy activity and urban form'. In the first edition of *The Global City*, she takes three leading examples of such 'global cities': London, New York and Tokyo. The point is that the concept of the global city is warranted because these three cities 'have undergone massive and parallel changes in their economic base, spatial organization and social structure' (ibid.: 4). The reason is that these cities are being influenced by 'a set of global processes' which she situates around four themes in relation to the nature and impact of these new functions being fulfilled.

Firstly, Sassen argues that 'the territorial dispersal of current economic activity creates the need for expanded central control and management' (ibid.: 4). In essence, top level control, she argues, has become concentrated in a few leading financial centres, notably London, New York and Tokyo (ibid.). These account 'for a disproportionate share of all financial transactions' and 'extremely dense business district agglomerations'. Second, global cities are about more than just nodal points of control, being also 'particular sites of production' of specialized services needed by complex (transnational) organizations and the production of financial innovations and the making of markets (ibid.). In this context, 'the things a global city makes are services and financial goods' (ibid.). Third, Sassen makes a series of arguments about 'the consequences of global city development for national urban systems and the relationship of global cities to nation-states' (ibid.: 7–8). In particular, she opens up the question of the extent to which 'development posited for London, New York and Tokyo are replicated "in a less accentuated form" in smaller cities at a lower level of the urban hierarchy' (ibid.: 8). Fourth, Sassen is very much concerned with the impact of global city development 'on the social order' (ibid.:9). Importantly, she argues that global city development has produced polarization in labour markets and consequently in the social form of these cities. The reason is that 'major growth industries show a greater incidence of jobs at high- and low-paying ends of the scale'. In addition, global city development is also linked to a 'vast supply of low-wage jobs required for high income gentrification' and in the proliferation of consumer services for high-paid workers.

Sassen develops these arguments using a substantial body of empirical data on the three cities and during the 1990s this book formed the basis for a large 'global city' literature that engaged and developed her ideas (Brenner and Keil 2005; Clark 2003; Short 2004). It is in this context that we need to consider the second edition of *The Global City*, published a decade later. The reason is that the second edition represents a significant revision and development of her theoretical arguments, and attempts to respond to the critical reception of the ideas in the first. In this new edition, Sassen extends her theoretical 'global city thesis' and reorganizes it around seven hypotheses, although it is useful here to group these seven into four revised strands that map onto those discussed in the first edition.

The first couple of hypotheses broaden her earlier argument about the simultaneous geographic dispersal and integration of economic activities. In the second edition, the general concern for command and control becomes much more focused on activities within firms. She argues in this respect that, as well as dispersal and integration being 'a key factor feeding the growth and importance of central corporate functions', 'the more dispersed a firm's operations across different countries, the more complex and strategic its central functions' (Sassen 2001: xx). She argues further that by the twenty-first century 'these central functions have become so complex that increasingly the head-quarters of large global firms outsource them' and 'buy a share of their central functions from highly specialized service firms' (ibid.).

Second, in relation to the production and market for specialized services, her contention is that 'those specialized service firms engaged in the most complex and globalized markets are subject to agglomeration economies' (ibid.: xx). Global cities are 'production sites' where the 'mix of firms, talents, and expertise from a broad range of specialized fields makes a certain type of urban environment function as an information center' (ibid.). Furthermore, 'the more [corporate] head-quarters outsource their most complex, unstandardized functions . . . the freer they are to opt for any location because the more the work actually done in the headquarters is not subject to agglomeration economies' (ibid.). In response to critics of the first edition which used the location of corporate headquarters as a measure for 'global city-ness', she is emphasizing that it is the location of specialized services that most defines the global city.

Third, Sassen argues in the second edition that 'specialized service firms need to provide a global service which has meant a global network of affiliates or some other form of partnership' (ibid.: xxi). Global cities are thus not isolated entities (as perhaps implied in the first edition), for 'there is no such entity as a global city' (ibid.). Rather, they are part of 'transnational urban systems' linked through a growing number of 'cross-border transactions and networks' (ibid.). This is an important elaboration and departure from the earlier edition, and in particular appears to be a response to Castells's criticism in the mid-1990s that the global city should be understood as a process and a network located in the 'space of flows', rather than a specific place that can be marketed (see Castells 2000a).

Fourth, she contends that 'the growing numbers of high-level professionals and high-profit making specialized services have the effect of raising the degree of spatial and socioeconomic polarization evident in these cities' (ibid.: xxi). She further suggests that this process is leading to 'the growing informalisation of a range of economic activities in these cities' (ibid.). This is a rather broader elaboration of the polarization arguments made in the first edition.

For Sassen, the key development to her arguments from the first edition of *The Global City* is that her approach, in focusing on the production of 'the capabilities of global operation, coordination and control', 'shifts the emphasis to the *practices* that constitute what we call economic globalization and global control'.

Conclusion: debates around the spatiality of globalization

In the final part to this chapter, I examine the critical reception to the spatialized thinking about globalization of both Dicken and Sassen. Both thinkers have provoked a response to their ideas over the last two decades in their own right, but I want to suggest that their highly empirical interventions into the globalization debate expose a number of crucial epistemological issues that remain to be resolved in future thinking about globalization.

It should be apparent that Dicken's work has made a heavyweight impact on debates about economic globalization and the emergence of a global economy. As Yeung and Peck (2003) indicate in their review of Dicken's work, *Global Shift* has been widely cited across the social science literature on globalization. They suggest three major strengths to his approach which have made his arguments so influential. First, Dicken's 'grounded' empirical approach has circumvented the generalist 'globaloney' that others have been so critical of elsewhere in the globalization literature. They further suggest his work 'manages to convey subtlety, intricacy and nuance, while avoiding the pitfalls of aimless empiricism' (ibid.: 20). Second, while Dicken is concerned with theorizing structures and processes, they suggest he does not fall 'into the trap of process fetishism', defined as 'an exaggerated concern with processes at the expense of due concern with the actors and outcomes of globalization' (ibid.). Third, they also suggest 'one of the real virtues of his work is the *explicit interdisciplinarity*' that other segments of the globalization literature have been less successful at.

Perhaps because of the empirical grounding to his ideas, Dicken's thinking has not been strongly critiqued. It is certainly hard to disagree with much of the empirical basis to his arguments. However, a number of potential limitations to his conceptual approach have emerged. First, despite the view of Peck and Yeung, Dicken's process-based framework for theorizing economic globalization provides little detailed explanation of specific relationships between actors and processes. Processes appear to be aggregate 'average' transformations in epistemological terms, but Dicken never really provides a theoretical discussion of how processes are constituted and where they 'begin' and 'end'. Second, the spatial concepts that he develops have also been criticized elsewhere in the social science literature for concealing power and agency, and providing too simplistic an explanation for the nature of relationships between actors. Both the concepts of global production networks and circuits perhaps are limited in this respect, with neither 'network' nor 'circuit' fully capturing the complex dynamics between different economic actors. Third, the concept of the geo-economy (in terms in particular of where production is located and the role of places) can be criticized for simplifying the relationship between material places and economic activity (see Jones 2008).

Such possible lines of critical engagement are in fact reflected in the criticisms that have been made more directly of Sassen's ideas about global cities. I have already discussed how Sassen reformulated her ideas during the 1990s about the nature of 'global city-ness', essentially redefining it as a process present to a greater or lesser extent in many cities around the world. However, Sassen's work remains vulnerable to similar conceptual issues as Dicken's concerning the relationship between economic power, practice and places. Elsewhere I have argued that the proposition that 'command and control' is centralized *within* the material spaces of global cities is neither entirely accurate nor especially useful in understanding how corporate power is exercised in the global economy (Jones 2002). Where power in the global economy is located, and where it is exercised, is rather more complicated than the simplistic idea that global cities act as control nodes. Furthermore, the extent to which Sassen's systemic conception of global city networks successfully captures the role played by urban centres – as well as the relationships between cities – in the global space economy remains an unresolved issue. Ultimately, the remaining weakness of the global city approach as a basis to theorize practices, control or even production is that a significant strand to the globalization literature questions whether or not any of these phenomena are exclusively *contained* within material places. Epistemologically, the interesting and key issue is whether a theoretical framework based around place (as opposed to space) is adequate to capture that complexity.

Overall, however, it is important to emphasize that both Dicken's and Sassen's thinking about globalization has made a substantial impact on the debate, and has brought a set of spatial concepts and theories to the discussion that – aside from Castells – was certainly oddly lacking in the mainstream of the literature. Their concepts of networks, circuits and embeddedness represent important attempts to develop in depth the generalized meta-theoretical basis to globalization theories around time–space distanciation that thinkers like

Giddens, Held, McGrew and even Castells only outline in the broadest of terms. Dicken's work certainly both challenges and pushes further Castells's concepts of the space of flows, as well as providing an empirically rich insight into production and economic practices in the global economy that complements Castells's concern with informationalism.

Further reading

Works by Peter Dicken

Dicken, P. (2003) 'Placing' Firms: Grounding the Debate on the 'Global' Corporation, in J. A. Peck and H. W-c. Yeung (eds), *Remaking the Global Economy: Economic-Geographical Perspectives*. London: Sage.

Dicken, P. (2004) Geographers and 'Globalization': (Yet) Another Missed Boat? *Transactions of the Institute of British Geographers* 29: 5–26.

Dicken, P. (2007) *Global Shift: Mapping the Changing Contours of the World Economy*. London: Sage.

Dicken, P. and Weidong, L. (2006) Transnational Corporations and 'Obligated Embeddedness': Foreign Direct Investment in China's Automobile Industry. *Environment and Planning A* 38: 1229–47.

Dicken, P., Coe, N., Hess, M., Yeung, H. and Henderson, J. (2004) 'Globalizing' Regional Development: A Global Production Networks Perspective. *Transactions of the Institute of British Geographers* 29: 468–84.

Dicken, P., Yeung, H. and Wiedong, L. (2006) Transnational Corporations and Network Effects of a Local Manufacturing Cluster in Mobile Telecommunications Equipment in China. *World Development* 34: 520–40.

Commentaries and critical engagements: Peter Dicken

Yeung, H. and Peck, J. (2003) Making Global Connections: A Geographer's Perspective, in J. Peck and H. Yeung (eds), *Remaking the Global Economy*. London: Sage, ch.1.

Works by Saskia Sassen

Sassen, S. (1991) *The Global City*. Princeton: Princeton University Press.

Sassen, S. (1996) *Losing Control? Sovereignty in an Age of Globalization*. New York: Columbia University Press.

Sassen, S. (1998) *Globalization and Its Discontents: Essays on the New Mobility of People and Money*. New York: The New Press.

Sassen, S. (2001) *The Global City* (2nd edn). Princeton: Princeton University Press.
Sassen, S. (2006) *Cities in a World Economy* (3rd edn). Thousand Oaks, California: Pine Forge.
Sassen, S. (2007) *A Sociology of Globalization*. New York: W. W. Norton.

Commentaries and critical engagements: Saskia Sassen

Brenner, N. and Keil, R. (2005) *The Global Cities Reader*. London: Routledge.
Clark, D. (2003) *Urban World /Global City*. London: Routledge.
Jones, A. (2002) The Global City Misconceived: The Myth of 'Global Management' in Transnational Service Firms. *Geoforum* 33: 335–50.
Short, J. (2004) *Global Metropolitan: Globalizing Cities in a Capitalist World*. London: Routledge.

8 POSITIVE THINKING: THOMAS FRIEDMAN AND MARTIN WOLF

Introduction

Having moved through a range of academic thinkers on globalization from several different disciplinary backgrounds, this chapter turns to a different segment of the globalization literature with consideration of the work of two distinguished journalists, one on each side of the Atlantic. These thinkers are Thomas Friedman and Martin Wolf, who are leading journalists on the *New York Times* and *Financial Times* respectively. In shifting our attention to these more 'popular' thinkers, this chapter represents a step-change in our critical journey. After the more conceptual and theoretical thinkers we considered in the earlier chapters of this book, each successive chapter is now tackling a more specific area of thought and a more discreet sub-component of the debate. I have entitled this chapter on Friedman and Wolf 'positive thinking' because both of these thinkers argue vigorously for the benefits of (neoliberal) economic globalization. Their works have thus been widely cited for presenting strong arguments in favour of furthering economic integration and that globalization presents an exciting opportunity for improving human welfare across the globe in the twenty-first century.

Both thinkers – at least in part – have also made major contributions that counter the arguments of radical critics in the anti-globalization movement (to whom we will turn in later chapters) and argued that the negative view of globalization that emerged during the 1990s is misguided and misplaced. Thomas Friedman is best known for his international best-selling book, *The World is Flat*, first published in 2005, which has won several prizes and is one of the most widely known 'popular' books on globalization. However, Friedman has been writing on globalization for over a decade in his readable journalistic style, developing his view that (economic-driven) globalization is a 'force for good' in every sphere of human concern from economy to politics, culture and the environment. Martin Wolf, similarly, is known for an influential popular book, *Why Globalization Works*, which was published in 2004. However, in contrast to Friedman's often hyperbolic style, Wolf is a much more sedate and sober proponent of the benefits to contemporary economic globalization. His goal is to make 'a powerful defence of the global market economy' and to develop a serious counter-critique of the criticism made by the anti- and alter-globalization movements. Yet both Friedman and Wolf share the underlying argument that contemporary globalization has been and can continue to be a hugely progressive transformation for human society.

The context from which both Friedman and Wolf have developed these positions has much in common – both are journalists with a career background in economics, policy and business. Born in Minneapolis in 1953, Friedman has spent most of his career at the *New York Times*. Interested in journalism and foreign affairs since he was at high school, he took a first degree in Mediterranean studies at Brandeis University in 1975. In the later 1970s he studied in the United Kingdom, receiving a Master of Philosophy degree in Modern Middle East studies from Oxford in 1978. On completing this latter degree, he joined the London bureau of United Press International and was soon despatched to Beirut, where he stayed until 1981. He spent most of the 1980s in the Middle East working for the *New York Times*, winning the Pulitzer Prize for International Reporting in 1983 and again in 1988 for his coverage of the first Palestinian Intifada. He won the Pulitzer for a third time in 2002, and, more recently, *The World is Flat* (his fourth book) won the inaugural Goldman Sachs/*Financial Times* Business Book of the Year award. In 2005 he was also given an Order of the British Empire (OBE).

Martin Wolf's background is similar. Born in 1946 – the son of an Austrian Jew who had fled the Holocaust – he grew up in Britain. Like Friedman, he studied at Oxford from 1965, taking a first degree in politics, philosophy and economics in 1968 and then a Master of Philosophy degree in economics in 1971. His father was a strong supporter of the Labour Party in Britain and Wolf remained a supporter under his influence until the 1970s. Upon leaving Oxford, he joined the World Bank's young professionals' programme, being promoted to the position of senior economist in 1974. Through this period his political views shifted as he became more convinced of the benefits of liberal market economies. In 1981, he left the World Bank to take up the role of Director of Studies at the Trade Policy Research Centre (London) where he stayed until the later 1980s. However, in 1987 he shifted career path into journalism by joining *The Financial Times* where he has been ever since. Wolf has been chief economics commentator at the paper since 1996 and is now associate editor. He is also a visiting fellow of Nuffield College, Oxford, a special professor at the University of Nottingham and an honorary fellow of the Oxford Institute for Economic Policy. He has also been a forum fellow at the annual meeting of the World Economic Forum in Davos since 1999. He was awarded the CBE (Commander of the British Empire) in 2000 and an honorary doctorate in economics by the London School of Economics in 2006.

In terming Friedman and Wolf 'positive thinkers', it needs to be made clear that they are positive about a certain form of globalization that can be characterized as the neoliberal economic globalization of the last thirty years or so. In this respect, their version of positive thinking about globalization is both powerful and contentious. In contrast to the academic thinkers we have thus far considered, both these thinkers are directly engaged with and central to the politicized nature of debate about globalization. And whilst their thinking certainly is informed by and develops theoretical perspectives about what globalization 'is' and should be, theorization largely takes second place to arguments about policy, practice and politics. This chapter therefore has a number of tasks before it. The first is to uncover and examine the theoretical arguments (and underlying epistemological assumptions) that underpin the popular contributions of these thinkers. I argue that both are grounded in a perspective that adheres to – or at least accepts – many of the tenets of the key post-Second World War school of neoliberalist thought (see Peck and Tickell 2006). Second, we will also explore the extent to which Friedman and Wolf's contribution represents new and innovative insight. Friedman in particular has been hugely influential in his arguments about 'a flat world', and his work is often considered to be highly original. Whilst there is some truth in this, this chapter also argues that many of his proposals are at best idealistic – or at worst simplistic – to the degree that there has to be serious doubt about whether many of his policy suggestions are feasible in reality. Furthermore, and third, they also both present a one-sided and sometimes utopian vision of global economic integration that glosses over both the complexity and downsides.

To some extent, I address these tasks through the analysis rather than in sequence, as it makes more sense to consider each of the thinkers in turn. The next section therefore begins by examining the thinking of Friedman, with a particular focus on his highly influential arguments in *The World is Flat*. The third section then turns to Wolf, again largely focused on his principal intervention in the globalization debate *Why Globalization Works*. In the fourth section, however, I evaluate the major critical challenges that have been made in the globalization literature which are relevant to both thinkers. One of the principal arguments to emerge here is that both Friedman and Wolf articulate a revised hyperglobalist account of globalization – albeit more sophisticated than that of the 1990s. The final section thus concludes by considering this issue.

Friedman and a 'flat' world

In comparison to much of the globalization literature, reading Thomas Friedman is easy and pleasurable. Friedman writes as an accomplished columnist (which he is) and in a style that is both interesting and colourful. Yet the key problem for any student of globalization who wishes to summarize his major thoughts on globalization is that this prosaic approach can make his key arguments hard to extract from the text. This section aims to cut through his prose to provide a commentary on how his ideas about globalization have been developed through his two principal works: *The Lexus and the Olive Tree* and *The World is Flat*.

The Lexus and the olive tree

In his first book written at the end of the 1990s, Friedman makes five key arguments about globalization. First, he sees globalization as having had distinct historical phases. His view is that the world entered a new and distinct phase of globalization after the fall of the Berlin Wall in 1989. This 10-year-old (as it was at that point) *era of globalization* is different to previous eras of globalization and in particular the one between the mid-1800s and 1920 which 'was blown apart by the successive hammer blows of World War I' (ibid.: xvii). Unlike political science thinkers like Held et al., however, he sees the immediate post-Second World War period as a hiatus in globalization. He argues that 'the formally divided world that emerged after World War II was then frozen in place by the Cold War'. For Friedman, the new era is thus 'Globalization Round II' – at least in terms of the last two centuries (ibid.). This is what he means by the idea that 'the world is ten years old' (ibid.: xvi).

Second, he argues that this new era is different to previous eras. His view is that 'what is new today is the degree and intensity with which the world is being tied together in a single globalized marketplace and village' (ibid.: xvii). Thus, contra the Hirst and Thompson critique, pre-1914 globalization 'may have been large in scale relative to its time' but was, he contends, 'minuscule in absolute terms compared to today' (ibid.: xviii). The contemporary era represents 'turbo-charged' globalization.

Third, this difference between contemporary globalization and those phases of the past is not only about 'degree' but also 'kind' in both technological and political terms. Friedman argues that previous phases of globalization were built around falling transport costs whereas the contemporary one is built around falling telecommunications costs. It is these new information technologies 'that are able to weave the world together tighter' (ibid.: xviii). This argument is clearly reminiscent of Castells. Politically, the difference with previous eras revolves around the shift from British to American power in the twentieth century. American power is central in that 'it drove the creation of the IMF [and] the GATT' (ibid.: xix).

Fourth, and following on, Friedman sees American power as behind the development of globalization as 'a new dominant international system' which has replaced 'the Cold War system' (ibid.: xx). Drawing on and reconfiguring the ideas of Paul Kennedy (Kennedy 1988), Francis Fukuyama (Fukuyama 1991) and Samuel Huntington (Huntington 1997), Friedman argues that 'to understand the post-Cold War world you have to start by understanding the international system that has succeeded it' (ibid.: xxi). Globalization is not just influencing events, 'it is the system'. Thus he is closest to Fukuyama in broadly agreeing that globalization represents 'the triumph of liberalism and free market capitalism as the most effective way to organize society' and, in that context, 'is a good thing' (ibid.: xxi).

The bulk of *The Lexus and the Olive Tree* is thus concerned to outline this systemic view of globalization. It does this in three phases, but for our purposes here we will focus on the first part of the book which outlines the major features of globalization as 'the new system'. Friedman proposes eight major features of this system. First, the contemporary globalization system is similar to the Cold War international system but, rather than being characterized by division, its overarching feature is integration captured in the concepts of interconnection and 'the web' (ibid.: 8). Second, the globalization system is not as static as the Cold War system but dynamic and is seen as 'an ongoing process' that essentially amounts to 'the inexorable integration of markets' (ibid.: 9). Third, in contrast to the Cold War, the globalized international system is driven by free market capitalism and its spread. Fourth, also 'unlike the Cold War system', the globalization system 'has its own dominant culture' (ibid.: 9). Friedman sees this most often as 'Americanization'. Fifth, the contemporary system has 'its own defining technologies: computerization, miniaturization, digitization, satellite communications, fibre optics and the Internet' which 'reinforce its defining perspective of integration' (ibid.). Sixth, Friedman argues that 'whilst the defining measurement of the Cold War was weight . . . the defining measure of globalization is speed' (ibid.: 10). Seventh, he suggests the globalization system 'has its own demographic pattern – a rapid acceleration of the movement of people from rural areas and agricultural lifestyles to urban areas and urban lifestyles' (ibid.: 13). Eighth, he suggests that the globalization system 'has its own defining structure of power which is more complex than the Cold War structure' (ibid.: 13). Where the Cold War was built around the balance between the USA and USSR, the globalization system 'is built around three balances which overlap and affect one another' (ibid.). These are, respectively, the traditional balance between nation-states, that between nation-states and markets and a (historically novel) balance between individuals and nation-states (ibid.: 14).

Friedman then develops a number of arguments about the nature of this system. The first – from which the book takes its title – is the tension between tradition, continuity and territoriality (the olive tree) and integration, change and modernization (the Lexus) (ibid.: 29–34). The 'wrestling' between these two sets of human values characterizes contemporary globalization in Friedman's view, and the consequent challenge 'in this era of globalization – for countries and individuals – is to find a healthy balance between preserving a sense of identity, home and community and doing what it takes to survive within the globalization system' (ibid.: 42). Second, he suggests that in this system a whole range of facets of the contemporary world have become 'democratized' (perhaps better understood as available to all) – technology, finance and information. Third, he suggests that – in part as a consequence of these democratization processes – the defining political-economic form for the globalization era is one of 'a Golden Straitjacket' which in essence amounts to a series of policies that countries must adopt to fit into the dominant free market capitalist model.

The next two sections in *The Lexus and the Olive Tree* develop and explore the implications of this globalization system for different countries, activities and aspects of contemporary human life. Friedman thus variously attends to questions of state form, international relations, corruption, resistance, key actors in the global economy, winners and losers and so on. Probably the most cited argument he makes in these later chapter is his 'Golden Arches' argument concerning conflict prevention which, simply put, states that no two countries in which there are McDonalds restaurants have ever gone to war. Interested readers may well wish to look at these parts of the book further but, in terms of understanding Friedman's more recent arguments about globalization, we need now to turn to his most recent contribution to the debate.

The flat world thesis

Five years after publishing *The Lexus and the Olive Tree*, Friedman produced his most recent and widely cited contribution to the globalization debate: *The World is Flat* (2005). The book has since been revised and republished twice, although the major arguments that Friedman develops in these editions do not change substantially. The central development from the arguments about globalization in his earlier book centres on the relationship between globalization and information and communications technology (ICT), and most particularly the internet. He argues that 'right around the year 2000, we entered a whole new era: Globalization 3.0' (ibid.: 10). The essence of this new phase to globalization is that it is 'shrinking the world from a "size small" to a "size tiny" and flattening the playing field at the same time' (ibid.). The consequence is that if 'Globalization 1.0' was about 'countries globalizing' and 'Globalization 2.0' about 'companies globalizing', then 'the dynamic force in Globalization 3.0 . . . is the newfound power for *individuals* to collaborate and compete globally' (ibid.). This phenomenon is 'enabling, empowering and enjoining individuals and small groups to go global so easily and seamlessly' and represents 'the flat world platform'.

At the centre of this conception of globalization is ICT. Friedman sees the personal computer, fibre optic cables and work-flow software (amongst other aspects of ICT technology) as central. He argues that this is a very recent phenomenon insofar as it really is only since around 2000 that these technologies have developed to a degree sufficient to enable individuals to 'go global'. The consequence is that everyone increasingly has to ask how they as an individual 'fit into global competition and opportunities' and how they 'can collaborate globally' (ibid.: 11). Thus, for Friedman, post-2000 globalization (Globalization 3.0) differs from previous eras also insofar as previous eras 'were driven primarily by European and American individuals and businesses' whereas now it is increasingly driven by 'non-Western, non-White' people. It therefore is conceived of as a more inclusive, diverse and potentially democratic phase of globalization. This individualization of globalization is the core of the flat world thesis which, Friedman argues, if it continues 'will be seen in time as one of those fundamental shifts or inflection points' akin to the 'invention of the printing press' or 'the rise of the nation-state' (ibid.: 49). Furthermore, he suggests that 'there is something about the flattening of the world that is going to be qualitatively different from the great changes of previous eras: the speed and breadth with which it is taking hold' (ibid.: 49). The flattening is happening 'at warp speed', and thus the faster and broader this transition to a new era, the greater the potential for disruption, as opposed to 'an orderly transfer of power from the old winners to the new winners' (ibid.: 49). The challenge is therefore 'to absorb these changes in ways that do not overwhelm people or leave them behind' since the flat world 'is inevitable and unavoidable' (ibid.: 50).

Friedman goes on to set out the key tenets of what the flat world entails. He does this by identifying ten forces 'that flattened the world'. First, he suggests that two developments – the fall of the Berlin Wall in 1989 and the launch of Microsoft Windows 3.0 in 1992 – marked the unleashing of key transformative forces. The fall of the Berlin Wall, aside from 'liberat[ing] all the captive peoples of the Soviet Empire', also 'tipped the balance of power across the world towards those advocating democratic, consensual, free-market oriented governance' (ibid.: 52). The fall of the Wall released 'pent-up' aspirations to develop market economies and allowed people 'to think about the world differently – to see it as more a seamless whole'. Almost concurrently, the release of Windows 3.0 in 1992 led to an unprecedented standardization of a key commodity – the Windows-powered personal computer. For the first time this enabled 'individuals to author their own content right from their desktops in digital form' (ibid.: 56) and then 'to disseminate their own digital content in so many new ways to so many more people' (ibid.: 56). This forms the basis for Friedman of how individuals now *globalize* themselves.

The second and third forces follow on from the ICT element of the first insofar as they correspond to the development of the World Wide Web and the internet since the mid-1990s and the subsequent development of 'work-flow software'. In relation to the former, Friedman suggests that internet browsers furthered the Windows 3.0 'flattening' by enabling 'me and my computer [to] interact with anyone anywhere on any machine' (ibid.: 77). Work-flow software then furthers the seamless integration of this development by allowing 'machines to talk to other machines over the Internet by using standardized protocols, with no humans involved at all' (ibid.: 84).This is in essence transforming the nature of work as it creates 'virtual global offices' which can access talent 'sitting in different parts of the world and have them complete tasks that you need completed in real time' (ibid.: 92). The fourth force also follows again from this in the guise of 'uploading' where Friedman argues that the 'flat world platform' has led to a range of community-developed software, freeware, Wikipedia and blogging which represents a profound empowering of communities, groups and individuals.

Fifth and sixth, Friedman's suggests that 'outsourcing' and 'off-shoring' respectively have been key forces in flattening the world. In relation to the former, he cites the Year 2000 bug (Y2K) as a crucial moment in stimulating the Indian ICT industry and giving it the capacity to become the globally competitive regional industry it now is. The latter force he equates largely to the rise of new production in China. The seventh flattening force is also related in the guise of 'supply chaining' for which he takes the US supermarket transnational Wal-Mart as the primary case study, pointing to its complicated global-scale sourcing of products, their distribution and the role of ICT in stock inventory management. The central role played by distribution in supply chains forms the eighth force where Friedman focuses on the development of the global logistics industry and takes the logistics firm UPS as his case study. Importantly, he argues that global logistics amounts to a process of 'insourcing' that represents 'a whole new form of collaboration and creating value horizontally' (ibid.: 169). Global logistics firms like UPS are providing supply chain possibilities to firms of all sizes, most of whom unlike Wal-Mart are not big enough to manage the complexity of these chains themselves.

The ninth force flattening the world is termed 'in-forming'. This is defined as 'the individual's personal analog to uploading, outsourcing, insourcing, supply-chaining and off-shoring' (ibid.: 178) and amounts to 'the ability to build and deploy your own personal supply chain – a supply chain of information, knowledge and entertainment' (ibid.). It is about 'self-collaboration' as people become their 'own self-directed, self-empowered researcher, editor and selector of entertainment' (ibid.: 179). This process involves 'searching for friends, allies and collaborators' and is 'empowering the formation of global communities across all international and cultural boundaries' (ibid.: 183).

Tenth, and finally, Friedman argues there are a range of 'steroids' that act to make all of the previous forces possible. These are essentially a key set of ICT capacities: the greater speed and processing capacity of computers, breakthroughs in instant messaging and file sharing, internet-based phone calls, video-conferencing, advances in computer graphics and new wireless technologies and devices. All of these developments have enormously increased the scope for people and machines to communicate with each other.

Overall, the flat world thesis is wide-ranging and the metaphor of flatness one which is deployed in a complex (and not necessarily coherent) set of meanings. In the later chapters of his book, Friedman elaborates at some length on the implications of these flattening forces in the contemporary world. Whilst I cannot review all of this argument here, what all of his analysis shares is a positive and progressive view of the era of Globalization 3.0 as liberating, empowering, democratizing and wealth-generating. We will return to possible lines of critique that intersect with this position shortly, but first we need to turn to the work of a similarly positive thinker: Martin Wolf.

Wolf on why globalization 'works'

In comparison to the hyperbole, anecdote-rich and metaphor-based 'blue sky' thinking of Thomas Friedman, Martin Wolf's book, *Why Globalization Works*, is a significant contrast. Wolf's book has received substantial critical acclaim, and rightly so because it is an erudite (if polemical) discussion about contemporary economic globalization that engages with both the general themes and specific details of the debate in impressive detail.

Wolf's perspective is best characterized as that of a liberal, pro-market political economist and the book is a vigorous defence of the progressive nature of a liberal global market economy. His thinking emerges very clearly from classical economics and political economy – notably in a lineage drawing on Adam Smith, David Ricardo and the twentieth-century (neo)liberal economic thinking of Friedrich von Hayek, Jagdish Bhagwati and Anne Krueger amongst others. I want to suggest that, whilst his arguments about the origins, nature and future direction of globalization are wide-ranging, Wolf's contribution in a nutshell revolves around three key contentions: first, that liberal market democracies are the best form of government; second, that liberal globalization is the best strategy for increasingly human wealth and ensuring world peace; and third, that the arguments of the anti-globalization movement are misguided. Such claims are not made lightly but with detailed reference to academic thinking, research and some data analysis. In the remainder of this section, I will focus on these three key lines of thinking in turn.

Markets, democracy and peace

Wolf's central contention is that market economy is a progressive phenomenon, and the most sophisticated and effective politico-economic system for 'satisfying [the] material wants of mankind [sic]' (ibid.: 46). An increasingly globalized market economy is thus highly desirable in his view. He argues the market 'is not a jungle, but among the most sophisticated products of civilization' (ibid.: 12). The reason is that 'self interest, co-ordinated through the market, motivates people to invent, produce, and sell a vast array of goods, services and assets' (ibid.: 44). This starts with the free society, underpinned by the valued worth 'of the active, self-directing individual' (ibid.: 24). Whilst individuals are unavoidably embedded within society, in the free society the central feature 'is voluntary action – the freedom to choose' (ibid.) Citing John Locke, he argues that 'the bedrock of a liberal society . . . is the right of all individuals to own and use property freely, subject to well-defined, law-governed constraints' (ibid.: 25). A liberal society is thus necessarily 'a commercial society', and also 'endemically restless' which means it is, furthermore, 'consequently insecure' because liberalism means 'perpetual and unsettling change'. However, complex free societies cannot exist without the rule of law because long-term investments require individuals to trust they will reap the fruits. Complex free societies thus need 'freedom under law' which means they need to be governed by some form of state authority.

Markets, however, are seen as far from perfect. Wolf dismisses the models and assumptions of neoclassical economics – perfect competition, universal rational behaviour, etc. – as unrealistic. Rather, his argument is that markets are of course imperfect and that market failures exists, and therefore there is a need for them to be governed and regulated. Many of the downsides to contemporary economic globalization can, he contends, be traced to the failure of governments to allow markets to either develop or work sufficiently well. The key issue thus is the nature of *governance* in the contemporary world. He argues that the best form of governance which produces the best form of markets is a constitutional democracy which has government accountable to the governed as well as an independent judiciary (ibid.: 28). This is progressive because 'a democratic elector-ate has . . . an interest in choosing institutions and policies that make society as a whole richer rather than seizing wealth from a minority' (ibid.: 29). Democratic societies are also 'the only societies where indi-vidual rights to private property and contract can be expected to last across generations' (ibid.: 30), and the existence of private property also represents 'a necessary condition for political pluralism' because a political entity which controls all a country's resources is unlikely to allow any opposition access to the means of mounting campaigns against it (ibid.). The consequence is that, for democracy to function, the political domain has to be circumscribed and market economies, based on private property, achieve this (ibid.). The bottom line is that the relationship between liberal democracy and the market economy is conceived as symbiotic: this means that the market underpins democ-racy, as well as democracy normally strengthening the market (ibid.). Perhaps most importantly, Wolf makes the argument that the pro-cesses of marketization and democratization are mutually reinforcing, producing a virtuous and progressive circle that has led to the situation where all the advanced liberal democracies share a range of positive features: they are constitutional democracies which are subject to the rule of law; they respect private property and the ability to make con-tracts; they protect freedom of speech and inquiry; they recognize a range of fundamental human rights; they have elected governments; they have independent and honest judiciaries, and finally they also have rational bureaucracies and armies subject to civilian control (ibid.: 33).

Wolf further argues that 'liberal democracy' is 'the only system of governance for which harmonious and cooperative inter-state rela-tions are a natural outcome' (ibid.: 33). This draws on the Kantian argument that 'liberal democracies may fight with other states but they have no reason to fight with one another'. Following the argument of Adam Smith's *Wealth of Nations*, there is an economic basis to these harmonious international relations because 'the prosperity of a nation derives not from the size of its territory or the population under its control but from the combination of internal economic development and international exchange' (ibid.). Wolf thus elucidates the classic arguments for free trade against mercantilism (state protectionism) and 'democratic peace' – that is that wars cease as more and more states become democratic. The globalization of liberal democracy thus will lead to an increasingly peaceful world.

The need for liberal globalization

The second (and closely related) strand to Wolf's thinking follows on from the argument that liberal democracy and market economies go hand in hand. It can be summarized thus: liberal globalization is a desirable phenomenon, that there is currently 'not enough of it' and there needs to be more not less. At least three points are important to specify in relation to this argument. First, Wolf echoes various thinkers including Held et al. in seeing (neo)liberal globalization as the latest manifestation of a long historical process of human economic and societal integration that has and continues to produce a wide range of benefits for humankind. The essential reason for this progressive trajectory, he suggests, is the 'almost limitless opportunities for positive-sum interaction among human beings'[4] (ibid.: 97). Contemporary globalization as this 'long historical process' must be therefore understood as 'ultimately a consequence' of the choice that the advanced economies made to become liberal democracies. Second, however, this does not mean liberal globalization will homogenize the world in economic or any other terms. He argues that the advanced liberal democracies are not all the same, nor is there a logic or need for them to become so. To the contrary, Wolf suggests 'there is still room for difference and that difference needs to be protected' (ibid.: 38). The key point though is that globalization is to be nurtured and supported as it has produced an unprecedented spread of democracy across the globe. In a vigorous attack on the anti-globalization critics, he argues that the task ahead revolves not around halting global economic integration, but rather making it work for more people than ever before (ibid.: 39). Third, the implication of Wolf's historical analysis of globalization as a long historical process (ibid.: 95–105) is that 'globalization is considerably more limited than critics suppose' (ibid.: 134) and that 'the pity is not that there has been too much globalization, but that there is too little' (ibid.: 95).

Such a conception of globalization is somewhat different to thinkers like Giddens, Held, McGrew and Castells. Wolf has little interest for general definitions of globalization such as those developed by Giddens or Held et al. Wolf suggests that the concept of globalization when defined as general societal integration becomes 'unmanageably broad'. Instead, he favours a narrower economic-centred definition of globalization 'as the integration of economic activities via markets' (ibid.: 19). However, despite his apparent 'economic' definition of globalization, his arguments have clear wider societal implications and at times the book alludes to progressive cultural and social transformation as a natural consequence of the processes of liberal globalization.

The folly of the anti-globalization movement

Wolf's third overarching theme in *Why Globalization Works* is 'the intellectual clash between liberal capitalism and its opponents' (ibid.: 4). He sees this clash as being manifest around the collectivist critique of a broad anti-globalization coalition 'who want to halt or reverse market driven globalization and destroy the international institutions that promote and oversee it' (ibid.: 4). He suggests these 'members of antiglobalization.com fall broadly into two groups: old fashioned economic interests . . . and single-issue, non-governmental organizations' (ibid.: 5). The central argument he develops is that the main tenets of the 'anti-globalization' critique of neoliberal globalization are misguided, and that the movement itself is seeking (perhaps inadvertently) to set a regressive rather than a progressive agenda. Wolf develops this argument by addressing what he sees as the five main lines of attack from the anti-globalization critique.

First, he seeks to counter the claim that neoliberal globalization is producing greater inequality. In assessing the last two decades, Wolf refutes the idea that globalization has increased poverty and inequality. He contends that 'human welfare, broadly defined, has risen' and that 'the proportion of humanity living in desperate misery is declining' (ibid.: 172). The 'problem of the poorest' in his analysis, 'is not that they are exploited, but that they are almost entirely unexploited' because 'they live outside the world economy'. Where economic globalization has occurred, the soaring growth of the developing economies has in his view transformed the world for the better (ibid.).

Second, to those globalization critics who attack free trade and the activities of the World Trade Organization (WTO), he argues that the idea that 'the rise of the developing countries threatens the livelihoods of the privileged citizens of high-income countries' are largely groundless (ibid.: 218–19). He suggests that deindustrialization – understood as an absolute negative in the global economy – is a myth and that the associated 'pauper labour'[5] argument is flawed. Furthermore, he describes the call for 'localization' as an absurdity which 'is both foolish and dangerous, particularly to the people of developing countries' (ibid.: 219). He does acknowledge that some of the criticisms of the WTO have validity but that this is largely because the WTO is an imperfect institution in need of reform.

Wolf's third counter to the anti-globalization critic concerns the argument that transnational corporations have too much power, and exploit people through the influence of malevolent brands. His argument here can be put succinctly: 'corporations are not more powerful than countries and do not dominate the world through brands' (ibid.: 247). Rather, corporations are positive agents insofar as 'inward investments benefit recipient countries, given the right policies' and 'above all, workers the corporations employ' (ibid.). He does acknowledge problems in relation to 'the role of corporations in democracy', but argues it must not be exaggerated. Central to this is his contention that the idea that the liberal economic policies of the past two decades or more are the result of a 'single-minded plot' by corporate interests is plain wrong (ibid.: 248). Wolf's position is that the essentially Marxist idea that we live in pseudo-democracies because of the power of money 'was wrong then and is wrong now' (ibid.).

Fourth, Wolf argues the anti-globalization movement is wrong to cast globalization as causing a situation where 'predatory market forces are making it impossible for beneficent governments to shield their peoples from the beasts of prey that lurk beyond their borders' (ibid.: 249). Rather, he suggests 'there is no evidence of the disappearance of a well-managed state's ability to tax and spend at levels it chooses' (ibid.: 277). Countries do not compete directly with one another 'as companies do', and their most important source of wealth and comparative advantage, namely people, is 'highly immobile' (ibid.). States are thus 'in no way any less necessary than before' (ibid.). Fifth, and finally, Wolf argues that attributing crises like the East Asian crisis to global financial integration is misguided. Blaming what he sees 'as a series of blunders' by states, the IMF and other actors in seeking to integrate markets into the global financial system, he argues that global financial integration over the last two decades has been and continues to be beneficial overall. The problem has been how integration is managed.

We will return to consider the arguments of the anti-globalization critics that Wolf engages with in more depth in chapter 10 but for the present I want to end this chapter by addressing the issue of how convincing Friedman and Wolf are in their positive conception of contemporary economic globalization.

Conclusion: progressive globalization or hyperglobalism revisited?

There can be no doubt that both Thomas Friedman and Martin Wolf have made high profile and influential contributions to the recent debate about globalization. Friedman's thinking has influenced a global audience and captured the imagination of policy makers, politicians, business leaders and academic thinkers. Similarly, Wolf's sensible and informed defence of globalization has attracted enormous attention for the considered manner in which he has countered some of the more extreme and ill-founded claims of anti-globalization critics. Taking the two together of course does each a disservice to some extent, but I want to argue in this final section that as leading positive advocates of neoliberal globalization and its benefits for global society, both share common strengths and weaknesses in their ideas. I identify four major areas of debate which have emerged in the critical response their work.

First is the issue of whether this is a hyperglobalist vision, more than an empirically grounded and intellectually rigorous argument. The hyperglobalists – in the language of David Held and others – paint a utopian vision of globalization as an unproblematic and unstoppable vehicle for integrating global society and economy, and tackling problems of poverty. Friedman's work more than Wolf's certainly echoes leading hyperglobalists of the 1990s like Kenichi Ohmae in terms of his enthusiasm for a conceptually ill-defined globalization. Friedman's 'flat world' thesis has been criticized for its reliance on selective case studies and anecdotes, more than on any generalized set of evidence. Whilst his cut on globalization is enthusiastic and certainly insightful as to the many positive transformations occurring in today's world, he also (sometimes perhaps naively) omits assessment of the downsides to some of these changes. Wolf is less rose-tinted in his view in this respect, and acknowledges the problems with globalization, but his counter-challenge to critics of globalization is more concerned to show how negative impacts are exaggerated than to offer detailed proposals for mitigating them.

Second, and probably more significant for many critics, is the unproblematic manner in which both Friedman and Wolf place their faith in liberal market economies and what can be loosely termed neoliberal theories. Friedman, for his part, rarely engages with the theoretical arguments which account for how economic globalization is producing positive outcomes, tending to take the positive effects of free trade, TNCs and economic integration for granted. Again it is Wolf who offers a far more theoretically sophisticated (and thus convincing) set of arguments for *why* neoliberal globalization creates wealth, reduces poverty, leads to international peace and encourages democracy. His arguments are founded in the classical market and trade theories of Adam Smith, David Ricardo and their lineage.

However, a range of social science critics from a variety of disciplines are less confident than Wolf in the conceptual and theoretical accuracy of markets and trading system. Perhaps most importantly, several leading thinkers including Joseph Stiglitz have questioned the veracity of this classical theoretical position on economic globalization. We will come back to consider his critique in some depth in the next chapter.

Third, Friedman's 'flat world' argument in particular can be criticized for lacking any clear conception of the role for social actors in this. *The World is Flat* is notable for the sense it conveys of multiple exterior processes and transformations driving forward globalization and producing solutions. Friedman's world is populated by his engaging and rich anecdotes about individuals, but he has little to say about how the many individuals he quotes are themselves part of the flattening process.

Fourth, and finally, Wolf's rebuttal of the anti-globalization movement's critique of neoliberal globalization almost certainly is guilty of caricaturing and generalizing radical critics of globalization in a manner that glosses over some of the more substantive criticisms. His argument about rising inequality, for example, is that the anti-globalization movement is wrong to criticize neoliberal globalization because aggregate figures show that parts of the developing world are narrowing the gap with the more developed economies. Such an argument is unlikely to impress many anti-globalization thinkers insofar as it to a large extent misses the subjective and politicized point that the growing gap between rich and poor is unacceptable, unjust and leading to social problems in wider society. Again Stiglitz's arguments are crucial here and it is therefore now the natural moment in our analysis to move on to his work.

Further reading

Works by Thomas Friedman

Friedman, T. (1999) *The Lexus and the Olive Tree*. London: Harper Collins.
Friedman, T. (2003) *Longitudes and Attitudes: The World in the Age of Terrorism*. (2nd edn). New York: Anchor Books.
Friedman, T. (2005) *The World is Flat: The Globalized World in the Twenty-First Century*. New York: Allen Lane.
Friedman, T. (2007) *The World is Flat: The Globalized World in the Twenty-First Century* (2nd edn). New York: Penguin.
Friedman, T. (2008) *Hot, Flat and Crowded: Why the World Needs a Disruptive Green Revolution*. New York: Allen Lane.

Website resources

A large number of Thomas Friedman's articles can be found on the *New York Times* website: www.nytimes.com

Works by Martin Wolf

Wolf, M. (2004) *Why Globalization Works*. Yale: Yale University Press.

9 REFORMIST THINKING: JOSEPH STIGLITZ

Introduction

There are few contemporary thinkers on globalization whose ideas have been more widely influential than Joseph Stiglitz. Since the publication of his international best-selling book *Globalization and Its Discontents* in 1999, Stiglitz has established himself as one of the leading thinkers on globalization and the future of this phenomenon in the early twenty-first century. The attention given by academics, politicians and policy makers to Stiglitz's ideas is largely accounted for by three factors: his academic prowess, the key policy job he held in the World Bank and US Clinton administration and his engaging, readable and clear writing style. He is certainly an academic with the highest credential – sharing the 2001 Nobel Prize for Economic Science with George Akerlof and A. Michael Spence – but also an individual who filled top jobs in key institutions at the very heart of the policy in the unfolding (economic) globalization of the late twentieth century. Stiglitz was the Chairman of President Clinton's Council of Economic Advisers during the 1990s and also the Chief Economist at the World Bank until 2000. Regardless of whether or not you share the ideological basis of Stiglitz's post-Keynesian thinking about the global economy, it is therefore hard to ignore the arguments of an individual with this track record.

It may seem a little strange that we only come to consider the ideas of Stiglitz at such an advanced stage of this book. Yet in the pathway I have mapped, it is most useful to turn to Stiglitz in light of having already considered both the more theoretical academic thinkers in the early chapters and the more applied policy arguments of thinkers like Friedman and Wolf. For in turning to Stiglitz, we arrive at someone who can be seen as the axiomatic thinker in our journey because in Stiglitz's work more than anywhere else there exists a detailed and wide-ranging set of both diagnoses of the problems with contemporary globalization, and also proposals for reforming the nature of globalization in the future. If earlier academic thinkers have helped us understand what globalization 'is', and the positive thinkers have made the classically grounded case for why it is a 'good' thing, then it is Stiglitz who can provide insight into the limits to the positive story about globalization and an explanation as to what needs to be done to improve how globalization develops to the benefit of a greater proportion of people on the planet. Stiglitz is not of course alone in offering arguments for 'alter-globalization', reformed global institutions or a critique of neoliberal economic globalization. It is not an exaggeration to suggest there are dozens of academic thinkers who make similar kinds of arguments or occupy similar 'reformist' positions in the globalization debate to Stiglitz. If this list were extended to popular commentators, it would doubtless run into hundreds. Yet for many 'pro-globalization' thinkers such as Friedman and Wolf, a large proportion of reformist contributions are either steeped in politicized ideology more than objective thinking or based on assertions supported by insufficient empirical evidence or intellectual rigour.

What sets Stiglitz apart, however, is that his arguments are much harder to refute in such a manner. His credentials both as an academic and senior policy adviser establish him as probably the most influential and heavyweight reformist thinker in the globalization debate. In this chapter, I argue that Stiglitz's thinking more than anyone else has pushed the globalization debate towards a new stage of sophistication. In particular, I suggest that it succeeds in transcending the simplistic and polarized 'pro' or 'anti' positions that much of the literature has struggled to escape. He does this by combining a detailed theoretical perspective on the nature of (economic) globalization and the global economy with a politically grounded and deeply pragmatic understanding of forces that have shaped the development of global interconnectedness since the end of the Second World War. Furthermore, I also argue that Stiglitz's balanced critique of both the neoliberal free market ideology behind economic globalization, and the anti-globalization response, represents one of the most comprehensive assessments of the nature of contemporary globalization and how it can and should be reformed. Thus, although there have been critiques to his intervention in the globalization debate – the main thrust of which being that his criticisms of neoliberal economic globalization are driven more by (neo-Keynesian) ideology than rigorous analysis – I suggest that much of this criticism is limited in scope and fails to substantially undermine his key arguments.

Before I examine these arguments further, however, it is important to provide some biographical background. Stiglitz was born in 1943 in the United States, and took his first degree at Amherst College. After a year at the University of Chicago, he went on to take a PhD in economics from MIT in 1967. Undoubtedly, the approach of MIT economics which focused on developing simple economic models that addressed 'big' relevant policy questions influenced his subsequent work. In 1969 he moved to Cambridge in the United Kingdom where he spent a year as a Fulbright fellow, before moving back to the United States to take a string of academic posts at Yale, Duke, Stanford and Princeton. He has also held a visiting professorship at Oxford University and currently holds a Chair in Economics at Columbia University where he also has simultaneous positions in the Business School and School of International and Public Affairs (SIPA). However, as already mentioned, since the late 1980s he has had a parallel career in public policy, notably serving in the Clinton Administration as the chair of the President's Council of Economic Advisers (1995–1997). This was followed by the period at the World Bank as Senior Vice-President and Chief Economist (1997–2000). Stiglitz is thus a relatively rare form of economist in that he combines a high degree of expertise in the more technical side of economics with a strong interest in broad and high profile policy questions. It is particularly significant to note in this respect, and in assessing his thought on globalization, that he was awarded the Nobel Prize for his joint work on asymmetric information in markets which is highly critical of many of the standard assumptions of neoclassical economics. His academic work therefore is quite heavily bound into the theoretical root of his arguments about the nature of neoliberal global economy.

The rest of this chapter now focuses on the sequential development of his ideas in his three key books published since the late 1990s. Thus, whilst it is relevant, it does not engage in any depth with his more specific academic research within economics. The next section outlines the main tenets of his arguments in the first of these – *Globalization and Its Discontents* – arguing that his diagnoses of some of the key problems of neoliberal globalization are hard to refute. The subsequent section then provides a brief oversight of the critical arguments made in the second book which are concerned with the more specific topic of the development of the US economy in the 1990s. Thereafter, the fourth section explores in depth the detailed proposals he outlines for reforming globalization in his third book, *Making Globalization Work*. Finally, the chapter ends by assessing the critical response and limitations of his thinking, and in particular considers whether Stiglitz's critics are right to fall back on the familiar criticism that his arguments are based more on ideological assertion than rigorous empirically informed analysis.

Globalization and its discontents

In late 1999 when the profile of globalization as an idea was becoming headline news around the world as a consequence of the protests at Seattle, Stiglitz published his first major book on the issue, *Globalization and Its Discontents*. Becoming a best-seller almost immediately, the book sought to critique the paradigm of American-led neoliberal globalization since the end of the Second World War, and especially of the preceding two decades. Stiglitz's focus is thus primarily on economic and political globalization, although other dimensions to the concept such as cultural globalization appear at times. His overarching proposition in the book is that, whilst globalization has brought many benefits in terms of development, poverty alleviation and the dissemination of new ideas, its proponents have been 'unbalanced' in proclaiming its universal success. While he thinks that 'those who vilify globalization too often overlook its benefits' (ibid.: 5), its proponents have seen globalization as progress per se with a view that 'developing countries must accept it if they are to grow and to fight poverty effectively' (ibid.: 5). Unfortunately, argues Stiglitz, 'to many in the developing world, globalization has not brought the promised economic benefits' (ibid.: 5); it has also failed to ensure stability and to protect the environment (ibid.: 6). Globalization is thus 'itself neither good nor bad', and 'has the power to do enormous good' but for some 'seems closer to an unmitigated disaster' (ibid.: 20). This then is the root of the discontent he seeks to diagnose, and his arguments in this respect can be divided into four main threads which I will deal with one at a time.

The global institutions

The primary contention of Stiglitz's critique is that the reason globalization has 'gone wrong' is because the supranational institutions that govern economic globalization are inadequate and in need of reform. His attention focuses on the three main global institutions in this respect: the International Monetary Fund (IMF), the World Bank and the WTO.

From the perspective of the later 1990s, Stiglitz argues that the IMF 'in its original conception was based on a recognition that markets often did not work well' and that there 'was a need for collective action at a global level for economic stability' (ibid.: 12). However, over the years 'the IMF has changed markedly' and 'champions market supremacy with ideological fervor' so that it pressures countries 'to engage in policies like cutting deficits, raising taxes, or raising interest rates that lead to a contraction of the economy' (ibid.: 13). This change occurred during the 1980s in the era of Thatcher and Reagan when, he argues, the IMF became a 'missionary institution'. His view is that 'whilst the IMF was supposed to focus on crises' it in fact became 'a part of life for most of the developing world' and took 'a rather imperialistic view' (ibid.: 14). The prognosis is that 'the IMF has failed in its mission' and 'not done what it was supposed to do – provide funds for countries facing an economic downturn' (ibid.: 15). Rather in the near hundred countries that have faced crises, 'IMF programs have not only failed to stabilize the situation, but have made matters worse, especially for the poor' (ibid.: 15). And whilst both the IMF and the World Bank have been concerned to provide countries 'with alternative perspectives on some of the challenges of development and transition', they were in fact 'both driven by the collective will of the G7' (ibid.: 14). With regard to the third institution – the World Trade Organization – the problem for Stiglitz is that the combination of neoliberal ideology and the lack of transparent representation in trade negotiations meant that trade agreements often reflected vested interests of countries in the global North rather than a fair set of regulations that would helping developing countries grow.

In sum, his contention is that all three of the global institutions that provide governance for globalization have failed to deliver economic growth and poverty reduction to a large proportion of the world. His view is that these organizations more often reflected the interests of the richer countries, and that the ideological basis of much of the policy and action was misguided. However, in fact the main force of this critique is directed towards one of the three: the IMF. To understand why he criticizes the IMF specifically, we need now to examine this neoliberal perspective and its accompanying policy framework in more depth.

Neoliberal ideology and the Washington Consensus

Stiglitz's argument in *Globalization and Its Discontents* is that the global institutions had become dominated by a misplaced neoliberal market fundamentalist ideology which became solidified in a set of policies known more widely as 'the Washington consensus'.

Considering the ideological issue first, I want to suggest there are three main features to this. First, ideologically the global institutions assumed that markets worked perfectly (when they did not) and thus attributed macroeconomic problems and crises with countries' economies such as unemployment or inflation to other factors – corrupt politicians or greedy unions for example (ibid.: 35). Drawing on his academic work in economics on imperfect information in markets, he argues the IMF in particular was mistaken in this view. Furthermore, he suggests that this ideology led to the abandonment of any notion of the IMF 'as a deficit financier, committed to maintaining economies at full employment'. The ideological position became obsessed with 'the pre-Keynesian position of fiscal austerity in the face of downturn' (ibid.: 38). Second, given the fundamentalist nature of this ideology, the IMF has been arrogant and tended 'to take a "one size fits all" approach'. Stiglitz argues that 'the problems of this approach became particularly acute when facing the challenges of the developing and transition economies' (ibid.: 34). In addition, the stance of the IMF was as 'the font of wisdom, the purveyor of an orthodoxy too subtle to be grasped by those in the developing world' (ibid.: 41). Third, this market ideology led the IMF 'to confuse means with ends, thereby losing sight of what is ultimately of concern' (ibid.: 27). In particular this applies to the relationship between inflation and unemployment where the IMF doggedly believed that inflation must be conquered at any cost for a country to grow, whereas Stiglitz contends it should have seen tackling inflation 'as a means to an end' which needed to be adjusted according to circumstances of the needs of developing economies.

In partial agreement with radical thinkers like Klein or Marcos (whose ideas we examine in the next chapter), his argument is that the ideological market fundamentalism outlined above produced a set of policies that were more hindrance than help in producing economic growth and development. Captured under the umbrella of the 'Washington consensus', Stiglitz suggests this policy framework has three major 'pillars', all of which 'became ends in themselves' (ibid.:

53), all of which were problematic and all of which should be regarded as 'failures'.

The first pillar was fiscal austerity. In its prioritization of containing inflation at any cost, Stiglitz argues that 'fiscal austerity [was] pushed too far' and often 'under the wrong circumstances'. Governments were pushed to cut public expenditure and during the 1980s the World Bank's *structural adjustment loans* became ideological tools to get developing countries to implement austerity measures. These measures, argues Stiglitz, 'can induce recession' and 'high interest rates may impede fledgling business enterprises' (ibid.: 54). Furthermore, as many other critics of structural adjustment have argued (e.g. Abouharb and Cingranelli 2007; SAPRIN 2004), the social hardships produced by fiscal austerity led to damaging civil strife, violence and worse in a number of developing countries. In sum, he argues that austerity 'pursued blindly, in the wrong circumstances, can lead to high unemployment and a shredding of the social contract' (Stiglitz 1999: 84).

Second was the pillar of privatization. Stiglitz argues that 'the IMF and the World Bank have approached the issue from a narrow ideological perspective – privatisation was to be pursued rapidly' (ibid.: 54). As a result, he suggests, it 'often did not bring the benefits that were promised' (ibid.). The problem was that 'the IMF simply assumed that markets arise quickly to meet every need when in fact many government activities arise because markets failed to provide essential services' (ibid.: 55). Rather than rapid privatization, he suggests that 'the moral is a simple one' – privatization needs to be part of a more comprehensive programme, which entails 'creating jobs in tandem with the inevitable job destruction that privatization often entails' (ibid.: 57). He argues that 'privatisation has made matters so much worse that in many countries . . . [it] is jokingly referred to "briberization"' (ibid.: 58). If the government is corrupt, argues Stiglitz, 'there is little evidence that privatization will solve the problem.'

Third, Stiglitz contends that liberalization – manifest as 'the removal of government interference in financial markets, capital markets and barriers to trade' (ibid.: 59) – has been pushed too far. In this respect, he argues that 'the liberalizing capital and financial markets contributed to the global financial crises of the 1990s and can wreak havoc on a small emerging country' (ibid.: 59). In particular, the IMF's ideological position on trade liberalization was misguided. With liberalization, this position assumes that, in line with theories of comparative advantage, liberalization will enhance a country's income by forcing resources to move from less productive uses to more productive ones. In this view, 'new, more productive jobs' will be created as inefficient industries close down and jobs are lost. Stiglitz argues that this is 'simply not the case' because countries lack capital and entrepreneurship to create new firms and jobs. In this respect, IMF liberalizing ideology has simply created unemployment (ibid.: 59–60). In addition, he points to 'the hypocrisy of those pushing trade liberalisation' as western countries push for liberalization for the products they exported whilst seeking to protect those sectors such as agriculture where developing countries might threaten their economies (ibid.: 60–1). However, if the problem with trade liberalization is the *way* that it has been implemented, then he argues that 'the case for financial liberalization was far more problematic' (ibid.: 64). He suggests that the consequences of the banking crises produced by overzealous deregulation are far greater for developing countries than developed ones, and the opening up of capital markets allowed speculative flows of money that prevented rather than facilitated development (ibid.: 65–7). In this respect, the IMF's simplistic belief that free markets are more efficient was highly problematic.

The need for reform

The mid-sections of *Globalization and Its Discontents* expand these key critical arguments about the failure of the global institutions to govern globalization effectively through consideration of several detailed examples. Stiglitz examines both the Russian transition to a market economy and the East Asian crisis in the 1990s, arguing that the lack of success in either managing this process or tackling the crisis respectively is bound into the limitations and ideology of the governance of globalization. However, for our purposes here it is more important to consider the arguments about what needs to change which he makes in this first book.

Stiglitz's argument in a nutshell is that 'globalization today is not working for many of the world's poor' (ibid.: 214) but that 'we cannot go back on globalization' and that 'it is here to stay' (ibid.: 222). In that respect, he is critical of the radical and anti-globalization critics who argue for abandoning globalization altogether. Rather, Stiglitz argues that globalization can be made to work better 'and not just for the well-off and the industrial countries, but for the poor and developing nations' (ibid.: 254). To do this, he contends that there needs to be four major areas of reform with respect to the global institutions and the governance of globalization.

The first dimension to reform concerns the IMF. He argues that the organization 'should limit itself to its core area, managing crises' and that 'it should no longer be involved [outside crises] in the economies of transition'. This is in part because 'other reforms that would enable it to promote democratic, equitable and sustainable development and transition are simply not forthcoming' (ibid.: 232). Forcing it back to its 'original mission' will partly solve the problem by making the IMF more accountable, but for Stiglitz it will not address the problems with its ideological and policy perspective.

The second dimension relates to economic stability. Stiglitz argues that 'something needs to be done to make the global economy more stable' (ibid.: 233). This involves a string of radical reforms to the international financial system which he groups into seven areas. The first is 'an acceptance of the dangers to capital market liberalization and short-term capital flows' and measures to restrict the huge cost externalities they impose (ibid.: 237). Second, he argues there is a need for bankruptcy reform 'that recognizes the special nature of bankrupt-cies that arise out of macroeconomic disturbances'. This amounts to a 'super Chapter Eleven' which represents 'a provision that expedites restructuring and gives greater presumption for the continuation of existing management' (ibid.: 237). This reform, he argues, would have the advantage 'of inducing more due diligence on the part of creditors' (ibid.). The third reform is that there needs to be 'less reliance on bailouts' which have not only failed to work but 'contributed to the problem' by 'reducing incentives for care in lending'. Improved bank-ruptcy arrangements should enable this to happen.

Fourth and fifth, he argues that there needs to be much improved banking regulation – 'both design and implementation' in developed and developing countries (ibid.: 238) – and that there must be improved risk management. With respect to the latter, he argues that exchange rate volatility poses 'an enormous risk' to countries, and that 'whilst the problem is clear, the solution is not' (ibid.: 238). Reform of the exchange rate system is thus needed and at the very least measures to help developing countries cope with this volatility such as a loan provision should be put in place. Sixth, there is also a need for 'im-proved safety nets' by which he means better unemployment benefits and welfare provision. Seventh, and finally, he argues that reform requires 'improved responses to crises' insofar as 'responses to future financial crises will have to be placed in a social and political context' (ibid.: 240). This entails a return 'to basic economic principles', rather than focusing on 'ephemeral investor psychology'. This would mean the IMF returning to 'its original mandate of providing funds to restore aggregate demand in countries facing an economic recession' (ibid.: 240).

The third dimension to reform that Stiglitz proposes is concerned with the role of the World Bank and development assistance. He argues that, in the past, governments largely only differed in their approach towards development around whether 'changes should be achieved through government-led planning or unfettered markets' but that 'in the end, neither worked' (ibid.: 242). For Stiglitz, 'development encompasses not just resources and capital but a transformation of society' (ibid.) and this requires a different approach. Development *assistance* needs in his view to abandon forms of *conditionality* that undermine the democratic process and shift towards *selectivity* that gives aid to countries 'with a proven track record, allowing them to choose their own development strategies and ending the micro-management of the past' (ibid.). Most significantly, he argued at this juncture that substantial debt relief is crucial if the poorest developing countries are to grow.

The fourth and final dimension of reform outlined in this first book concerns a need for substantial reform of the WTO and the trade agenda. Stiglitz suggests that the past bias and hypocrisy of the global North, and the US in particular, must end in favour of a fairer trade regime which opens markets up – especially in areas like agriculture and textiles – to the developing countries in order that they might grow (ibid.: 244).

We will return to Stiglitz's reforming agenda in his later work shortly but first we need to briefly consider his more specific arguments about the problems that 'market fundamentalism' created for both the US and wider global economy in the 1990s.

The roaring nineties

Stiglitz published *The Roaring Nineties* in 2003 as a direct critique of the bad governance of what he terms 'the greediest decade in history'. The target is 'market fundamentalism' and its subsequent consequences for the US – and by wider implication – the global economy. Much of the book is concerned with a detailed discussion of the 1990s' technology boom, corporate greed, the ideology of the Federal Reserve and the financial system in the US and is not of direct concern here. However, in terms of Stiglitz's wider thinking about globalization, we need to consider the way in which his arguments develop in this book. This centres around the argument that the US promoted 'the wrong kind of globalization' that served its own and not the global common interest – it therefore amounted to 'mismanaged globalization'. At least three key points are important.

First, he emphasizes the widely made point (Harvey 2003; Juhasz 2007; Smith 2005) that the US – particularly under the Bush adminis-tration – adopted a unilateralist approach to globalization which failed to recognize that 'globalization meant there was a need for countries of the world to work together, to address common problems' (ibid.: 333). Despite the mistakes of Clinton, Bush was thus 'a thousand times worse' (ibid.) as he 'walked away from treaty after treaty' and 'a disdain for the rule of [international] law' (ibid.: 334).

Second, regarding economic globalization, the Bush administration did not learn from the mistakes made by Clinton in the 1990s but rather 'made matters worse' (ibid.). It failed to develop effective cor-porate governance in the new era of globalization, allowing the con-tinuation of non-transparency and offshore financial centres which act as tax refuges in the global economic system (ibid.: 335) and enable companies and individuals to avoid regulations (ibid.: 336). For Stiglitz, perhaps worst of all was that 'America seemed to have suc-ceeded *in spite of bad corporate governance*' (ibid.: 339), setting a bad example to the rest of the world and developing nations in particular.

Third, in terms of the trade agenda, it 'built on discontent', not redressing it, and has shown little concern for global social justice. For example, the Bush administration bowed to the continued pressure for agricultural subsidy in the US (in complete contradiction to the sup-posed free market ideology of the Republican administration) and sought to protect its domestic markets in industries like steel (ibid.: 334). The Bush administration also 'stood adamant against the world in agreeing reform' of an unfair intellectual property regime (ibid.: 336). Thus, the Doha development round of negotiations stalled, although in part admittedly to equal resistance from Europeans.

Overall, in terms of his thinking about globalization, in *The Roaring Nineties* Stiglitz opens up a critical space to consider 'what kind of market economy' states might want to become in the global economy. He contests the notion that American capitalism since the 1990s and under the Bush administration is the best path for achieving growth and development and presents 'an alternative perspective to the view that there is a single form of market economy'. It is, however, in his next contribution that the shape of this other possible world is outlined in depth.

Making globalization work

In 2006, Stiglitz returned his attention to globalization as an issue per se with the publication of *Making Globalization Work*. The critical arguments concerning the problems with contemporary globalization remain broadly similar, if updated, to those made in earlier works, but in this book his arguments for the specific nature of the reforms needed are far more detailed. We will spend most of this section examining the latter, but there are a few aspects of his updated critique of globalization which need mentioning first.

Updating the critique of globalization

In this third book, Stiglitz reiterates his view that he believes 'globalization has the potential to bring enormous benefits to those in both the developing and developed world' (ibid.: 4), but that 'it has failed to live up to its potential' (ibid.: 4). And the issue he argues is one of politics. The ongoing discontent can thus be summarized across five issues. First, 'the rules of the game have largely been set by the advanced industrial countries' and 'they have not sought to create a fair set of rules'. Second, 'globalization advances material values over other values', such as a concern for the environment or life itself. Third, its management has 'taken away much of the developing countries' sovereignty' and 'undermined democracy'. Fourth, whilst advocates of globalization 'have claimed that everyone will benefit economically, there is plenty of evidence from developed and developing countries that there are many losers in both', and fifth, 'the economic system that has been pressed on the developing countries . . . is inappropriate and often grossly damaging' (ibid.: 9). Globalization 'should not mean the Americanization of either economic policy or culture, but it often does – and it has caused resentment' (ibid.).

For Stiglitz, one of the most pressing problems that is linked to this last issue is the way in which globalization has failed to make significant inroads in tackling global poverty. In essence, he says that income growth amongst the poorest people in the world has not been sufficient, and where there has been most success it is in fact not down to market fundamentalism or trickle-down economics, but in countries like China where economies are significantly managed (ibid.: 10–11). The task therefore is to make globalization work better.

Reforming Globalization II – the sequel

The lack of progress in reforming globalization is, for Stiglitz, understandable. The reason is that 'those who benefit from the current system will resist change, and they are very powerful' (ibid.: 13). He identifies only limited progress on this issue since his first call for reform in *Globalization and Its Discontents*, and refines his argument for reform around six areas: reducing poverty; aid and debt relief; fair trade; the limits to liberalization; protecting the environment; and, perhaps most importantly, tackling the 'flawed system of global governance' (ibid.: 13–19). Central to this final issue is the question of the future form of nation-states that have been overtaken by globalization. Stiglitz argues that globalization 'has resulted in the need for more collective action, for people and countries to act together to solve their common problems' (ibid.: 21). Too many issues – 'trade, capital, the environment – can be dealt with only at the global level'. Nation-states have been weakened, but 'there has yet to be created at the international level the kinds of democratic global institutions that can effectively deal with the problems globalization has created' (ibid.: 21). The issue is simply this: 'economic globalization has outpaced political globalization.' There is a need for 'strong global institutions' and this will require 'a change in mindset if we are to change the way globalization is managed'. He argues this change is already underway insofar as 'the debate is, to a large extent, no longer "anti" or "pro" globalization' (ibid.: 22) but rather how to 'restructure' globalization (ibid.: 24).

The arguments for reform he develops are detailed but broadly cover six areas, all of which in one way or another will require better global governance. First, he argues that there is a need for a new attitude to development. He suggests that successful development arises from a comprehensive approach that is concerned not just with 'providing resources and capital' and nurturing markets, but also creating 'the right mix of governments and markets' (ibid.: 47–9). This cannot be achieved without placing people and communities at the core of development with effective policies around, for example, education and health (ibid.: 50–3). However, it must also be coupled with the capacity of countries 'to use resources well' and 'take advantage of new opportunities' (ibid.: 54–5). The major factor influencing this is governance and he argues the West needs to help developing countries by doing two things: 'not undermining democracy' and 'doing more to reduce the opportunities for corruption, by limiting banking secrecy, increasing transparency, and enforcing anti-bribery measures' (ibid.: 56).

The second area of reform that is still needed concerns trade. Whilst Stiglitz acknowledges some progress in creating a fairer international trading regime, he argues there is further to go to shift both ideology and policy. For Stiglitz, the Doha development round has failed (ibid.: 81). Current trade arrangements 'are still not fair' and he proposes what he terms a series of 'pro-poor and pro-development reforms' so that 'a true development round' of trade measures can be created (ibid.: 83). Stiglitz argues that developing countries 'should receive "special and differential treatment"' whereby, for instance they are permitted 'to deviate from the most favoured nation principle by allowing lower tariffs on imports from developing countries'. The most important reform, however, he argues is simple: 'rich countries should simply open up their markets to poorer ones, without reciprocity and without economic or political conditionality' (ibid.: 83). He couples this with the contention that 'since the vast majority of those living in developing countries depend directly or indirectly on agriculture . . . eliminating agricultural subsidies and opening agricultural markets . . . would be of enormous benefit' (ibid.: 87). Aside from removing tariff barriers for developing countries (ibid.: 87–96), he further argues for reducing restrictions on labour migration, restricting bilateral trade agreements and addressing the failure of effective enforcement in the trading system by 'allowing developing countries, at least, to sell their [WTO] enforcement rights' (ibid.: 99).

The third area of reform is a familiar one: debt. *Making Globalization Work* reiterates and refines the argument of this earlier work. He reaffirms the persistent problem that 'developing countries borrow too much – or are lent too much – and in ways that force them to bear most or all of the risk of subsequent increases in interest rates, fluctuations in exchange rate or decreases in income' (ibid.: 212). He suggests that 'often the debtor country is blamed for borrowing too much when, in fact, the lenders share the blame' and 'the imbalance between sophisticated lender and the less knowledgeable recipient could not be starker'. The answer he argues is 'an expedited process of restructuring for private debts – money owed by private firms to foreign creditors – and a new, more balanced approach for public debts'.

This entails reform in five areas in relation to debt. First, Stiglitz argues for rich countries shifting to a principle of 'doing no harm' to developed countries in dealing with their debt (ibid.: 234–6). Second, there needs to be a return to counter-cyclical lending to offset the pro-cyclical pattern of private lending (ibid.: 236). Third, the risk of borrowing needs to be reduced so that developing countries should 'be able to do so in ways that shift the risk – including the risk of exchange and interest rate fluctuations – to developed countries' (ibid.). Fourth, borrowing must become conservative. Debt forgiveness must also be accompanied by a shift in borrowing by developing countries – they 'should borrow less – much less – than they have in the past' (ibid.: 213). Fifth, and finally, he argues for significant reform to international bankruptcy laws involving the creation of an international bankruptcy organization in the long term.

The fourth broad area of reform concerns natural resources and the environment. With regard to the former, Stiglitz argues globalization to date has locked developing countries in a 'natural resource curse'. The rich countries are more powerful than poorer developing ones and have thus won the fight to gain control over these resources. Often in the process, however, conflict and violence has been the consequence and democracy has been stifled in resource-rich poor countries (ibid.: 133–44). He argues that reform around a range of issues can reverse this situation, proposing an action agenda for the international community that involves making the extractive industries more transparent in their activities; reducing arms sales; the development of certification for resources like tropical hardwood; targeted financial assistance for developing country governments to provide incentives against corruption; a role for an international body to set norms to assess what fraction of the net value is going to a developing country; better incentives for transnational corporations to limit the environmental damage they do; and as with other areas, better enforcement against bad practice (ibid.: 155–9).

A further chapter of the book is devoted to the specific issue of global environmental problems which Stiglitz argues 'is unlike the other problems of globalization' (ibid.: 161) because it affects developed and developing nations alike. He suggests that 'the tragedy of the commons' that is eroding the earth's natural resources must be addressed, and most urgently with respect to global warming. He makes proposals for reform in two respects. First, he argues, if the Kyoto agenda of reducing emissions is to be pursued, then three things need to happen: 'if the US is to be to be brought along, then . . . developing countries must be included also' in a 'fair system of targets'; there needs to be a way of enforcing these targets; and that 'compliance will be much easier if the cost of reducing emissions is lowered' (ibid.:

174). However, Stiglitz proposes a second 'alternative framework' for reducing emissions. He argues that a system using the market mechanism will have a better prospect of engaging the US. His solution is 'make people pay for the full cost of what they do' by having 'all the countries of the world impose a common tax on carbon emissions' (ibid.: 181). This transfers the responsibility for reducing emissions onto firms and households and avoids the problems associated with national targets.

A fifth broad area concerns the need to reform the intellectual property regime. He argues that intellectual property 'is not an end in itself' (ibid.: 118) and that critics of globalization have been right to argue that the existing Trade Related Aspects of Intellectual Property regime (TRIPS) 'reflected the triumph of corporate interests in the US and Europe over the broader interests of billions of people in the developing world' (ibid.: 105). What is needed, he argues, is a regime that will 'enhance societal well-being by promoting innovation' (ibid.: 118). To achieve this, reform is needed around three issues. The first is to tailor intellectual property to the needs of developing countries which would involve 'separate intellectual property regimes for the least developed, the middle-income and the advanced industrial countries' (ibid.: 119). Second, life-saving drugs and medicines should be provided 'at cost' to developing countries, a system of 'compulsory licenses' should be extended to cover many drugs so they can be produced generically at low cost. Research into developing world diseases should also be supported by a 'global innovation fund' and 'purchase guarantees' from developed world governments to drugs companies to incentivize the development of drugs that will benefit developing countries (ibid.: 120–4). Third, he argues that the intellectual property of developing countries needs to be protected by developing a regime that prevents biopiracy and protects traditional knowledge with an international agreement and all countries signing up to the biodiversity convention (ibid.: 127).

Finally, the sixth broad area corresponds to an urgent need to better regulate TNCs and the global financial system. He contends that whilst corporations 'have been at the centre of bringing the benefits of globalization to the developing countries', they can also 'be blamed for much of its ills' (ibid.: 188). The issue is therefore 'what can be done to minimize their damage and maximize their net contribution to society' (ibid.: 188). He proposes a five-pronged agenda in this respect underlined by 'a simple objective: to align private incentives with social costs and benefits' (ibid.: 198). First, there needs to be stronger regulation of companies – corporate social responsibility is not enough (ibid.: 199). Second, and related, globalization has produced a 'globalization of monopolies' which 'requires a global competition law and a global competition authority to enforce it' (ibid.: 203). Third, corporate governance needs to be improved by making officers liable for their actions, improving the scope for firms to be sued outside their home territories and making judgements in foreign courts against reckless corporations enforceable worldwide (ibid.: 203–5). This should entail 'working toward the creation of international legal frameworks and international courts' (ibid.: 207). Fourth, and finally, advanced industrial countries need to take several actions 'to make it more difficult for corporations to get away with the worst kind of misdeeds' (ibid.: 208). This includes in particular removing scope for bank secrecy.

In relation to the global financial system, Stiglitz reignites an old argument made by Keynes in the 1930s in relation to the need for a global reserve system. He argues that the era of floating exchange rates where the US dollar has acted as the global reserve currency has created global financial instability (ibid.: 254–60). Instead, he proposes there is a need for the international community to 'provide a new form of fiat money to act as reserves' (ibid.: 260). This new 'global greenback' would solve 'the destructive self-logic of the current system, where the reserve currency country [the US] becomes increasingly in debt, to the point where its currency no longer serves as a good reserve currency' (ibid.:263).

Stiglitz and his critics: heavyweight theorist or neo-Keynsian ideologue?

It is not the task of this book to present a final position with respect to the major debates around the nature of globalization, nor to side with one perspective to the exclusion of all others. In this respect, whilst I have argued that Stiglitz represents one of the most influential and 'axiomatic' of globalization thinkers, this is not to suggest his thinking is either unquestioned or unproblematic. However, it is fair to state that the critical response to Stiglitz's many interventions in the globalization debate has largely been characterized by the ideological position of the audience. For many radical and reformist critics of globalization, Stiglitz is little short of a hero. His career and authority as a leading academic economist have given his thinking enormous influence in both academic and policy spheres. In contrast, many of his critics occupy a pro-market ideological position similar to Martin Wolf or Jagdish Bhagwati (Bhagwati 2004; Wolf 2004). Leading figures within the global institutions including the IMF have responded to the criticisms he levels at both their record and their ideological position. Other academic critics suggest that the popular and politicized interventions of the three of his books focused on in this chapter are based more on assertion and generalization than on the rigorous analytical work he won the Nobel Prize for (e.g. Stiglitz and Greenwald 1992; Stiglitz and Grossman 1980; Stiglitz 1985, 2000). Given Stiglitz's prominence, it is impossible to explore every criticism made here, but I want to end this chapter by identifying five broad lines of argument that share some common ground between different critics in both the academic and policy literature.

The first has just been mentioned – that his popularist thinking on globalization is more politicized assertion than argument based on rigorous research or evidence (Flanders 2002). To some extent this is valid. It is undoubtedly true that much of his writing on globalization is couched in subjective perspectives for which there is no final social scientific answer. Whether global social justice is desirable or not is a value judgement and doubtless some would not share it. However, Stiglitz does sometimes err into generalized claims about the failures of markets that probably need closer analysis. Certainly IMF respondents to his critique have pointed out that his presentation of a unified view of 'market fundamentalism' (supposedly dictating the actions of the institution) misrepresents the level of sophisticated understanding of the strengths and weaknesses of markets in the institutions. Others have questioned his representation of the cause of the problems with the Russian transition or the reasons for the success of China (Dabrowski et al. 2000).

Second, and related, it has also been suggested he underplays the complexity of politics and policy-making in development and the capacity for the global institutions to influence outcomes. Again, IMF respondents have argued that issues such as Russia's difficult transition from communism and the Argentine collapse were 'all very complex situations on which there was, and remains to this day, plenty of disagreement about the right policy response' (Dawson 2002). Whilst the IMF may share the blame for mistakes, many other actors were involved.

Third, a number of critics see Stiglitz's neo-Keynesian position as itself dogmatic. Many of these occupy a pro-market position, but the criticism again highlights the complexity of debates about the nature of markets themselves, and what role government and regulation need to play. Stiglitz's pro-interventionist stance is viewed by some as too crude and as overstating the benefits of intervention.

Fourth, as perhaps with many who propose reforms to globalization, some of Stiglitz's arguments have been criticized for being idealist, or at least politically unrealistic. This may be unfair criticism, but it is hard to find much discussion in his work of some of the more ambitious reforms such as his alternative agenda for tackling climate change or the global reserve system. His generalized calls for such reform lack much detail on how such systems would work in practice, and thus lack realism with respect to the nature of supranational policy-making.

Whether these lines of criticism are valid is debatable. What is certainly true overall is that, despite the protestations of some IMF figures, there has been surprisingly little rebuttal of the overarching arguments about the need for reforming globalization. At the time of writing, it is also true to say, in light of the deadlock in the Doha round of trade negotiations and the financial downturn and banking crises during 2008, many of his arguments look more timely than ever. It is also true that several of his proposed reforms – for example, tighter financial regulation, tackling offshore tax havens and even a global reserve currency – have been adopted or at least discussed at the 2009 meeting of the G20.

Further reading

Key texts on globalization by Joseph Stiglitz

Stiglitz, J. (1999) *Globalization and Its Discontents.* London: Penguin.
Stiglitz, J. (2003) *The Roaring Nineties: Why We are Paying the Price for the Greediest Decade in History*. London: Penguin.
Stiglitz, J. (2006) *Making Globalization Work*. London: Penguin.
Stiglitz, J. and Bilmes, L. (2008) *The Three Trillion Dollar War*. New York: W. W. Norton.

Website resources

Look at Stiglitz's own website of papers and other commentary pieces: www2.gsb.columbia.edu/faculty/jstiglitz/index.cfm

Commentaries and critical engagements

Dabrowski, M., Gomulka, S. and Rostowski, J. (2000) Whence Reform? A Critique of the Stiglitz Perspective. Available online at http://eprints.lse.ac.uk/20167/

Dawson, T. (2002) Stiglitz, the IMF and Globalization. Text of speech available at www.imf.org/external/np/speeches

Flanders, S. (2002) Is Stiglitz Right? *Prospect Magazine* (August).

10 RADICAL THINKING: NAOMI KLEIN, GEORGE MONBIOT AND SUBCOMANDANTE MARCOS

Introduction

If Joseph Stiglitz has 'become a hero of the anti-globalization movement', then its original heroine is undoubtedly Naomi Klein. In terms of our understanding of thought on globalization, her position is one of considerable importance as probably the highest profile 'radical' thinker in the global North. I use the term 'radical' of course with a degree of caution insofar as it is used in much of the globalization literature to describe a certain ideological position, usually informed by Marxism. Such a definition holds to some extent but the degree to which radical thought necessitates significant difference from other strands of reformist or alter-globalization thinking is more complicated. We will address this issue shortly, but what is clear to begin with is that Naomi Klein is a central figure in this critical strand to the globalization literature, witnessed by the fact that she has both championed and been to some extent active in the anti-globalization movement. Certainly her best-selling book, *No Logo: Taking Aim at the Brand Bullies* (2000), attracted enormous attention and has been viewed as one of the key readings for the anti-globalization movement.

The task of this chapter is thus to address how 'popular' radical thinking such as that of Klein fits into the jigsaw of different perspectives that have been covered thus far in this book. After the academic analyses in the earlier chapters, the last two chapters have been concerned with thinking that has been journalistic in its written style and aimed at a wide popular audience. Whilst Stiglitz is an academic, I argued that his major contributions to globalization thought fall into this more popularist category. In that respect, we continue here down a path followed in the preceding two chapters as we move through popular thinking based around a broadly pro-market, pro-globalization Wolf–Friedman position to Stiglitz's more critical 'middle ground' reformist position. It is therefore a natural progression to next consider radical popular thinking which occupies a more overt 'anti-globalization' position. Hereafter, we will continue to consider radical thinking on globalization, but will return to more academic thought in the next chapter in considering the work of the Italian Marxist thinkers, Michael Hardt and Antonio Negri.

Having suggested, however, that Naomi Klein will be the entry point for this chapter, I want to adopt an explicitly broader remit in this chapter than in earlier ones by also considering the work of several other popularist 'radical' thinkers. The reason for this relates to the diffuse nature of radical popular thought on globalization, and to the fact that, if I focused purely on Klein's thinking, the breadth and scope of radical thought on globalization would be misrepresented. In this respect, this chapter also tries to broaden its discussion of radical thinking by considering the ideas of the journalist/writer George Monbiot and the Zapatista spokesman-leader Subcomandante Marcos. Both of these thinkers have made a significant 'popular' contribution to this diffuse field of radical thinking on globalization and to the ideological basis that informs the equally diffuse (and indeed questionable) 'anti-globalization' movement. Put in its most succinct terms, the ideological common thread which runs thorough all of these thinkers' work is strong opposition to neoliberal economic globalization, its institutions and effects in recent decades. Whilst different thinkers have different foci for this strong critique – for example, social injustice, environmental degradation, development or poverty – all have argued in one way or another for a radically different form of globalization than currently exists. Often united under the anti-globalization movement's caption 'another world is possible' (George 2004), each of these thinkers has sought to argue that contemporary globalization has produced some highly undesirable consequences and that world society and economy need to follow a different path in the future.

The key issue that emerges from such radical thinking is, of course, what kind of alternative world is both possible and indeed desirable. I will argue in this chapter that whilst this general position unites much radical thinking on globalization, such radical thinking has to date struggled to provide a feasible blueprint for this other world. Despite several attempts to overcome this issue, one of the key problems is that much radical thinking finds it difficult not to draw the conclusion that the global capitalist economy should be replaced by another kind of system. Yet few detailed proposals for an alternative to the global market economy have emerged and, in that sense, much radical thinking on globalization often tends to slip back to some kind of reformist position. There is in other words a general consensus amongst many thinkers on the nature of the problems with globalization, but rather less on what kind of alternative is needed.

We begin therefore by considering in depth the arguments made by Naomi Klein. The next section provides an overview of the principal elements of her propositions in *No Logo* before the third section turns to examine her more recent work which has been more directly focused on critiquing (economic) globalization around the ideas of 'disaster capitalism' and 'the shock doctrine'. In the fourth section, the chapter moves on to examine the arguments of George Monbiot and Subcomandante Marcos. It examines Monbiot's proposition about the 'age of consent' and his radical proposals for new forms of global governance. In turning to the ideas of Marcos, the focus is the development of his Marxian arguments in his capacity as the leading spokesperson for the Zapatista movement in southern Mexico. In particular, the section focuses on his critique of neoliberalism and the impact of economic globalization on the world's poorest people. The final section then seeks to draw together a general critical appraisal of all three thinkers, identifying a number of ongoing potential difficulties in their thinking.

Naomi Klein and *No Logo*

Naomi Klein was born in Montreal in 1970 and has a family history of broadly left-wing activism. Her grandfather was sacked for union organizing activity at Disney in the US and her father was an active campaigner against the Vietnam War. She was educated at the University of Toronto where she edited the university student newspaper and began a career in journalism. Her first position was on *The Toronto Star* where she wrote *No Logo,* published in 2000. Having risen to international prominence, she now writes for a wide range of newspapers as a columnist in North America and Europe, including the *New York Times, The Nation* and the *Guardian* in the UK. She has also since held an academic position as a Miliband Fellow at the

London School of Economics in 2002, and is regularly a guest lecturer at universities around the world. Aside from written journalism, she has also branched into film-making with an award-winning documentary on Argentine factory workers which was released in 2004.

The central argument that Klein proposes in *No Logo* is that transnational corporations have too much power and influence and that through the power of brands they are producing a version of globalization that is leading to 'the surrender of education and culture to marketing' and 'an assault on the three pillars of employment, civil liberties and civil space' which amounts to 'corporate rule' (ibid.: xxi). A key facet of this is the way in which corporations, 'far from levelling the global playing field with jobs and technology for all', are rather 'in the process of mining the planet's poorest back country for unimaginable profits' (ibid.: xvii). Furthermore, she suggests that this corporate power is producing 'an anti-corporate politics' which is 'capturing the imagination of the next generation of troublemakers' (ibid.: xix). This activism is 'sowing the seeds of a genuine alternative to corporate rule' (ibid.: xxi).

The book is divided into sections that tackle this argument around four dimensions which make use of a wide range of anecdotes, examples and case studies to support her contentions. The first of these sections is entitled 'No Space' and it provides a historical account of the role of brands in the rise of corporate power. For Klein, brands are invidious and negative cultural vehicles that in effect dupe (especially young) people to lead 'a sponsored life' with 'ingenious gimmicks' (ibid.: 12). Brands have developed into a 'virus' form which companies send 'out into the culture via a variety of channels' that sell people a lifestyle experience often disconnected from the actual product (ibid.: 22). Nineties-style branding, she argues, increasingly seeks to associate brands with 'a lived reality' that has led 'to the branding of entire neighbourhoods and cities' (ibid.: 38). The media, film, pop music, sport and youth culture have thus been overrun and recruited to the branding activities of large corporations, producing a 'loss of space' which 'happens inside the individual; it is a colonization not of physical but mental space' (ibid.: 66). Klein is in effect arguing that (young) people's identity is being repressed in a near Orwellian (or Althusserian) nightmare of corporate control through branding. She develops this argument through an analysis of the incursion of branding in North American schools and universities (ibid.: 87–105), and contends that they need to be 'protected' in much the same way as 'national parks and nature reserves' (ibid.: 105). The final chapter in the first section turns its attention to the way in which branding has reinforced a regressive attack on the civil rights and feminist movements.

In the second part of the book, the argument moves to the impact of the growing concentration of corporate power in large transnational firms on individual choice. She argues that 'market-driven globaliza-tion doesn't want diversity but in fact quite the opposite' (ibid.: 129). This 'assault on choice is taking place on several fronts at once' in a 'structural' sense through 'mergers, buyouts and corporate synergies' and locally as 'a handful of superbrands use their huge cash reserves to force out small and independent businesses' (ibid.: 130). It is also 'happening on the legal front, with entertainment and consumer-goods companies using libel and trademark suits to hound anyone who puts an unwanted spin on a pop-cultural product' (ibid.) For Klein, this is an 'Orwellian' oppression of 'cultural production and public space'. Communities watch as 'lively downtown[s] hollow out, as big box discount stores with 70,000 items on their shelves set up in the periph-ery' (ibid.). Such transformations, she argues 'are much more than changes to the way we shop' (ibid.: 140), rather representing a key shift as culture is overtaken by brands and the corporations. In essence this is consumption run amok, as 'brand-obsessed shoppers have adopted an almost fetishistic approach . . . in which the brand name acquires a talismatic power' (ibid.: 141).

The third part of *No Logo* turns to consider the impact of corporate and brand power on employment and the nature of jobs. Klein's central contention here is that the rise of brands has devalued the 'actual manufacturing process' and by association those jobs that are involved in this process. The people making branded goods in the logic of the corporations 'are likely to be treated like detritus' (ibid.: 197), made all the worse by processes of outsourcing and off-shoring. She points to manufacturing plant closures in North America and other developed economies, arguing the corporations are not interested in maintaining or creating jobs at all (ibid.: 202), and to 'export produc-ing zones' (EPZs) in developing countries in Asia and Central America. She argues that, far from generating wealth for developing nations, these EPZs have poor work conditions and wages which have 'concen-trated and isolated' manufacturing in the global economy 'as if it were toxic waste' (ibid.: 203). Thus, 'rich and supposedly law-abiding mul-tinational corporations' have regressed 'to nineteenth-century levels of exploitation' (ibid.: 212). She also cites evidence of exploitation of workers in these 'sweatshop' zones, especially of women, and repres-sion of attempts at labour and union organization. Thus, for Klein, the idea that the shift of manufacturing to developing nations is a 'myth' where real development as a consequence of this globalization is a 'mirage' (ibid.: 226). Furthermore, in producing global branded goods, many firms 'have escaped the need to pay a living wage' to the workers who produce those goods (ibid.: 236–7). However, the final stage to Klein's argument is to argue that the transition to service sector jobs in America and other advanced economies has also been a negative one for many workers. Her argument in essence is that many service sector jobs are casual, low paid and low quality, filled disproportionately by young people (ibid.: 232–45). Overall, Klein expresses the negative perspective on EPZs and the new international division of labour that Wolf in particular has sought to counter.

In the fourth and final part of the book, Klein completes her analysis with what is in effect both an analysis of existing resistance to these forces of corporate and brand rule, and also a call to arms. She begins with a discussion of 'culture jamming' and 'adbusting', arguing that this undercurrent represents an ongoing form of resistance to the advance of the brands and corporate rule. The book also discusses street protests in the US and Europe, suggesting that, as 'anti-corporate' rage takes hold, 'the resistance will be as transnational as capital' (ibid.: 322). There will be more direct attempts at action 'to take on multinational corporations' through shareholder lobbying and campaigns (ibid.: 325–43) and, most effectively in Klein's view, there will be 'anti-brand campaigns' that 'have succeeded in rattling their corporate targets, in several cases pushing them to substantially alter their policies' (ibid.: 365). In discussing the cases of Nike, Shell and McDonalds respectively, Klein's conclusion at the end of *No Logo* is that anti-corporate campaigns have their limits. Alternative brands run the risk of being subsumed by the very thing they wish to resist, and so any solutions to the problem of corporate power have to be political. Thus, 'political solutions – accountable to people and enforceable by their elected representatives – deserve another shot before we throw in the towel and settle for corporate codes, independent monitors and the privatization of our collective rights as citizens' (ibid.: 442). This entails thinking about 'the possibilities for a truly globally minded society, one that would include not just economics and capital, but global citizens, global rights and global responsibilities as well' (ibid.: 442). How this is to be achieved, however, is not developed further in this first book.

Klein's subsequent critiques of globalization

It is not an overstatement to suggest that the impact of *No Logo* has been substantial in the last decade. Aside from establishing Klein as one of the leading anti-globalization spokespeople, it also became an emblematic text for the anti-globalization movement. Yet the scope and emphasis of *No Logo*, with its primary concern for brands and a subtext of the cultural oppressiveness of globalization, does not in many ways make it an engagement with the mainstream of the globalization debate. It is striking that, as a globalization 'best-seller' published at a similar time to Stiglitz's *Globalization and Its Discontents*, it addresses virtually none of the same themes or topics. However, Klein has subsequently consolidated and widened her thinking to what we might understand to be the full breadth of the globalization debate in two further books and it is these I now want to examine.

Fences and windows

Klein's (2002) book *Fences and Windows* carries the subtitle, *Dispatches from the Front Lines of the Globalization Debate*, but is not, she suggests, 'a follow-up to *No Logo*'. Rather the book is a collection of her articles and speeches which, whilst diverse, she suggests share several common themes. The first is captured in the idea of the fence, both as something desirable and also undesirable. Undesirable fences are manifest in the 'barriers separating people from previously public resources, locking them away from much needed land and water' and 'restricting their ability to move across borders'. Furthermore, there are barriers to expressing 'political dissent', to demonstrating on public streets and which even keep 'politicians from enacting policies that make sense for the people who elected them' (ibid.: xviii). She argues that 'some of these fences are hard to see, but they exist all the same' and that 'fences have always been part of capitalism' (ibid.: xix), but that 'the double standards propping up these fences have, of late, become blatant' (ibid.). Conversely, however, the latter category of 'necessary fences are under attack' (ibid.: xix). In this group, she includes 'the barriers that once existed between many public and private sector spaces – keeping advertisements out of schools . . . profit-making interests out of healthcare, or news outlets for acting purely as promotional vehicles for their owner's other holdings' (ibid.).

The consequence of these fences becoming more blatant, Klein argues, is that 'globalization is now on trial because on the other side of all these virtual fences are real people, shut out of schools, hospitals, workplaces, their own farms, homes and communities' (ibid.: xxi). 'Fences of social exclusion . . . can discard an entire industry . . . write off an entire country' or 'in the case of Africa, essentially an entire continent can find itself exiled to the global shadow world'. She argues that in fact 'remarkably few of globalization's fenced-out people turn to violence', preferring to move, only then to face real fences 'in the gated factories and refugee detention centres' (ibid.: xxiii). For her, the 'seductive borderless world' is 'a brutal model of globalization' and anti-globalization (or whatever it is termed) represents the opening up of what Subcomandante Marcos terms a 'crack in history' – new windows for a different kind of world (we will consider more of Subcomandante Marcos's thinking shortly).

The rest of the book gathers articles that address these arguments around four themes. The first is concerned with what is happening to democracy in the era of globalization, examining the negative consequence of free-trade agreements, IMF policies and attacks on trade unions. It also includes a range of pieces dealing with the problems of marketization, and in particular the loss of the 'global commons' through genetic modification, patents and intellectual property legislation favouring large corporations. The second part then turns to what Klein argues is an attempt to criminalize and suppress dissent against (neoliberal) globalization, examining border policing, growing surveillance and infiltration of resistance organizations. In the third part, the articles included focus more specifically on what she sees as the assault on civil liberties and freedoms in the supposed fight against terrorism in the post-9/11 world. The final part then moves on to examine what she suggests represents the potential window for change, in particular considering how the anti- or alter-globalization movement might be democratized through the World Social Forum and how the call to action instigated by the Zapatistas in Mexico can be repeated across the globe as a means to create 'another world'.

Disaster capitalism

If *Fences and Windows* represents a wide-ranging set of thoughts on different aspects of how contemporary (neoliberal) globalization needs to be resisted and changed, then her most recent book, *The Shock Doctrine: The Rise of Disaster Capitalism* (2007), represents a consolidation of her thinking around the nature of contemporary globalization and the ideological position that underpins it. The central thesis of the book – somewhat concealed in hyperbole – is essentially a critique of right-wing conservative politics and neoliberal economic ideology taken in combination. The inspirational target for Klein in this critique is the Chicago School and its leading guru, the recently deceased economist Milton Friedman. It is to Friedman she attributes 'the core tactical nostrum' which she terms 'the shock doctrine' (ibid.:

6). It is based on Friedman's (famous) argument that 'only a crisis – actual or perceived – produces real change' and that when that crisis occurs 'the actions that are taken depend on the ideas that are lying around' (ibid.: 6). Her central thesis is that 'for three decades Friedman and his colleagues had been perfecting this very strategy' so that when a major crisis occurred they could perpetrate market fundamentalism by 'selling off pieces of the state to private players while citizens were still reeling from the shock, then quickly making their "reforms" permanent' (ibid.: 6). She argues Friedman and his Chicago School learnt this tactic from his experience advising the Chilean dictator General Pinochet, coining the phrase 'economic shock treatment'. This shock therapy, she argues, has become 'the method of choice' when governments 'have imposed sweeping market-reform programmes' (ibid.: 7). The most recent example is the Bush administration's approach to Iraq since 2003. Her contention is therefore that, 'seen through the lens of this doctrine, the past thirty-five years look very different' (ibid.). The shock doctrine thesis thus represents a recasting of Klein's conception of the nature of contemporary globalization.

The key argument that Klein develops from this analysis is ambitious and far-reaching. Put simply, she contests the idea 'that the triumph of deregulated capitalism has been born of freedom' and 'that unfettered free markets go hand in hand with democracy' (ibid.: 18). Rather, she argues, 'this fundamentalist form of capitalism has consistently been midwifed by the most brutal forms of coercion, inflicted on the collective body politic as well as on countless individual bodies' (ibid.). In this view, 'the history of the contemporary free market – better understood as the rise of corporatism – was written in shocks' (ibid.: 19). She is careful to qualify the use of the term 'shock' in this hypothesis. Notably, she states that she is 'not arguing that all forms of market systems are inherently violent' and that 'it is eminently possible to have a market-based economy that requires no such brutality and demands no such ideological purity' (ibid.: 20). The target then is market fundamentalism, manifest as 'a desire for unattainable purity, for a clean slate on which to build a re-engineered model society' (ibid.: 20).

The book develops this contention at some length through seven parts which tackle different aspects of her thesis. The first part suggests that this ideological position was influenced by the science of shock interrogation which was developed by the CIA in the Cold War and which has become an established paradigm that informed the rationale behind the Guantanamo Bay detention camp after 9/11. She argues that the idea behind this form of shock interrogation method was that 'by shocking . . . patients into a chaotic regressed state' it would 'create the preconditions' for a 'rebirth into healthy model citizens' (ibid.: 47). The contention developed is that this underlying idea has permeated the ideology of disaster capitalism and interventions like the Iraq War – 'the fervent belief in the redemptive powers of shock' (ibid.: 48). The problem, suggests Klein, is that it does not work and just leads to destruction. She then integrates this discussion of shock interrogation methods into her analysis of the economic ideology of Friedman and the Chicago School, arguing that in a similar vein Friedman believed that 'when the economy is highly distorted, the only way to reach [the] prelapsarian state was to deliberately inflict painful shocks' (ibid.: 50). This fundamentalist idea is based on the 'closed loop' faith that 'the free market economy is a perfect scientific system' so that if something goes wrong, 'it has to be because the market is not truly free' (ibid.: 51). This ideological perspective had its moment when the Keynesian interventionist state appeared to enter crisis in the 1970s, and the Chicago School advocated economic shocks to the system of rapid deregulation, privatization and free market radicalism. Significantly, she argues that the political and economic arguments of shock ideology came together to produce the US-backed coup in Chile in 1973, as a first experiment in shock-based regime change (ibid.: 66–71).

This 'road-testing' for the shock doctrine is the concern of the second part of the book. In assessing the Chilean coup led by General Pinochet in the early 1970s, Klein points to the key role of Friedman and the Chicago School in advising Pinochet on how to run the Chilean economy. Her point is that, despite the fact that the shock treatment did not work – 'in the first year of Friedman-prescribed shock therapy, Chile's economy contracted by 15 percent' (ibid.: 83) – Pinochet's team were undeterred and used Chile as a laboratory to test Friedman's 'more experimental theories'. Klein argues that Chile's subsequent success was mythological and 'the facts behind the "Chilean miracle" remain a matter of intense debate' (ibid.: 85). What is worse still, she suggests, is that the Chilean laboratory soon became the seed for a spreading of shock-doctrine ideas. Klein contends that this ideology was linked by implication to the Argentine junta's killing and torturing of opponents to the regime in the late 1970s. In this respect, she argues, 'the Chicago School Project in Latin America was quite literally built on the secret torture camps where thousands of people who believed in a different country disappeared' (ibid.: 115). Yet she also argues that neoliberal ideology 'was cleansed of its crimes' by a separation of 'the shock of the torture chamber' from 'economic shock treatments' (ibid.:

118). The issue was that 'by focusing on human rights abuses and not the reasons behind them, the human rights movement also helped the Chicago School ideology to escape from its first bloody laboratory virtually unscathed' (ibid.: 118). The consequence for Klein is that 'these days, we are once again living in an era of corporatist massacres, with countries suffering tremendous military violence alongside organized attempts to remake them into model "free market" economies' and that 'once again the goals of building free markets, and the need for such brutality, are treated as unrelated' (ibid.: 128).

The third part turns then to examine how this shock doctrine was transmitted to advanced western democracies where it was much harder to implement. Klein contends that, in the case of the UK in the early 1980s, Margaret Thatcher was able to introduce neoliberal policies as a consequence of the shock effect of the Falklands (Malvinas) War. Klein argues that the poll boost the Thatcher government gained turned around its political fortunes (although in fact the electoral evidence for this is highly debatable). The contention is that 'Thatcher's successful harnessing of the Falklands War was the first definitive evidence that a Chicago School economic program did not need a military dictatorship and torture chambers in order to advance' (ibid.: 139). This was reinforced by the advice received by the Bolivian government in the mid-1980s from Harvard economist Jeffrey Sachs on how to tackle the country's hyperinflation. The lesson that emerged from this, and from tackling the 1980s' debt crisis in Latin America, was that this neoliberal shock doctrine could work in democracies if it moved 'deftly from crisis to crisis, expertly exploiting the desperation of economic emergencies to push through policies that would tie the hands of fragile new democracies' (ibid.: 168).

The fourth part draws the Tiananmen Square massacre in China in 1989 and Poland's transition to a free market economy in the early 1990s into this narrative. In the case of the former, she argues that 'in China, democracy and Chicago School economics were not proceeding hand in hand; they were on opposite sides of the barricades surrounding Tiananmen Square' (ibid.: 184). This was in direct contradiction to Francis Fukuyama's claim 'that democratic and "free market reforms" were a twin process, impossible to pry apart' (ibid.: 184). With respect to the latter, shock therapy 'caused a full blown depression' and many policies were reversed but yet Poland was 'still held up as a model' (ibid.: 193). The rest of the chapters in this section variously argue that the shock thesis can be equally applied to South Africa, Russia and the Asian economies.

The remaining three parts of the book turn to more recent history and expound the central arguments about the ideological nature of contemporary disaster capitalism. In many ways, aside from the first couple of chapters, this is the heart of the book with much that precedes acting as a preamble for arguments that are most clearly articulated here. At least six key arguments emerge across these chapters, and I will try to summarize them briefly. First, she argues that in the US, the Bush administration (with Donald Rumsfeld as a key architect) used the aftermath of 9/11 to instigate a new homeland security regime that 'forms the basis for a disaster economy' (ibid.: 288–300). This represented a kind of perverse Keynesian intervention where the homeland security industry facilitated 'a domestic form of shock therapy'. The Bush administration 'moved quickly . . . to push through its radical vision of hollow government in which everything from war fighting to disaster response was a for-profit venture' (ibid.: 298). Although the stated goal was to fight terrorism, 'the effect was the creation of the disaster capitalism complex – a full-fledged new economy in homeland security, privatized war and disaster reconstruction' (ibid.: 299).

Second, this new economy represented 'a corporatist state' where 'you have big business and big government combining their formidable powers to regulate and control the citizenry' (ibid.: 307). This is intrinsically bound to the global dimension, because it is impossible 'to separate the military project – endless war abroad – and a security state at home from the interests of the disaster capitalism complex'.

Third, Klein finds no clearer evidence to support this contention than the war in Iraq. She argues that 'the invasion and the occupation were two part of a unified strategy' where 'the initial bombardment was designed to erase the canvas on which the model nation could be built' (ibid.: 331). The fact that this has not worked in terms of creating a peaceful Iraq 'cannot be reduced either to the incompetence and cronyism of the Bush White House or to the sectarianism or tribalism of Iraqis' (ibid.: 351). For Klein, it was rather 'a very capitalist disaster' (ibid.: 351) with contemporary Iraq 'a creation of the fifty-year crusade to privatize the world'.

Fourth, one of the key consequences of the Iraq War was that 'the longer it wore on, the more privatized the foreign presence became, ultimately forging a new paradigm for the way wars are fought and how human catastrophes are responded to' (ibid.: 377).

Fifth, of particular relevance in relation to globalization, Klein suggests this model 'for privatized war and reconstruction' quickly became 'export ready'. In the final part of the book she thus argues that the international response to the East Asian tsunami, Hurricane Katrina in New Orleans and ongoing crises in the Middle East peace process have all been shaped by this model.

Sixth, and finally, in the conclusion to the book, Klein argues that there has been a globalized backlash to the shock doctrine in recent years and that it is 'wearing off'. This backlash has taken on a 'hopeful form' in Latin America where people are 'picking up the project that was so brutally interrupted' in the 1970s and early 1980s (ibid.: 453). Aside from the elections of progressive leaders like Chavez in Venezuela and Morales in Bolivia, she contends that the regions' 'most significant protection from future shocks . . . flows from the continent's emerging independence from Washington's financial institutions' (ibid.: 455). She suggests that this transformation reaches further as both the credibility and capacity to intervene of the IMF, World Bank and WTO have now been undermined. This 'revolt against neoliberalism' (ibid.: 458) offers a different model for reconstruction in the aftermath of events like the Boxing Day tsunami that does not seek 'to wipe the slate clean' and 'build model states', but rather use 'the rubble that is all around' (ibid.: 466). This alternative to disaster capitalism is 'radical only in [its] intense practicality, rooted in communities' and involves 'taking what's there and fixing it . . . making it better and more equal' (ibid.). It is the basis for ongoing radical resistance to neoliberal disaster capitalism and provides the context for her vision of 'another possible world'.

More radical thinking: George Monbiot and Subcomandante Marcos

We will come to consider the potential problems with Naomi Klein's thinking about globalization shortly, but first I want to briefly consider a couple of other significant contributions to radical thinking about globalization. The rationale for this relates to the wider goal of covering a broader set of radical ideas on globalization than just Klein's. As I suggested at the start of the chapter, whilst Klein's radical thinking on globalization has been widely disseminated, she does not address the full diversity of issues addressed in radical thought. It is therefore important to consider at least a couple of contrasting radical thinkers in order to gain an understanding of the scope of radical thought more generally. In this section, I therefore examine the ideas of two further thinkers. The first, George Monbiot, is another journalist writer based in the United Kingom who has made a number of interventions in the globalization debate, taking a rather different ideological perspective from Klein. The second, Subcomandante Marcos, is one of the leading radical thinkers on globalization from the Global South and, as a former leading Zapatista activist, he comes from a rather different background to that of Naomi Klein.

Monbiot – radical idealism about 'another world'

The British journalist writer George Monbiot has made several significant contributions to radical thinking in the globalization debate, although here I want to focus on his arguably most influential and sustained contribution concerning how the political order needs to be reformed in the contemporary world. Monbiot was born and grew up in Britain, taking a first degree at Oxford. Much of his work reflects his strong environmental interest, and in this respect he has also held a series of academic positions as a visiting fellow or professor at the universities of Oxford, Bristol, Keele and East London. He is currently a visiting professor of planning at Oxford Brookes University.

His most important contribution to thinking about globalization came in his 2003 book, *The Age of Consent: A Manifesto for a New World Order*. In this book, Monbiot outlines what he admits – in political terms to most people – amounts to a set of 'repulsive proposals' about how the world political system needs to be reformed to deal with the nature of contemporary world economy and society. The arguments made are by any measure considerably more radical and far-reaching than those made by a reformist thinker such as Stiglitz. The overarching argument he develops is that 'everything has been globalized except our consent' insofar as 'democracy alone has been confined to the nation-state' (ibid.: 1). The result is that for Monbiot in the present world 'a handful of men in the richest nations use the global powers they have assumed to tell the rest of the world how to live.' This amounts to 'an age of coercion' which needs to be replaced by 'an age of consent' (ibid.).

Monbiot starts with what should now be a familiar position in the globalization debate that on the one hand 'globalization is establishing a single, planetary class interest' as well as 'breaking the local bounds which sustained local communities' and destroying 'geographical loyalties', whilst on the other 'it has placed within our hands the weapons we require to overthrow the people who have engineered it and assert our common interest' (ibid.: 9). The 'global dictatorship of vested interests has created the means of its own destruction' because 'by expanding its own empire through new communication and transport networks, it has granted the world's people the means by which they can gather and coordinate their attack' (ibid.: 9). For Monbiot, those in the anti-globalization movement who adopt an 'anti-power' position are misguided as 'global governance will take place whether we participate in it or not' (ibid.: 12). The answer is 'to harness the power of globalization' by 'overthrowing its institutions and replacing them with our own' (ibid.: 15).

Monbiot argues therefore that what is needed is 'a global democratic revolution' (ibid.: 23). This, however, is not a call to localization as some radical thinkers such as Colin Hines have argued for (Hines 2000). Rather, it is about a democratization of globalization through a radical reform of the global institutions. This is three-pronged. First, Monbiot contends that – hard as it will be – there is a need now to establish 'a world parliament'. As a consequence of the vetoes exercised by the advanced western economies, the UN, he argues, is undemocratic and essentially 'unfit for purpose' (ibid.: 68–82). This parliament 'would need to be big enough to represent a wide range of views, but small enough to make decisions with efficiency' (ibid.: 87). He argues that six hundred representatives is a suitable size. Members would need to be 'seen to have no connection to the governments of the nations from which they come' (ibid.: 88) and thus this would not be 'an assembly formed by nation-states, but an assembly formed by the world's people' (ibid.: 88). And whilst he argues there is a need 'to dis-invent the United Nations Security Council', there would be a need 'to develop another organization, with a similar mandate' which is more democratic (ibid.: 132).

The second of Monbiot's prongs is the establishment of a new international clearing union to replace the IMF and the World Bank. Monbiot argues both 'are inherently unreformable and destined to fail'. Using Stiglitz's critique of both institutions, Monbiot essentially argues for a resurrection of Keynes's argument for an international clearing union that is 'a global bank with a global currency' (ibid.: 160–80). Such an organization is argued to be the only effective way to permit development, manage debt in the global economy properly and retain stability in the global economic system without skewing power in favour of the powerful nations. The third prong is the replacement of the WTO with 'a fair trade organization' that recognizes, 'in some areas of global governance, the possibility of an equality of outcome can be admitted only by unequal opportunity' (ibid.: 181). Currently he argues 'trade is a feeble, often regressive means of distributing wealth amongst nations' (ibid.: 185). His arguments in this respect follow much of what Stiglitz (2006) argues: permitting poorer countries to protect industries with tariffs until they achieve a certain level of wealth (ibid.: 216–19), banning agricultural subsidies by rich nations and creating an organization that effectively tackles corruption (ibid.: 219–20).

Monbiot ends *The Age of Consent*, like Klein, with a 'call to arms' in suggesting that achieving any of these reforms depends on individual democratic participation. He has applied similar calls in his thinking on how to tackle climate change, which interested readers may wish to explore further (Monbiot 2006). Radical reform will of course not happen spontaneously. It is this call for activism which much radical thinking on globalization shares and which, perhaps more than for any other, characterizes the ethos of our third radical thinker: Subcomandante Marcos.

Marcos – radical thinking from a front-line activist

In contrast to the developed world background of Monbiot, there is also a considerable volume of radical thinking on globalization that has originated from thinkers in the developing world. Contributors like the Indian academic Vandana Shiva (Shiva 2001, 2007, 2009) and Indian writer Arundhati Roy (Roy 2004) have been important in this respect. However, given the limited space within this chapter, it is one thinker in particular that I want to consider briefly: Subcomandante Marcos (also known as Delgado Cero). His arguments concerning globalization have especial resonance given his unique position as a leading figure in the 1994 Zapatista uprising in the southern Mexican state of Chiapas – a movement which we should remember is seen by Castells as a key development in the nature of the network society and political globalization. However, the Zapatista uprising in both its military and political forms is also often seen as an axiomatic event in the birth and development of the so-called 'anti-globalization' movement, and for that reason Marcos's arguments are of particular interest.

Given that Marcos is as much activist as 'thinker', his ideas about globalization are not gathered in one text but have been disseminated over the last fifteen years through numerous books, essays and articles. From 1992 through 2006, he wrote more than 200 essays and stories and published 21 books. His writings, whilst academically informed, are not explicitly designed to be academic analyses of globalization. Many are stories or other forms of fiction. Much of his writing also needs to be understood more as a political 'call to action', designed to provide a basis and commentary on the Zapatista and wider anti-globalization movement. It is certainly Marxian in its ideological basis, although there is some debate about to what extent Marcos reconfig-ures Marxism (Higgins 2005). However, through his writings a variety arguments concerning globalization emerge. Here I want to outline a series of arguments he has made equating globalization with what he terms 'a fourth world war'. The purpose is to provide an example of the nature of his radical thinking about globalization, rather than offer some comprehensive analysis of his many contributions.

First, Marcos argues that the era of globalization represents a phase after the 'third world war' which corresponded to the Cold War period. The effect of the 'defeat' of the USSR 'should have been a unipolar world – one single nation which dominated a world where there were no rivals' (Marcos 2002) but in order to be effective 'this unipolar world would have to reach . . . globalization'. He thus conceives the process of globalization as a process of war 'seeking to conquer terri-tory' and based on 'neoliberalism'

Second, he argues that computers and global communications tech-nologies mean that 'there are no longer any borders or constraints of time or geography'. Marcos suggests that it 'is thanks to computers that the process of globalization began' and that information and com-munications technologies, more than any other factor, have eroded 'separations, differences [and] nation-states' to create the global village.

Third, he sees neoliberalism as 'a new religion' which 'is going to permit this process to be carried out' (ibid.). In this context, the 'fourth world war' is 'destroying humanity as globalization is universalizing the market'. It is a war where 'everything human which opposes the logic of the market is an enemy and must be destroyed'. In this sense, Marcos suggests 'we are all the enemy to be vanquished: indigenous, non-indigenous, human rights observers, teachers, intellectuals, artists.'

Fourth, globalization then is a coercive way of 'doing away with people's ways of being'. The fourth world war and its globalization thus 'destroys' and then rebuilds new places and territories 'which the laws of the market' determine. He argues that this 'is what is driving globalization'. Neoliberalism is a process that is seeking to force 'one single market, in which the same person can consume the same product in any part of the world' and where 'the same person acts like a citizen of the world, and no longer as a citizen of a nation-state'. In that sense, he sees this aggressive globalization much as Klein does insofar as it is 'homogenizing' and about 'hegemonising a lifestyle'. It is what he terms 'a global life' (ibid.).

Marcos's thinking is certainly radical, and clearly confrontational and combative in nature. Where many academic theorists have argued that contemporary globalization is characterized by neoliberal ideas that produce contemporary 'global transformations', Marcos forcefully provides an account that focuses on power and resistance. His conception of globalization as a 'war' and a struggle provides a radically different interpretation of agency to much academic globalization theory which has often conceptualized globalization as some kind of neutral or abstract process.

Critical engagements with radical thought

The final task of this chapter is to consider critical engagements with radical thought on globalization. It is important to assess each of the three thinkers discussed separately, but in so doing I will also draw out some common potential problems that this diverse field of thought shares. At the outset, however, it is also important to appreciate that the critical reception to the radical thinkers discussed here has very much been shaped by underlying ideological and political perspectives. Many of the pro-liberal globalization thinkers such as Martin Wolf occupy a position of direct opposition to, for example, the ideas of Klein. Whilst some of their criticisms may have merit, this can potentially be seen as too dogmatic a response. I therefore want to try to avoid the polarized critiques caught up in the pro–anti debate around globalization, and to adopt a more objective approach to considering the strengths and weaknesses of the radical thought discussed in this chapter. I therefore will identify in turn a series of debatable issues within the ideas of each of the three thinkers, also pointing to common threads of critical engagement that span radical thinking more generally.

Klein: difficulties with culture, domination and the role of ideology

Taking Klein's thinking to begin with, I want to identify four key issues. First, the conception of corporate power, hegemony and domination which is outlined in *No Logo* but which pervades all of her work is undoubtedly questionable. Klein attributes significant agency and power to corporations without systematic or detailed empirical analysis to back it up. The result is that her account of corporate power is vulnerable to criticism in that it overestimates both the coherence of corporate (and state) strategy, and the capacity of these entities to control and dominate. *No Logo* in particular paints a picture of the relationship between corporate action and cultural domination through the power of brands that is highly problematic, largely because of its relatively simplistic understanding of the relationship between brands, consumer culture and wider society. Appadurai's thinking – which we will consider in chapter 12 – presents a significant challenge to her arguments in this respect. In particular, many cultural theorists would question whether brands can produce cultural homogenization in the way she describes, as well as the pervasiveness of this process (see Hopper 2007; Tomlinson 1999).

Second, *No Logo*'s arguments about the nature of resistance to global corporate power, along with its arguments for alternatives, have been criticized for being overstated, idealist and lacking in concrete proposals. Klein suggests there is evidence of an almost spontaneous resistance movement that is both democratic and anti-corporate if not anti-capitalist. Whilst the anti-globalization movement that has developed since the late 1990s clearly represents a loose correspondence to this resistance, *No Logo*'s claims about its nature are arguable. In common with the ideas of Hardt and Negri about the 'multitude' considered in the next chapter, Klein presents a rather vague set of claims about both the specific goals of democratic or spontaneous opposition to globalization, as well as the capacity of this movement to achieve change.

Third, Klein's argument concerning the nature, role and coherence of neoliberal ideology in relation to globalization are highly debatable. There is a substantial political science literature which argues that neoliberalism is an incoherent, precarious and inconsistent ideological perspective that has been deployed differently in different contexts over the last three or four decades (e.g. Harvey 2003; Leitner et al. 2006; Saad-Filho and Johnston 2004). Klein's account tends thus to present coherence where none necessarily exists, and overall weaves a conspiratorial account of the interconnections between different components of 'disaster capitalism' that relies on much historical assertion. Whilst Klein's analysis of market fundamentalism and 'shock' ideology is certainly at times insightful in relation to the case of the recent US Bush administration, her contention that this represents a coherent and pervasive globalized perspective that actively informed political decisions in the post-Second World War period has to be questionable.

This leads to a fourth and closely related issue: that Klein's thinking comes close to reducing globalization to a narrowly defined and

US-centric project. Such a perspective is replete with problems in light of the wider academic debate about global interconnectedness. In particular, *The Shock Doctrine* presents an essentially US-centric account with most of the examples Klein uses to support her argument being focused on one specific US government (the second Bush administration) within the last decade. There is only very limited evidence of other US governments (for example, the Clinton administration) fitting this argument, let alone examples that support the wider collusion of European or Asian governments in this project. Furthermore, many of the events and political developments that Klein uses as evidence for her thesis are in reality highly complex and involve many actors who were motivated by a range of rationales and ideologies. In short, even if some aspects of the disaster capitalism thesis hold, this is more an account of a specific moment in US ideological approach to globalization than a universal phenomenon.

Monbiot: idealism and an unfeasible reform agenda?

The strengths of George Monbiot's thinking about globalization – on which his work has built a reputation – centre on his capacity to outline in some depth proposals for alternative kinds of democratic and political structures to those that exist presently. However, at least two substantial (and by now hopefully familiar) areas of difficulty exist with his thinking.

First, as with other radical thinkers, Monbiot finds it hard to escape the challenge that his proposals are idealistic and far from what is politically achievable. In developing the concept of a global parliament, he does not address in any detail how this new institution is to relate to existing nation-states and other supranational institutions, or how power will be divided between this new institution and others. The nature of this institution's jurisdiction is thus at best vague. Likewise, the same applies to the role of the new elected six hundred representatives and their capacity to act. In reality, the current debate about the problems with the UN, the Security Council and the constitution of entities like the EU suggests that founding this institution and getting it to work in the way Monbiot proposes is likely to be very difficult, if not impossible, because of the realities of global politics. In short, his thinking in this respect appears idealistic, if not utopian, and far removed from the historical reality of political globalization processes.

Second, and following on, there is the issue of what mechanisms for change could possibly lead to this new institutional governance structure emerging in the global economy. Monbiot's proposals in respect of how this new world order might be created are thin, particularly in explaining how individuals can go about collectively mounting his proposed 'global democratic revolution'. As political scientists have considered at length (e.g. Cohen and Sabel 2005), there is a significant risk that greater global scale democracy will produce political paralysis and inaction. If I suggested in chapter 5 that Held's more detailed and nuanced proposals for reforming the world political order were vulnerable to criticisms of idealism, then in comparison Monbiot's thinking is much more prone to this problem.

Marcos: the limited scope for true revolution?

This latter issue with Monbiot leads us neatly on to consider areas of difficulty within Marcos's thinking. Whilst Marcos's writing is not intended to be so programmatic and academic in his radical thinking about globalization, at least two key issues pervade any critical engagement with his ideas. The first is a similar issue to that we encountered with Klein: Marcos is strong on critiquing neoliberal globalization but has much to less to contribute with respect to alternatives. Hidden behind the headline slogan of 'another possible world', Marcos (like many other radical thinkers) does not develop any detailed outline of what an alternative economic and social system to the global capitalist economy might look like. His arguments in this respect are restricted to a general sense of collectivist democracy and a revised form of international socialism. Such a proposition inevitably continues to be open to the critiques long levelled at socialist systems of governance for producing insufficient levels of growth and for stifling individual freedoms.

Second, it is clear that Marcos's strongly negative view of neoliberal globalization, like Klein's, also simplifies the nature of the phenomenon and reduces it to a unified and coherent political project. It is easy to argue that his combative conception of globalization as a form of 'war' overstates the coherence and capacity to dominate of the actors he seeks to resist. Likewise, his notion that globalization is homogenizing is vulnerable to the same criticisms as others that see it as a process suppressing difference (whether cultural or otherwise). In short, our journey through thinking on globalization thus far suggests Marcos's focus on domination and resistance produces a relatively narrow interpretation of what globalization 'is'.

Conclusion: truly radical thinking?

The aim of this chapter has been to provide some insight into a broad body of thinking that adopts what can be loosely termed a radical approach to globalization. The undoubted commonality that spans much of this thinking is its oppositional perspective towards contemporary neoliberal economic globalization. Klein, Monbiot and Marcos all share this worldview, albeit with different emphases, and provide strong critiques of what is 'wrong' with contemporary globalization. However, like many other radical thinkers, what they also share is a call for some kind of alternative to globalization as currently experienced. I have argued that Klein and Marcos are rather weak, however, in developing detailed proposals for this alternative world. Conversely, although Monbiot provides a more detailed and programmatic set of ideas for reform, they remain abstracted from political reality. This problem – a lack of detailed alternative proposals – represents one of the most fundamental challenges for the wider body of thinking about globalization. It therefore also represents an appropriate juncture to turn to our next two thinkers – Michael Hardt and Antonio Negri – who definitely also fall within the radical approach. However, their work is far more forthright in prescribing what kind of political action is needed and how this is to be achieved – namely, revolution. It is to this issue of what revolutionary thinking about globalization might look like that we now turn.

Further reading

Works by Naomi Klein

Klein, N. (2000) *No Logo*. New York: Flamingo.
Klein, N. (2002) *Fences and Windows: Dispatches from the Front Lines of the Globalization Debate*. New York: Flamingo.
Klein, N. (2007) *The Shock Doctrine: The Rise of Disaster Capitalism*. London: Penguin.

Website resources

Klein's website: www.naomiklein.org/main

Works by George Monbiot

Monbiot, G. (2004 [2003]) *The Age of Consent: A Manifesto for a New World Order*. London: Harper Perennial.
Monbiot, G. (2006) *Heat: How to Stop the Planet Burning*. London: Allen Lane.

Other radical literature

Kingsnorth, P. (2003) *One No, Many Yeses*. London: The Free Press.

Website resources

Monbiot's website: Monbiot.com

Works by Subcomandante Marcos (in English)

Marcos, S. (2002) *Our Word is Our Weapon*. London: Serpent's Tail.
Marcos, S. (2006) *The Other Campaign* (bilingual edn). San Francisco: City Lights Books. Subtitled *The Zapatista Call for Change from Below*.

Commentary on Subcomandante Marcos

Higgins, N. (2005) Zapatista Poetics and Cultural Humanism, in C. Eschle and B. Maiguashca (eds), *Critical Theories, International Relations and 'The Anti-Globalization Movement'*. London: Routledge, pp. 87–102.

11 REVOLUTIONARY THINKING: MICHAEL HARDT AND ANTONIO NEGRI

Introduction

In examining the work of Michael Hardt and Antonio Negri, I want to return to two pervasive problems that we have encountered on a number of occasions in this journey through thinking about globalization. The first is the question of whether globalization is 'one thing' or 'one system' in conceptual terms which has occupied a range of academic theorists and remains unresolved. To a considerable extent, this issue has not troubled many radical thinkers whose ideas assume globalization is one phenomenon without ever justifying this assumption. Hardt and Negri are, in contrast, important in representing a type of radical thinking that goes to great lengths to theorize exactly how globalization is systemic in a sinister and negative way. Likewise, they are equally unequivocal about a second issue we discussed earlier in the book: whether or not globalization can be theorized (as many academic thinkers have) as a neutral objective phenomenon rather than a heavily politicized and contested project, analysis of which is hard to separate from different political ideologies. For Hardt and Negri there is no doubt that that globalization is far from some neutral phenomenon beyond the control of individuals or small groups. Rather it is an orchestrated form of imperialism and something that needs to be resisted vigorously with the ultimate goal of overthrowing it. Their contribution is thus arguably amongst the most radical of the radical engagements with globalization because it advocates strong resistance and complete rejection of many of the central features of contemporary globalization – so much so that this chapter addresses what I cautiously term 'revolutionary thinking' on globalization.

Hardt and Negri are both best described as political philosophers, certainly for the purposes of their ideas about globalization. Both are – or have been – professional academics of sorts, and have written extensively as individuals and together. Most of their thinking, and their major contributions to the globalization debate, are however joint efforts and these works will be the focus of our analysis here. Hardt was born in 1960 in the United States and grew up in Maryland. He took a first degree in engineering at Swarthmore College in Pennsylvania. He was actively involved in college politics during the late 1970s, campaigning for the development of alternative energy which led him to work for solar energy firms after graduation in 1983. He then worked for a number of NGOs in El Salvador, and moved to Seattle to study comparative literature, taking a Master of Arts degree in 1986 and a PhD in 1990. It was during a period in Paris that he met Antonio Negri and began to write with him. He is currently Professor of Literature and Italian at Duke University.

Negri is an Italian and is 27 years older than Hardt, born in Padua in 1933 where he was educated at the university and promoted to full professor at a young age in the field of 'dottrina dello Stato' (state theory). Throughout his life, Negri has, however, had a parallel career as a political activist. This began in the 1950s when he joined the militant Roman Catholic youth organization, Gioventù Italiana di Azione Cattolica (GIAC). He joined the Italian Socialist Party in 1956 and remained a member until 1963, while at the same time becoming more and more engaged throughout the late 1950s and early 1960s in Marxist movements. Negri's life and career has thus not just been one of an academic. He has always been a politicized and political activist, often of radial groups. In the late 1960s, for example, he founded a communist worker organization called Potere Operaio. This organization disbanded in 1973 but led to the formation of another in which he was involved – Autonomia Operaia Organizzata (Organized Worker's Autonomy). Negri was controversially alleged to be associated with the Italian 'Red Brigades' in the 1970s, and was accused of being the mastermind behind the assassination of Aldo Moro, the leader of the Christian Democrat Party in 1978.

Whilst Negri was later cleared of links with the assassination and the Red Brigades, he was given a long prison sentence on controversial charges of 'association and insurrection against the state'. Michel Foucault famously said of his imprisonment, 'Isn't he in jail simply for being an intellectual?' In 1983, four years after his arrest and whilst still in prison awaiting trial, Negri was elected to the Italian legislature as a candidate of the Radical Party. Although the provision in Italian law that freed him to serve in the parliament was revoked shortly afterwards, Negri had by this time gone to France where he remained for 14 years, writing and teaching at the Université de Vincennes (Paris-VIII) and the Collège International de Philosophie. He was protected from extradition although his refusal to return to Italy was widely criticized by Italian media and by some in the Italian Radical Party. In 1997, he did voluntarily return to serve the end of his sentence and was eventually released from prison in the spring of 2003. He now lives between Venice and Paris with his partner, the French philosopher Judith Revel.

Negri's biography in relation to his work on globalization is particularly important, given his controversial radical pedigree and the fact that the key text, *Empire*, was written with Michael Hardt whilst he was still in prison. Probably more than any thinker about globalization, Negri represents a heavyweight intellectual radical who forms a link between the left-wing Marxist radicalism of the 1960s and 1970s and the contemporary globalization debate. Negri and Hardt writing together have thus been regarded as an important exception to the body of radical globalization thinking which has struggled to produce a vision of how 'another world' can be achieved. For Hardt and Negri are very clear about the need for what they call 'the multitude' to resist contemporary neoliberal globalization (conceived as 'empire'). Theirs is not just a critique lacking a programme of action, or a diffuse and unfocused 'call to arms' as might be the case with thinkers like Naomi Klein. Hardt and Negri argue that the current system needs to be overthrown, and they outline in considerable conceptual depth how that political movement needs to take shape. Theirs is a critique with clear purpose.

Yet I also want to argue in this chapter that *Empire*, whilst undoubtedly a sophisticated neo-Marxist critique of the contemporary world order, remains deeply problematic as a thesis. I will argue that Hardt and Negri's thesis about globalization does not escape from an overdetermined conception of power and agency in global society and economy that owes much to its neo-Marxian roots. In that sense, for all its novelty, 'globalization as empire' is an unconvincing theorization that is limited by its understanding of how global interconnectedness has reconstituted what we might understand 'sovereignty' and 'capitalism' to be. In the context of this overarching argument, the chapter will also assess the extent to which Hardt and Negri's thinking is 'revolutionary' insofar as how (and indeed whether or not) their arguments are different from other radical thinkers on globalization.

The next section thus begins by outlining the major architecture of their critical analysis of globalization which is set out in the first half of *Empire*. The third section then addresses the latter part of the book where they consider the limits of both (global) capitalism and imperialism in relation to their ideas about sovereignty and capitalist production. In the fourth section, I consider the original arguments for resistance and what a new world order might look like that they set out in *Empire* itself, with the fifth section briefly providing an overview of how they develop these arguments in the 2003 book, *Multitude*, and other more recent contributions. The final section then considers the limitations and problems with their thinking, along with a number of critical responses to *Empire* and Hardt and Negri's other works.

The 'Empire' thesis

It is impossible to understand the epistemological foundations of the 'global empire' thesis – set out in their first book, *Empire*, in 2000 – or indeed its limitations, without some appreciations of the philosophical lineage that it draws upon. As we have already discussed, Negri was a contemporary of many of the leading post-structuralist philosophers of the 1960s and 1970s – Michel Foucault, Jacques Derrida, Gilles Deleuze and Félix Guattari. This post-structuralist epistemological position is evident in Hardt and Negri's arguments about empire, most notably in their relational conception of power, their concept of 'biopower' and their 'genealogical' approach which owes much to Foucault (Foucault 1976, 1984b) and their conceptual emphasis on multiplicity that clearly bears the mark of the thinking of Deleuze and Guattari (Deleuze and Guattari 1972, 1982). Yet Hardt and Negri remain Marxian as well, more specifically in a revised Gramscian[6] (Italian) Marxist mode of thinking concerned with how political and cultural hegemony is achieved. Gramscian Marxism in particular has long been concerned with a less economically determinist conception of class formation, power and social transformation than Anglo-Germanic 'classical Marxism', arguing that working-class revolution has been avoided in capitalist societies since the mid-twentieth century through cultural dominance by capitalist interests.

Empire itself is in this respect a readable but not always particularly accessible text. It uses the language of Marxism as well as adopting a sometimes 'playful' style that falls within aspects of the 'post-' approach in order to set out its complex array of arguments. It is also important to note that it has a potentially misleading title. As a review in *Political Science Quarterly* suggests, the main theme of the book is not in fact imperialism conventionally conceived, but globalization conceived as 'an imperial postmodernity' (Ninkoich 2000). I want to suggest in this section that the first part of the book develops this theory around three major components.

Globalization-as-Empire

For Hardt and Negri, 'empire is materializing before our eyes' (Hardt and Negri 2000: xi). The central argument is that 'over the past several decades . . . we have witnessed an irresistible and irreversible globalization of economic and cultural exchanges' which have been accompanied by not only 'a global market and global circuits of production' but also 'a new global order' (ibid.: xi). This they suggest represents 'a new form of sovereignty' where the concept of 'Empire' represents 'the political subject that effectively regulates these global exchanges, the sovereign power that governs the world' (ibid.: xi).

The consequence for understanding what globalization 'is' in this analysis is substantial for Hardt and Negri. Rather than meaning that 'economic relations have become more autonomous from political controls' along with an associated decline of political sovereignty, they argue that 'the decline in sovereignty of nation-states . . . does not mean that sovereignty as such has declined.' In contrast, therefore, to propositions that the global political system has become liberalized and freer of controls, they suggest that 'throughout the contemporary transformations, political controls, state functions and regulatory mechanisms have continued to rule the realm of economic and social production and exchange' (ibid.: xii). The 'basic hypothesis', therefore, is that 'sovereignty has taken a new form, composed of a series of national and supranational organisms united under a single logic of rule' (ibid.: xii). It is this 'new global form of sovereignty' that they define as the concept of 'Empire'.

This concept 'is characterized fundamentally by a lack of boundaries' as Empire's rule 'has no limits'. They make three definitional points in this respect. First, that the concept 'posits a regime that effectively encompasses the spatial totality, or really rules over the entire "civilized" world' (ibid.: xiv). Second, it presents itself not as 'a historical regime originating in conquest' but rather as 'an order that effectively suspends history and thereby fixes the existing state of affairs for eternity' (ibid.). Third, 'the rule of Empire operates on all registers of the social order extending down to the depths of the social world.' The point is that 'Empire not only manages a territory and a population but also creates the very world it inhabits.' This manifestation of 'bio-power' amounts not only to a desire 'to regulate human interactions' but to a seeking 'to rule directly over human nature' (ibid.: xv).

Their conception of the development of Empire has a distinct historical narrative. Hardt and Negri argue that 'the sovereignty of the nation-state' was 'the cornerstone of the imperialisms that European powers constructed through the modern era' (ibid.: xii). Empire, however, 'is something altogether different to "imperialism"' which was 'really an extension of the sovereignty of the European nations beyond their own boundaries' (ibid.). In contrast, Empire has emerged from what they term 'the twilight of modern sovereignty' and has 'no territorial center of power and does not rely on fixed boundaries or barriers'. Empire is 'a *decentred* and *deterritorializing* apparatus of rule' which is progressively incorporating 'the entire global realm within its open, expanding frontiers' (ibid.). It manages 'hybrid identities, flexible hierarchies, and plural exchanges through modulating networks of demand' (ibid.: xiii). This historical shift from 'a modern imperialist geography' to global Empire marks 'a passage within the capitalist mode of production'. The world which was based on sovereign nation-states in the political sphere and on external forms of discipline in the social has thus disappeared to be replaced by a 'global empire'.

A key geographical feature of this is that 'the spatial divisions of the three Worlds (First, Second and Third) have been scrambled so that we continually find the First World in the Third, the Third in the First, and the Second almost nowhere at all' (ibid.: xiii). Wallerstein's core, semi-periphery and periphery have been swept away in this view. This is a world defined not by old territorial borders but rather 'by new and complex regimes of differentiation and homogenization, deterritorialization and reterritorialisation' (ibid.). Importantly, Hardt and Negri argue that this 'globalization-as-Empire' cannot be understood as Americanization or a new era of American imperialism. Rather, they suggest that the US 'does not, and indeed no nation-state can today, form the center of an imperialist project' (ibid.: xiv). Old-fashioned imperialism 'is over'. Empire-as-globalization thus understood has succeeded in producing 'a fundamentally new form of rule' and a new world order where industrial modernization has been supplanted by a postmodern form of capitalism so all-embracing that 'capitalism has become a world' (Hardt and Negri 2000: 386). The 'passage' to this state of affairs has been one involving multiple processes of globalization which are not 'one thing' nor 'unified or univocal' (ibid.: xv). The consequence is that Empire is sustained through global processes by 'a multitude' and any resistance to it 'capable of constructing a counter-Empire' must also organize around 'an alternative political organization of global flows and exchanges' (ibid.: xv).

Finally, as implied in the concept of biopower, the 'postmodernisation of the global economy' has an important social dimension. Unlike earlier historical phases of capitalism, Hardt and Negri argue that in the contemporary period 'the creation of wealth tends ever more toward . . . biopolitical production' which amounts 'to the production of social life itself, in which the economic, the political and the cultural increasingly overlap with each other' (ibid.: xiii). This is significant, for Hardt and Negri's contribution explicitly links the world order and the global economy with society and culture in one intimately inter-woven framework. The separation between the economic sphere and other aspects of global social life that marks many positive, reformist and even some academic thinkers on globalization is dismissed in their approach.

The political constitution of the present

In the first part of *Empire,* Hardt and Negri outline their conception of 'the political constitution of the present' that forms the basis for the globalization-as-Empire thesis. This has three components with the first being the issue of the contemporary world order. Their argument, put simply, is that 'there is a world order' which has neither 'risen spontaneously out of the interactions of radically heterogeneous global forces' in line with the Wolf–Friedman neoliberal free market perspec-tive, nor been 'dictated by a single power and a single center of ratio-nality' which sees globalization as Klein does as something 'like a conspiracy theory' (ibid.: 3). Rather – and contrary to a world systems approach – the shift to Empire represents a 'juridicial' transformation to a world order that is shaped by a common ethico-political dynamic with two tendencies: first, it is based on 'a notion of right . . . that envelops the entire space of what is considered civilization' and, second, that it 'encompasses all time within its foundation' (ibid.: 11). This logic of what they term 'imperial right' may look like 'governance without government' (ibid.: 14), but is better understood as an order-ing mechanism under which the development of the global system is akin to the development of a machine that imposes procedures and seems to predetermine the exercise of authority and action across 'the entire social space' (ibid.: 14). The world order in the era of Empire is thus based on consensus and also seeks 'to enlarge the realm of con-sensuses that support its own power' (ibid.: 15).

The second component to their argument in effect corresponds to the mechanism by which Empire works. For this they draw on two of Foucault's concepts in relation to power: 'biopower' and the 'society of control'. In relation to the former, the concept refers to 'a form of power that regulates social life from its interior' (ibid.: 23) whereas the latter corresponds to the kind of society that 'is able to adopt the biopolitical context as its exclusive terrain of reference' (ibid.: 24). It is a society where power is expressed 'as a control that extends through the depths of the consciousness and bodies of the population' (ibid.: 24). Their argument is that contemporary global society is such a form of society where TNCs are amongst the key agents that 'construct the fundamental connective fabric of the biopolitical world' as they 'directly structure and articulate territories and populations' (ibid.: 31). Other institutions such as the IMF and World Bank are also part of this complex as the great industrial and financial powers produce not only commodities but also subjectivities (ibid.: 32). New commu-nications technologies are a key contributor to the capacity of achiev-ing this as a means of transmitting and shaping the imaginative constitution of this form of biopower. The consequence is that Empire is formed not only on the basis of its powers of accumulation and global extension, but also around a capacity to develop itself more deeply. This amounts to it being able to be reborn and to extend itself through the latticework of world society (ibid.: 41).

Third, for Hardt and Negri the contemporary world order in the era of globalization-as-Empire is not an entirely negative situation. They argue that 'the construction of Empire is good *in itself* but not *for itself*' (ibid.: 42). By this they mean it has played a role in ending colonialism and imperialism, but that it 'nonetheless constructs its own relationships of power based on exploitation that in many respects are more brutal than those destroyed' (ibid.: 43). It is thus better in the same way that Marx insisted that capitalism is better than the forms of society and modes of production that came before it (ibid.). Their conclusion from this is that resistance to globalization-as-Empire based around place or *localization* 'is both false and damaging' (ibid.: 44). Rather they suggest what needs to be addressed is 'the production of locality' defined as 'the social machines that create and re-create identities and differences that are understood as local' (ibid.: 45). Globalization is thus understood as 'a regime of the production of identity and difference' where it is impossible 'to (re)establish local identities that are in some sense outside and protected against the global flows of capital and Empire' (ibid.). Resistance to Empire has to come from within in order to 'confront its homogenizing and heterogenizing flows in all their complexity' (ibid.: 46). They further suggest that globalization-as-Empire is sustained by many existing forms of resistance because it is these resistance struggles that define the 'limits and opportunities to recalibrate Empire's own instruments' (ibid.: 59). The processes of globalization in this argument to some extent rely on resistance as currently conceived. This leads Hardt and Negri to argue that truly effective resistance to globalization-as-Empire must take a different form. We will examine this shortly, but first we need to consider their arguments about sovereignty and production in the second and third parts of the book.

The 'passages' of sovereignty and production

Hardt and Negri's central argument about sovereignty is that it is intrinsically bound into the historical development of capitalism, and that it is a product of various 'machines of power' which were 'constructed to respond to crisis' and in so doing 'led to the development of the modern sovereign state' (ibid.: 93). Central to this contention is the point that the modern concept of the nation has inherited the 'patrimonial body' of the monarchic state and then reinvented it in a new form (ibid.: 95). The consequence is that the nation-state is both a vehicle of repression and a potentiality for progressive social change. In relating this analysis to the twentieth century and the emergence of new nationalisms and nations, their conclusion is thus that 'the very concept of a liberatory national sovereignty is ambiguous if not completely contradictory' (ibid.: 133) because whilst 'nationalism seeks to liberate the multitude from *foreign domination*, it erects *domestic* structures of domination that are equally severe' (ibid.) National liberation and sovereignty are not only powerless against the global capitalist hierarchy but they themselves contribute to its organization and functioning (ibid.). What they suggest has arisen in more recent times is a transformation of sovereignty from its 'modern' nation-state basis to an 'imperial' post-national form. This imperial form seeks to manage hybridity and difference in the contemporary (post-colonial) world (ibid.: 186–204).

Coupled with this historical account of the 'passage' of sovereignty is a concomitant passage of production from an earlier "formal subsumption" of labour under capital (in Marxist terms). In short, they argue that where earlier capitalist development gradually drew in non-capitalist territories and peoples through expansion, more recent history has been marked by a 'real subsumption' that involves an 'integration of labour into capital' that is more intensive and produces 'a society that is ever more completely fashioned by capital'. They see earlier twentieth-century Taylorism and Fordism as markers along this path, but most pertinently to their argument suggest – drawing on the ideas of Castells – that the rise of network informational capitalism is the most recent manifestation of this process of real subsumption (ibid.: 284–300). This new form of production is not administered through TNCs who are its prime actors but through a complex of state and capital – hence, the dual passage of production *and* sovereignty. The nexus relationship between the two produces 'the apparatus of control' in the contemporary global disciplinary society (ibid.: 339–43).

Decline and fall: their road to revolution

What I have not discussed so far is how in *Empire* Hardt and Negri constantly point to the internal contradictions and opportunities for resistance that exist within their modern imperial world order. For I want now to consider a second goal of the globalization-as-Empire thesis which is to provide the theoretical basis for creating resistance and progressive social transformation in the contemporary world. This begins with their persistent argument through the first book that 'the theory of the constitution of Empire is also a theory of its decline' and that an alternative potential for political power exists within the 'multitude'. In this section I will consider first this argument as articulated in *Empire,* and then turn to assess how it is developed in the subsequent book *Multitude: War and Democracy in the Age of Empire* (2004).

The decline and fall of Empire

In order for the 'multitude' to resist, the key question for Hardt and Negri is how it 'can become a *political subject* in the context of Empire' (ibid.: 394). The answer they propose is that 'the action of the multitude becomes political primarily when it begins to confront directly, and with an adequate consciousness, the central repressive operations of Empire' (ibid.: 399). The key to this is that it should recognize and engage with imperial initiatives and not allow them 'to continually re-establish order'; that it must cross and break down 'the limits and segmentations that are imposed on the new collective labour power'; and that it gathers together these 'experiences of resistance' and wields them 'in concert against the nerve centres of imperial command' (ibid.). However, they also acknowledge in *Empire* that this task, 'although it is clear at the conceptual level, remains rather abstract' (ibid.: 399). What is more, they suggest in *Empire* that they are not able to elaborate 'the specific and concrete practices that will animate this political project' (ibid.: 400). Rather, they restrict themselves to a more abstract 'political program' for the global multitude.

The first of element of this is a demand for 'global citizenship'. This entails the multitude gaining 'control over the movements' of people – i.e. migration. The multitude thus 'must be able to decide if, when, and where it moves', as well as having 'the right to stay and enjoy one place rather than being forced constantly to be on the move' (ibid.: 400). This amounts for Hardt and Negri to the multitude's power 'to re-appropriate control over space' (ibid.). The second element is 'a social wage and guaranteed income for all' (ibid.: 403). This social wage should extend 'well beyond the family to the entire multitude, even those who are unemployed, because the entire multitude produces' (ibid.). The implication is that this 'extends to the entire population the demand that all activity necessary for the production of capital be recognized with an equal compensation' (ibid.). Thirdly, Hardt and Negri argue that the global multitude's political project entails 'a right to re-appropriation' (ibid.: 406). This is a right first of all 'to the re-appropriation of the means of production' that transcends its traditional (communist) sense. They argue the multitude must 'configure itself as a telos' – essentially a kind of consciousness – that 'not only uses machines to produce, but also becomes increasingly machinic itself' as the means of production are increasingly integrated into the minds and bodies of the multitude. (ibid.: 406). This re-appropriation thus means 'having free access to and control over knowledge, information, communication and affects' (ibid.: 407).

Hardt and Negri end *Empire* with the proposition that the multitude 'must live and organize its political space against Empire, and also within the "maturity of times" and the ontological conditions that Empire presents' (ibid.: 407). They state that they 'do not have any models to offer' because 'only the multitude through its practical experimentation will create the models and determine when and how the possible becomes real' (ibid.: 411).

Multitude and democracy

In their subsequent book, *Multitude: War and Democracy in the Age of Empire* (2004), Hardt and Negri elaborate further their concept of the multitude and how it will play a role in generating a radical new world political order, as well as how 'true' democracy can emerge in the contemporary world. They argue that only now at the start of the twenty-first century is 'the possibility of democracy' emerging 'for the very first time' (ibid.: xi). The premise of this book is that 'the project of the multitude not only expresses the desire for a world of equality and freedom, but also provides the means for achieving it' (ibid.). The problem, however, is that 'the primary obstacle to democracy is the global state of war' (ibid.). They argue that the current state of war 'is both global in scale' and 'long-lasting' (ibid.: xii). The focus therefore in this later work is on how the multitude – defined as 'the living alternative that grows within Empire' (ibid.: xiii) – can be understood as 'a new global class formation' (ibid.: xvii).

The analysis in the book sets out three further elements to Hardt and Negri's thinking about the contemporary globalized world. First, they elaborate a thesis that a global state of war exists, that global terrorism linked to 9/11 is part of this general state 'that erodes the distinction between war and peace' (ibid.: 5) and that 'the traditional military power structure is no longer capable of defeating or containing its enemies' (ibid.: 63). Second, they expand the concept of the 'multitude' as a new global class formation that supplants previous ideas of the international proletariat. Importantly, they suggest that it 'is also a concept of race, gender and sexuality differences' (ibid.: 101), and that it is 'the common subject of labor . . . the real flesh of postmodern production'. When this 'flesh' is 'imprisoned and transformed into the body of global capital, it finds itself both within and against the processes of capitalist globalization' (ibid.). Third, they argue that despite the fact that 'the end of the Cold War was supposed to be the ultimate victory of democracy . . . today the concept and practices of democracy are everywhere in crisis' (ibid.: 231). This crisis is 'not only to do with the corruption and insufficiency of its institutions and practices' but also 'with the concept itself' (ibid.: 232). Furthermore, they contest the 'social democratic' argument that 'democracy is threatened or debilitated by globalization' (ibid.: 233–4), arguing instead that it is more a failure of existing democratic forms 'to represent the opinion' of the multitude. What is needed, they argue, is a new form of democracy that draws on 'the decision-making ability in common' of the multitude (ibid.: 340) which should be based around principles that 'must counter the force of violence' (ibid.: 341).

Multitude and Democracy thus proposes overall that 'a new project for democracy' arising from the global multitude will both provide the 'radical insurrectional demand' to transform 'the long season of violence . . . [and] civil war' (ibid.: 358) and also the ideological and practical capacity to deliver a new kind of governance 'beyond sovereignty, beyond authority, beyond every tyranny' (ibid.: 354). Such an argument is likely to appear at best idealist to even the most dedicated supporter of Hardt and Negri's 'call to arms'. However, in the next section I want to argue that the problems with this development of the globalization-as-Empire thesis run far deeper than just idealism as we consider critical engagements with their work.

Hardt and Negri's libertarian pessimism? Problems with the Empire thesis

It is not an exaggeration to suggest that *Empire* and subsequent follow-ups have turned Hardt and Negri into something of celebrities. The first book was a best-seller globally, notably in the US, and they represent for many the leading champions of a revised Marxian basis for the anti-globalization movement. However, their Empire thesis has (perhaps consequently) not gone unchallenged. What is more, some of the criticisms which have been levelled are far from marginal or superficial. There is a substantial literature that has developed around the 'Empire' debate, and interested readers would be advised to delve further (e.g. Passavant and Dean 2004). However, for our purposes here, I want to focus on what is almost certainly the most substantial and sustained of the critiques developed: that of the Argentinian political scientist Atilo Boron. Other thinkers, including Alex Callinicos (Callinicos 2002) and Samir Amin (Amin 2005), have raised some of these critical points to a greater or less extent, but it is this contribution which most comprehensively critically engages with every dimension of their thinking about globalization-as-Empire.

In 2005, Boron published a book entirely devoted to a withering critical engagement of Hardt and Negri's Empire thesis, and this critique I will also argue resonates with wider ongoing problems we have already identified in this book in our journey through globalization thought. In *Empire and Imperialism*, Boron effectively seeks to dismiss the main tenets of Hardt and Negri's thesis. His critique has considerable force given both his respected position as a professor of political science writing from the global South, and also the fact that he has long been concerned in his career with the nature of imperialism and new social movements. Implicit in much of his criticism of *Empire* is the view that it ignores both the experience and intellectual analysis of thinkers from the South. The critique can be summarized around at

least seven major problems Boron identifies at the conceptual level
with Hardt and Negri's account of globalization-as-Empire. I can only
provide the main architecture of these points here, but that should be
sufficient.

First, Boron argues that the conception of imperialism that Hardt
and Negri develop is flawed. Central to this is the contention that it is
far too narrowly a 'juridicial' conception of imperialism that relies
heavily on the role of the United Nations and international law. In
Boron's view, this represents 'a gross exaggeration' of their importance, and Hardt and Negri 'naively take for granted the democratic
appearance of multilateralism and the UN system' (ibid.: 8). In contrast, he argues they are unable to see that the UN is often extremely
weak and essentially is ignored by the US (as in the case of the Iraq
War). This is US imperialism renewed (in some form) and Hardt and
Negri are thus essentially confusing the *rhetoric* of supranational juridicial rule with the *reality* of US power and new forms of state-based
imperialism. What is more, he suggests that Hardt and Negri pay little
attention to the (enormous) literature concerned with the *material
basis* of imperialism (ibid.).

Second, and related, Boron argues that they misconceive 'the supposedly de-territorialized and decentred character of imperialism'
(ibid.: 10). He argues that recent wars like that in Afghanistan and
Iraq only serve to show how 'illusory' such a claim is. Rather, he
argues strongly that 'there is nothing "de-territorialized" or immate-
rial' in contemporary imperialism. For Boron, these recent wars are
'the old practice of conquest and plunder repeated . . . by the same
actors wearing new clothes' (ibid.: 12). Furthermore, he suggests
'nothing can be more inaccurate than the image [in Empire] . . . in
which Washington becomes militarily involved all over the world in
response to a universal clamour for the imposition of international
justice and legality' (ibid.). This (often US-led) world order relies very
heavily on some forms of state-based national sovereignty and Hardt
and Negri are being nothing less than 'idyllic' in their view of the US
transferring power 'to a chimerical empire' (ibid.: 13). The nation-
state, far from weakening, remains a crucial agent of capitalism,
deploying a large arsenal of economic weaponry to protect and extend
its position, actively promoting globalization in its own interests.

Third, he argues that 'old-style' imperialism is far from dead as
Hardt and Negri claim, and that multiple events of the last decade
reinforce this criticism. In particular, contra to Hardt and Negri,
Boron suggests that 'access to strategic resources' (such as oil and
water) remain crucial and central to global capitalism. His argument

is thus that 'against what Hardt and Negri induce us to believe in their sublimated . . . view of empire, one of the possible future scenarios of the international system is that of heightened inter-imperial rivalry' (ibid.: 14).

Fourth, he argues that Hardt and Negri adopt a naive and very limited conception of what transnational corporations are and how they wield power in the global economy (or not). The problem is they 'endorse the vision of the capitalist world assiduously cultivated by the main US and European business schools' (ibid.: 14), where TNCs have 'entirely sloughed off the last vestiges of their national ascription' (ibid.: 15). As we know from the discussion of the work of thinkers like Dicken, this is a gross simplification. Boron reinforces this argument against Hardt and Negri, pointing to the relative rarity and limited power of 'truly global corporations', all of whom have a territorial basis in national state and institutional contexts.

Fifth, Boron argues that Hardt and Negri's concept of the 'multitude' and its relationship to new social movements opposed to neoliberal globalization is deeply problematic. For Boron, the multitude concept 'throws together' a plethora of incongruous groups who in no way represent any kind of new global class interest. Most important, however, is his argument that the democratic aspect of this movement is far less important than the 'capitalist' aspect. His view is that Hardt and Negri 'celebrate as the real hero of the struggle against the empire the anonymous and uprooted migrant, who abandons his or her homeland in the Third World to penetrate the belly of the beast' (ibid.: 18). Boron argues that, in contrast, the reality is that most of the movements lumped together in the multitude have 'solid roots in the social structures of metropolitan capitalism'. Hardt and Negri's key revolutionary actors in the multitude are in fact marginal.

Sixth, Boron is highly critical of Hardt and Negri's use of Foucaldian 'biopower' to understand the nature of power in the contemporary world order. Boron in essence contends that they present an idealized view of 'biopower' that lacks the novelty and sophistication of Foucault's more specific arguments on this subject, and which is used to provide a weak alternative explanation for power relations in the contemporary world. For Boron, this emphasis on a kind of Gramscian/ Foucaldian 'power in the background' misses the point that much more significant material and institutional structures of power continue to dominate contemporary global politics – the vested interests of nation-states, the owners of capital, etc..

Finally, Boron's view is that the analytical misconceptions around which Hardt and Negri's Empire thesis is based has unfortunate

implications for political resistance to imperialism. It is little exaggeration to suggest, he contends, that the Hardt and Negri position in
which the multitude represents the basis for a new kind of global
democracy is an entirely misconceived argument. It emerges from the
plethora of epistemological failures in empire: the 'blindness' of Hardt
and Negri to 'the inherently imperialist nature of the international
system'; 'the extremely formalist and legalistic point of departure'; 'the
weakness of the instruments used to analyse political economy', the
'lack of basic economic data'; the 'naive acceptance of several neoliberal and postmodern axioms', the 'confusing heritage of structuralism';
and the 'unsettling effects of a radically mistaken theory of the state'
(ibid.: 100). Yet most of all, the central problem is that their 'libertarian pessimism' (to use Terry Eagleton's term) focuses on 'the marginal
and the ephemeral' in a way that implicitly accepts that the system
(empire) is 'omnipotent and overbearing' (pessimism). They 'dream'
of marginal outsiders to overthrow the system (libertarian) (ibid.:
103), suggests Boron, and consequently become lost in 'impenetrable'
syntax and 'unnecessarily difficult' language in a desperate attempt to
construct an argument for how these marginal actors will produce
societal transformation. For Boron, of course, they cannot and will
not be the source of revolution because Hardt and Negri ignore all the
main, powerful actors of imperialism in the contemporary global
system who have certainly evolved but have by no means
disappeared.

Conclusion: imperial overstretch?

Atilo Boron's critique of Hardt and Negri is at times overly rhetorical,
and perhaps also overblown or at least unfair in attributing 'naivety'
where in fact it may be more a question of language and semantics.
However, at root, it does represent a powerful, well-informed and
incisive critique of their arguments about globalization-as-Empire (as
I have termed it in this chapter). Furthermore, given the high profile
of *Empire* and its authors, Boron is not alone in identifying many of
the criticisms outlined above. A range of political scientists, philosophers and social theorists have echoed many of his points (Amin
2005; Callinicos 2002; Okur 2007). To readers of this book, it should
also be apparent that some of his significant epistemological and conceptual lines of criticism, notably of Hardt and Negri's enthusiasm for
a post-national world and powerful TNCs and even their understanding of the nature of information and communications technologies,

have variously been levelled at other tranches of the globalization literature,

The argument I want to make by way of conclusion, therefore, is that Hardt and Negri's 'globalization-as-Empire' thesis overall lacks credibility as a meta-theoretical position for understanding contemporary global economy and society, as well as the processes that are creating societal interconnectedness. I would also add that the same applies for its Marxian-inspired propositions about how a future more equitable and democratic society will come about. That does not mean, of course, that they are universally 'wrong' nor that their contribution does not push the debate about how radical (or even revolutionary) resistance to neoliberal economic globalization might come about. Their analysis of how biopower (re)produces 'false consciousness', for example, is both stimulating and thought-provoking. What I would argue, though, is that *in toto* their contention that power now resides with a territorially freed 'empire' is misguided. It lacks both a conceptual and empirical appreciation of the nature of power and the types of actors that wield it in the contemporary world. Their argument that the multitude (which is never clearly enough defined) as a coalition of marginal (class) interests of resistance is also unconvincing for the same reason – a lack of understanding of the very material, territorial and institutional dimensions to power in the contemporary world.

In that sense, whilst the Hardt and Negri globalization-as-Empire thesis suffers from a different set of more predominantly conceptual problems to the radical thinkers considered in the previous chapter – and despite superficially appearing otherwise – it does still share a failure to produce a detailed feasible programme for a political project that will produce 'a radically alternative globalized world' to the one we have now. One of the reasons for this failure, and that of many of the globalization thinkers we have discussed in this book, is perhaps an epistemological narrowness that still has not got to grips with what globalization 'is'. Central to this narrowness is a lack of appreciation for how globalization probably needs to be understood and theorized as something more than just 'economic' – or economically driven in this case – and that even in seeking to conceptualize neoliberal institutions, TNCs or class formation, socio-cultural factors are of great significance. In that respect, the contribution of our final thinker considered in the next and penultimate chapter of this book is important in its key influence on debates about culture, society and other 'non-economic' features of globalization. It is to the work of the culturally informed thinker Arjun Appadurai that we now turn.

Further reading

Works by Michael Hardt and Antonio Negri

Hardt, M. and Negri, A. (2000) *Empire.* Cambridge, MA: Harvard University Press.

Hardt, M. and Negri, A. (2004) *Multitude: War and Democracy in the Age of Empire.* New York: Penguin.

Works by Antonio Negri

Negri, A. (1999) *Insurgencies: Constituent Power and the Modern State.* Translated by Maurizia Boscagli. Minnesota: University of Minnesota Press.

Negri, A. (2003) *Time for Revolution.* Translated by Matteo Mandarini. New York: Continuum.

Negri, A. (2004) *Negri on Negri: In Conversation with Anne Dufourmentelle.* London: Routledge.

Negri, A. (2008) *Reflections on Empire.* Cambridge: Polity.

Commentaries and critical engagements

Boron, A. (2005) *Empire and Imperialism: A Critical Reading of Michael Hardt and Antonio Negri.* London: Zed Books.

Passavant, P. and Dean, J. (eds) (2004) *Empire's New Clothes: Reading Hardt and Negri.* London: Routledge.

12 CULTURAL THINKING: ARJUN APPADURAI

Introduction

One of the most conceptually tricky areas of the globalization debate is that which deals with culture. Many students I have encountered begin by regarding the question of the relationship between 'culture' and 'globalization' as one similar to that between the 'economy' of a nation-state, a government or firm. The natural inclination is to treat 'culture' as some kind of entity that has escaped from territorial borders, transcended boundaries and become global in reach. It is only after some period of engaging with the conceptual side of the globalization debate that they realize such an approach is fraught with difficulties. The central problem is, of course, epistemological. We have already spent much time in this book assessing various thinkers' understandings of what 'globalization' might be understood to be as a phenomenon – along with the many associated definitional and conceptual problems these positions entail – but now we need to enter what in some ways represents a culminating 'difficult' stage. For long before 'globalization' became established as a problematically ambiguous and fuzzy concept, 'culture' was widely held to warrant such a label (Williams 2005). Defining culture has been the subject of a long and often protractedly confusing debate in the social sciences (Barker 1999; Storey 2008), and so, as we seek to assess the relationship to it of the phenomenon captured by the concept 'globalization', the risk of confusions and ambiguities proliferating is considerable. However, in this chapter I argue that in turning our attention to this issue, an engagement with 'cultural thinking' about globalization provides some important clarification of many of the problems identified with various earlier forms of thinking discussed in this book. And the focus for this argument will be our final key thinker: the Indian-born social anthropologist Arjun Appadurai.

On several of his book covers, Appadurai is described as 'a contemporary social-cultural anthropologist focusing on modernity and globalization', but his disciplinary identification with social anthropology was something that evolved in the course of his education career path. Appadurai was born and grew up in Bombay (Mumbai), India, in 1949 where he went to school before studying for a first degree in Intermediate Arts at the University of Bombay. After receiving this in 1967, he went to the United States to take a BA in History from Brandeis University in 1970. This was followed by an MA in Social Thought in 1973 which was when he became more clearly grounded within an anthropological disciplinary approach. After the Master's degree, Appadurai moved to the University of Chicago for his doctoral research which was concerned with a car festival held in the Parthasarathi temple in Triplicane, Madras. After receiving his PhD in 1976 (also in Social Thought), he was appointed as assistant professor of Anthropology at the University of Pennsylvania where he became a full professor of Anthropology in 1987.

Since the early 1990s he has held a string of academic positions in the United States, many of which have been linked to the developing significance of globalization as an object of concern within the academy. The first of these posts was at the University of Chicago where he took up a Chair in 1992, but he has also held professorial posts at Yale and the University of Pennsylvania. He is a former Director of the Center for Cities and Globalization at Yale University and has held visiting appointments at the École des Hautes Études en Sciences Sociales (Paris), the University of Michigan, the University of Iowa, Columbia University and New York University. He currently holds the John Dewey Professorship in the Social Sciences at the New School in New York where he also served for a period as Provost. Appadurai is also a fellow of the American Academy of Arts and Sciences and has founded several academic and policy networks concerned with globalization. Most notable is the Interdisciplinary Network on Globalization which is a consortium of institutions in various parts of the world devoted to the study of global politics and culture.

As a 'key thinker' on globalization, Appadurai represents an unusual case since he can be argued to be simultaneously a central and marginal figure in the (academic) globalization literature. His centrality is unquestionable, given the relatively early stage at which he made a very widely cited and important contribution to the debate at the very start of the 1990s with his arguments about 'disjuncture and difference' in the 'global cultural economy' (Appadurai 1990). We will come to consider this work in depth shortly. Yet he is also marginal insofar as his thinking and its implications has consistently been largely absent from (or at least ignored by) what is considered to be the 'mainstream' globalization debate. Appadurai has regularly been cited by many of the 'review' contributions of the last fifteen years (Held et al. 1999; MacGillivray 2006; Scholte 2005), but few thinkers engage at any length with his concepts or theoretical propositions. In this respect, to take one of the most recent examples, neither the periodization of the globalization debate nor the classification of globalization theories in Nick Bisley's review mentions Appadurai (Bisley 2007: 17; 23). This may be an omission, but I would suggest it is more because he does not fit into the classification developed. Furthermore, most of the academic literature has always to a large extent 'talked past' Appadurai's contribution (to take another of Bisley's terms).

It is therefore appropriate that we come to consider Appadurai as the final thinker in this book, a little of an 'outsider' to the mainstream debate. My proposition is that this is a consequence of more fundamental issues than the discomfort the dominant political science strand of the globalization literature may feel with contributions within the cultural and anthropological frameworks. My argument is that the reason Appadurai has been regarded as a 'parallel thinker' to the mainstream academic discourses about globalization is that his thinking (and cultural thinking more generally) presents some serious problems for many of the conceptual claims found in mainstream positions within the debate if it is engaged with in any depth. This stems from the way in which Appadurai's thinking about 'cultural globalization' presents a series of conceptual challenges that any attempt to theorize globalization in general needs to engage with. Central to this is the way in which cultural phenomena are shown to be intrinsic to many of the 'entities', 'processes' and 'transformations' that other segments of the literature focus upon. Furthermore, any attempt to absorb many of Appadurai's propositions concerning the relationship between cultural forms and global societal interconnectedness immediately problematizes many of the accepted discourses concerned with how globalization is affecting nation-states, firms, governments or institutions. Worst of all – for some of the more structural theories of globalization – it destabilizes accepted definitions of the nature of both actors and agency in the context of increasing societal interconnectedness.

In short, much mainstream thinking about globalization lacks any explicit engagement with cultural issues (or at least has done until recently) and Appadurai's work leads quickly to the conclusion that this is a significant problem. Ultimately, I will suggest Appadurai and other cultural thinkers about globalization lead us back to key epistemological issues about the nature of space, place and the spatiality of societal interconnectedness and in so doing provides important insights into one of the key future directions that thinking about globalization needs to take.

These arguments require a good understanding of the central ideas developed about 'cultural globalization' through Appadurai's work over the last two decades, and the chapter thus follows our normal path of tracking different stages and components of this thinking. The next section begins by providing an overview of his seminal argument on 'disjuncture and difference' in the global cultural economy. This has by far been the most widely cited and influential of his contributions. In the third section, I turn to consider further elements of his arguments about the cultural dimensions to globalization, largely drawn from his book, *Modernity at Large*. The fourth section then examines more recent contributions he has made around the concept of 'grassroots globalization' and the relationship between violence and globalization. The fifth task of the chapter is to consider the critical reception to his work, as well as its strengths and limitations. It is here that I develop the arguments concerning the implications of Appadurai's work that have yet to be absorbed by the mainstream of globalization thought. The final section then draws together some conclusions.

Disjuncture and difference in the global cultural economy

Appadurai's best known contribution to the globalization debate forms the second chapter to his 1996 book, *Modernity at Large*. It appeared in an earlier form as a journal article in 1990 but here we will focus on the book chapter. The central argument he makes is that 'the world we live in today is characterized by a new role for the imagination of social life' (ibid.: 31). For Appadurai, 'the image, the imagined, the imaginary – these are all terms that direct us to something critical and new in global cultural processes: *the imagination as a social practice*' (ibid.: 31; emphasis in original). This is to suggests that the imaginary 'is no longer mere fantasy (opium for the masses whose real work is somewhere else), no longer simple escape (from a world defined principally by more concrete purposes and structures), no longer elite pastime (thus not relevant to the lives of ordinary people), and no longer mere contemplation (irrelevant for new forms of desire and subjectivity)' (ibid.). Instead he suggests that the imagination has taken on a range of new attributes: 'an organized field of social practices', 'a form of work', 'a form of negotiation between sites of agency (individuals) and globally defined fields of possibility' (ibid.). The imagination in this view 'is now central to all forms of agency' and is itself 'a social fact' and a key component of a new global order (ibid.).

He proposes a fivefold framework for exploring the 'disjunctures' that exist in the 'new global cultural economy' that seeks to conceptualize 'the relationship among five dimensions of global cultural flows' (ibid.: 33). This derives from his view that this global cultural economy 'has to be seen as a complex, overlapping, disjunctive order that cannot any longer be understood in terms of existing center-periphery models (even those that might account for multiple centers and peripheries)' (ibid.: 32). Its complexity is 'to do with certain fundamental disjunctures between economy, culture and politics' which can be captured by five '-scapes'.

The '-scapes' of the global cultural economy

First, *ethnoscapes* represent 'the landscape of persons who constitute the shifting world in which we live: tourists, migrants, refugees, exiles, guest workers and other moving groups and individuals' (ibid.: 33). These people constitute an essential feature of the world and they appear to affect the politics of (as well as between) nations to a degree that is unprecedented (ibid.: 33). Appadurai is not arguing against the continued existence of 'stable communities and networks' but that everywhere now 'the warp of these stabilities is shot through with the woof of human motion' (ibid.: 34). The outcome is that more individuals and groups have to deal with either the realities of having to move or the fantasies of wanting to (ibid.). A key aspect of this phenomenon is that 'as international capital shifts its needs, production and technology generate different needs' and 'nation-states shift their policies on refugee populations', then 'these moving groups can never afford to let their imaginations rest too long' (ibid.).

Second, Appadurai proposes that *technoscapes* consist of the global configuration of technology as well as the fact that technology (in what he sees as high, low, mechanical and informational forms) now moves at high speeds across various kinds of boundaries that were previously impervious (ibid.). A central role is played in this by TNCs but Appadurai argues the peculiarities of these technoscapes are increasingly driven not by any obvious economies of scale, of political control or of market rationality but rather by increasingly complex relationships amongst monetary flows, political possibilities and the availability of all forms of labour (ibid.).

The difficulty in theorizing these complexities suggests the third concept: *finanscapes*. These he defines as 'the disposition of global capital' which is a landscape composed of currency markets, national stock markets and commodity speculations and is 'more mysterious, rapid and difficult' than ever before. The 'critical point', however, is that the relationship between these first three '-scapes' is 'deeply disjunctive and profoundly unpredictable' because each of the landscapes 'is subject to its own constraints and incentives . . . at the same time as each acts as a constraint and a parameter for movements in the others' (ibid.: 35).

The fourth concept of *mediascapes* refers 'to the distribution of the electronic capabilities to produce and disseminate information (newspapers, magazines, television stations, and film production studios)' which are now available to 'a growing number of public and private interests throughout the world'. Importantly, the concept also covers 'the images of the world created by these media' which Appadurai argues now 'involve many complicated inflections, depending on their mode (documentary or entertainment), their hardware (electronic and pre-electronic), their audiences (local, national or transnational), and the interests of those who own and control them' (ibid.). The implication of this is that 'many audiences around the world experience the media themselves as a complicated and interconnected repertoire of print, celluloid, electronic screens and billboards'. The consequence of this is that 'the lines' between 'realistic and fictional landscapes' are blurred. *Mediascapes* are 'image-centered' and 'narrative-based accounts of strips of reality' which tend to offer 'a series of elements out of which scripts can be formed of imagined lives, their own as well as those of others living in other places' (ibid.: 35). An important attribute of the complexity of these scripts is that they 'can and do get disaggregated into complex sets of metaphors by which people live' (ibid.: 36).

Mediascapes are 'closely related landscapes of images' (ibid.: 35), as is also the fifth concept of *ideascapes*. This refers to 'concatenations of images' that are 'often directly political and frequently have to do with the ideologies of the state and the counter-ideologies of movements explicitly oriented to capturing state power or a piece of it' (ibid.). For

Appadurai, these ideascapes are most commonly composed of 'elements of the Enlightenment world-view, which consists of chains of ideas, terms and images', including *freedom, welfare, rights, sovereignty, representation* and the master term *democracy* (ibid.). As a 'master term', democracy 'sits at the center of a variety of ideascapes, composed of distinctive programmatic configurations of rough translations of other central terms from the vocabulary of the Enlightenment' (ibid.: 37). Thus, *ideascapes* are most definitely fluid. However, in the case of the master term, that fluidity is complicated by the growing diasporas (both voluntary and involuntary) of intellectuals who continually inject new meaning-streams into the discourses that surround democracy in different part of the world (ibid.: 37).

Overall, Appadurai suggests that the concept of the '-scape' suffix in this typology aims 'to point to the fluid, irregular shapes of these landscapes, shapes that characterize international capital as deeply as they do international clothing styles' (ibid.: 33). It also indicates that 'these are not objectively given relations that look the same from every angle of vision' but that 'they are deeply perspectival constructs, inflected by the historical, linguistic and political situatedness of different sorts of actors' (ibid.). These actors range, for Appadurai, from 'nation-states, multinationals [firms], diasporic communities' to 'substantial groupings and movements (whether religious, political or economic) and even intimate face-to-face groups, such as villages, neighbourhoods and families' (ibid.). And it is these five landscapes that form 'the building blocks of . . . *imagined worlds*'. This is a concept that he develops from Benedict Anderson (see Anderson 1991) that seeks to capture 'the multiple worlds that are constituted by the historically situated imaginations of persons and groups spread around the globe'. His contention is that 'an important face of the world we live in today is that many persons on the globe live in such imagined worlds'. These worlds are much more than Anderson's imagined communities (which are seen as the basis for nation-state formation).

The implications of disjuncture

The next stage of Appadurai's argument is to suggest that these five terms '[set] the basis for a tentative formulation about the conditions under which current global flows occur' – namely through the growing disjunctures amongst these '-scapes'. (ibid.: 37). Five issues emerged. First, he contends that central to the growth in the nature and scope of 'disjunctures' is the process of deterritorialization which he conceives in much the same way as Giddens or Held et al. He argues this process forms one of the central forces of the contemporary world because it brings populations of workers into the lower-class sectors and spaces of relatively wealthy societies and is creating exaggerated and intensified critical discourses or attachment to politics in the home state (ibid.). Deterritoralization is thus at the heart of fundamentalism, including Islamic and Hindu fundamentalism. However, at the same time, it 'creates new markets for film companies, art impresarios and travel agencies, which thrive on the need of the deterritorialized population for contact with its homeland' (ibid.: 38). Such 'invented homelands' which 'constitute the mediascapes of deterritorialized groups' can 'often . . . provide the material for new ideascapes in which ethnic conflicts begin to erupt' (ibid.). He also argues that it is in the 'fertile ground of deterritorialization, in which money, commodities and persons are involved in ceaselessly chasing each other around the world, that the mediascapes and ideascapes of the modern world find their fractured and fragmented counterpart' (ibid.) The point is that the ideas and images produced by the mass media are only partial guides to the benefits and experiences that deterritorialized populations transfer to one another (ibid.).

Second, Appadurai argues that his framework for understanding global cultural flows has important implications for nation-states and how the 'impact' of globalization is understood. In his view, 'the relationship between states and nations is everywhere an embattled one' (ibid.: 39). In deconstructing the concept of the nation-state, he suggests that in the contemporary world 'in many societies the nation and the state have become one another's project'. By this he means that nations (conceived as 'groups with ideas about nationhood') are seeking 'to co-opt states and state power' whilst simultaneously states 'seek to capture and monopolize ideas about nationhood' (ibid.: 39). In this battleground, national and international mediascapes are exploited by nation-states to pacify separatists and to suppress all ideas of difference (ibid.). An important feature of this global cultural politics is that 'state and nation are at each other's throats, and the hyphen that links them is now less an icon of conjuncture than an index of disjuncture' (ibid.). He identifies two levels to this disjuncture. Firstly, at the level of any given nation-state 'there is a battle of the imagination' which represents 'the seedbed of brutal separatisms'. Secondly, at another level the disjunctive relationship is deeply entangled with other global disjunctures including the 'scaling-up' of ideas of nationhood and the 'threads of transnational diaspora'.

The third issue concerns the nature of *ethnoscapes*. Appadurai argues that 'the central paradox of ethnic politics in today's world is that primordia (whether of language or skin colour or neighbourhood or kinship) have become globalized' (ibid.: 41). The consequence is that 'sentiments', whose greatest strength relates to their ability to 'ignite intimacy' in a political state and turn locality into a 'staging ground for identity', have become spread over 'vast and irregular spaces as groups move yet stay linked to one another through sophisticated media capabilities' (ibid.). Ethnicity has become 'a global force' which is 'forever slipping through the cracks between states and borders'.

Fourth, Appadurai argues that 'the relationship between the cultural and economic levels of this new set of global disjunctures is not a simple one-way street' in which the terms of global cultural politics are structured around international flows of technology, labour and finance (ibid.: 41). Rather, he argues (drawing on a Marxian perspective) that 'commodity fetishism' has been replaced in the contemporary globalized world by two descendants. The first of these is *production fetishism* which represents an illusion 'created by contemporary transnational production loci that masks translocal capital, transnational earning flows, global management, and often faraway workers . . . in the idiom and spectacle of local . . . control, national productivity and territorial sovereignty'. Production has itself 'become a fetish, obscuring not social relations as such but the relations of production, which are increasingly transnational' (ibid.: 42). In this viewpoint, the locality becomes 'a fetish that disguises the globally dispersed forces that actually drive production processes' (ibid.). The second 'descendant' is the *fetishism of the consumer* which indicates how the consumer 'has been transformed through commodity flow (and the mediascapes, especially advertising, that accompany them) into a sign'. This is a sign in the sense that Baudrillard used it of a 'simulacrum' that 'only asymptomatically approaches the real form of social agency' (Baudrillard 1994) and is 'a mask for the real seat of agency which is not the consumer but the producer'.

Fifth, Appadurai states quite unequivocally that 'the globalization of culture is not the same as its homogenization.' Such a position strongly contradicts the contention of radical thinkers such as Klein and Marcos, as pointed out at the end of the last chapter. Rather, Appadurai suggests, the process of globalization involves the use of a variety of what he terms 'instruments of homogenization' (armaments, advertising techniques, languages, hegemonies, and clothing styles) that are 'absorbed into local political and cultural economies'. This represents a dilemma for nation-states in which they must be delicate. If they are 'too open' to global cultural flows, they run the risk of being 'threatened by revolt' but if they have too little openness, they 'exit the stage' (ibid.: 41). He argues, therefore, that the state has become 'the arbitrageur in the *repatriation of difference*' where difference exists in the multiple forms of 'goods, signs, slogans and styles' (ibid.). The critical point in seeking to theorize the nature of cultural globalization is that 'both sides of the coin of global cultural process today are products of the indefinitely varied mutual contest of sameness and difference' (ibid.: 43). This contest takes place on a stage that is 'characterized by radical disjunctures between different sorts of global flows and the uncertain landscapes created in and through these disjunctures' (ibid.).

The production of locality

Whilst Appadurai develops his arguments about global cultural flows in depth through several case studies in much of the rest of *Modernity at Large*, it is his arguments concerning the nature of locality that warrant most attention here. His propositions in this respect have significant implications for understanding the future prospects for nation-states and what we might understand a 'locality' to be in the contemporary period of 'transnational destabilization' (ibid.: 178). Appadurai contends that locality – in terms of understanding global cultural flows – needs to be conceptualized as 'relational and contextual rather than as scalar or spatial' (ibid.). He defines it as 'a complex phenomenological quality, constituted by a series of links between the sense of social immediacy, the technologies of interactivity and the relativity of contexts'. This phenomenological quality expresses itself, he suggests, in certain kinds of agency, sociality and reproducibility whereas he uses the term *neighbourhood* to refer to 'the actually existing social forms in which locality, as a dimension of value, is variably realised' (ibid.: 179). That is, a neighbourhood in this definition is 'situated communities characterised by their actuality, whether spatial or virtual, and their potential for social reproduction' (ibid.).

Social life and the context of locality

Appadurai suggests the first issue which must be addressed in seeking to understand the relationship between social life, locality and globalization is that of subjectivity. His point is that anthropological studies show that the historical production of locality 'is not simply a matter of producing local subjects as well as the very neighbourhoods that contextualise those subjectivities' (ibid.: 180). Rather, for Appadurai, space and time are themselves 'socialised and localized through complex and deliberate practices of performance, representation and action' (ibid.). Locality is thus too often problematically conceived as territorial rather than social, as 'ground' rather than 'figure'. In contrast, Appadurai sees it as both 'fragile' and a 'property of social life' which represents 'a structure of feeling that is produced by particular forms of intentional activity and yields particular sorts of material effects' (ibid.: 182).

Having outlined this conception of locality, he argues that the production of neighbourhoods is always something that is historically grounded and thus contextual. This 'social part' to the 'context of neighbourhoods' is similar to an *ethnoscape* and the process of 'locality building' always entails 'a moment of colonisation' where locality is wrested from 'previously uncontrolled peoples and places' (ibid.: 183). In other words, 'the transformation of spaces into places requires a conscious moment' and thus the production of a neighbourhood 'is inherently an exercise of power' (ibid.: 184). Neighbourhoods are therefore contexts for locality insofar as they provide a kind of setting within which various kinds of human action can be initiated and meaningfully conducted. This 'context-generative' property of neighbourhoods is important, argues Appadurai, because 'it provides the beginnings of a theoretical angle on the relationships between local and global realities' (ibid.). Key to this is the fact that, in the contemporary world, the production of neighbourhoods increasingly occurs under conditions where the nation-states system represents the normative 'hinge' for the production of both local and translocal activities (ibid.: 188).

The global production of locality

In developing his conception of locality – conceived as a structure of feeling, a property of social life and an ideology of a situated community – Appadurai's next step is to consider the task of 'producing' it. He suggests that this is a struggle composed of at least three 'interactive' dimensions: first, there is the steady increase in the efforts by modern nation-states to define all neighbourhoods under the sign of their forms of affiliation; second, there is a growing disjuncture between territory, forms of subjectivity and the organization of collective social movements; and, third, there is the erosion of the relationship between the spatial and virtual neighbourhoods (ibid.: 189).

The central problem is that in the contemporary globalized world these dimensions dictate that the production of locality 'is more than ever shot through with contradictions, destabilized by human motion, and displaced by the formation of new kinds of virtual neighbourhoods' (ibid.: 198). He concludes by suggesting, therefore, that locality is 'fragile': by this he means that the many displaced, deterritorialized and transient populations that for him constitute today's 'ethnoscapes' are engaged in the construction of locality 'in the face of erosion, dispersal and implosion of neighbourhoods as coherent social formations' (ibid.: 199). This disjuncture between 'neighbourhoods as social formations' and 'locality as a property of social life' is not new. What is new is the disjuncture between these processes and mass-mediated discourses and practices (and this includes things like economic liberalization, multiculturalism, human rights and refugee claims) that now surround the political-territorial entity that is the nation-state (ibid.)

Grassroots globalization and the globalization of violence

Two more recent and interrelated contributions by Appadurai to his thinking about cultural globalization need briefly examining. The first comes from his edited collection, *Globalization* (2001), and relates to a series of arguments about 'grassroots globalization'. He argues that globalization needs to be 'democratised' in the context of 'certain dominant forms of critical knowledge' which have 'come to be organized by the social sciences of the West' (Appadurai 2001: 4). He suggest three issues which he terms 'optical peculiarities': first, there is 'a growing disjuncture between the globalization of knowledge and the knowledge of globalization'; second, there is 'an inherent time lag between the processes of globalization and our efforts to contain them conceptually'; third, globalization as an uneven economic process creates 'a fragmented and uneven distribution of those resources for learning, teaching and cultural criticism' that are most vital for 'the formation of democratic research communities that could produce a global view of globalization' (ibid.). The consequence is that 'globalization resists the possibility of just those forms of collaboration that might make it easier to understand or criticise' (ibid.).

Developing this line of argument, he contends that globalization 'is not simply the name for a new epoch in the history of capital or in the biography of the nation-state' (ibid.: 14). Rather, he develops his

earlier arguments about the nature of the imaginary to suggest globalization 'is marked by a new role for the imagination in social life'
(ibid.). This he applies to the issue of the developing imaginary of the
'reformist', 'anti-' or 'counter-' globalization movements, arguing that
'the single greatest obstacle to this "grassroots globalization" – in relation to the power of global capital – is the lack of a clear picture among
their key actors of the political, economic, and pedagogic advantages
of counter-globalization' (ibid.: 19) His criticism is that 'grassroots
organizations that seek to create transnational networks . . . have not
yet seen that such counter-globalization might generate the sorts of
locational, informational and political flexibility currently monopo-
lized by global corporations and their national-civic allies'. This is
down to a lack of education about what globalization 'is', and one that
needs to be addressed if these movements of resistance are to succeed
in representing 'the poor, the vulnerable and the marginal' in global
society (ibid.: 19–20).

Second, Appadurai's most recent contribution to this developing
thinking about globalization is concerned with 'the globalization of
violence'. In *Fear of Small Numbers* (2006), Appadurai in part appears
to be responding to critics of *Modernity at Large* who saw it as 'insuf-
ficiently attentive to the darker sides of globalization, such as violence,
exclusion and growing inequality' (ibid.: x). However, he also suggests
that the research presented in the book into 'the harshest results of
globalization' also led him to 'grassroots globalization' which represented 'an entirely new phenomenon' (ibid.). *Fear of Small Numbers*
thus expands the arguments developed in the earlier edited collection
by seeking to better theorize the relationship between globalization
and violence. Appadurai does this around three interlocking ideas.
First, he argues that 'there is a fundamental, and dangerous, idea
behind the modern nation-state, the idea of a "national ethos"' (ibid.:
3). National sovereignty is always built upon 'some form of 'national
genius' which is never a 'natural outgrowth of this or that soil' but
rather has been 'produced and naturalized at great cost, through rheto-
rics of war and sacrifice, through punishing disciplines of educational
and linguistic uniformity', as well as 'through the subordination of
myriad local and regional traditions' (ibid.: 4). The problem is that in
the contemporary era of globalization 'some essential principles and
procedures of the modern nation-state' have 'come unglued'. Above
all, he suggests, 'the certainty that distinctive and singular peoples
grow out of and control well-defined national territories has been
decisively unsettled by the global fluidity of wealth, arms, people and
images' (ibid.: 7).

Second, and following on, he suggests that globalization 'exacerbates these uncertainties and produces new incentives for cultural purification as more nations lose the illusion of national sovereignty or well-being' (ibid.). This is leading to greater violence in the contemporary world because 'large-scale violence is not simply the product of antagonistic identities' but rather 'one of the ways in which the illusion of fixed and charged identities is produced' (ibid.: 7). Globalization thus 'exacerbates the conditions of large-scale violence' because 'it produces a potential collision course between the logics of uncertainty' and what Appadurai calls 'incompleteness' (Appadurai 1996). This refers to the way in which 'some minorities (and their "small numbers") remind . . . majorities of the small gap which lies between their condition as majorities and the horizon of the unsullied national whole' (ibid.: 8). Anxiety about incompleteness can lead to 'a runaway form of mutual stimulation' which is 'the road to genocide' (ibid.: 9).

A third idea relates to how globalization has brought about what he calls 'the narcissism of minor difference'. In the fourth chapter of the book, he argues that the 'growing rage against minorities' is articulated through a narcissistic process in nationalism whereby 'majorities can be mobilized to think they are in danger of becoming *minor*' and 'to fear that minorities, conversely, can become *major*' (ibid.: 83). Contemporary globalization intensifies 'the possibility of this volatile morphing' so that 'the naturalness that all group identities seek and assume' is perennially threatened 'by the abstract affinity of the very categories of majority and minority' (ibid.). Minorities in a globalizing world 'are a constant reminder of the incompleteness of national purity' (ibid.: 84).

Metaphorical limits: cultural flows and '-scapes' in question

In assessing the critical response to Appadurai's thinking about globalization, the first point to highlight is the widespread influence (at least in citation terms) of his work far beyond social anthropology. Across the social sciences Appadurai's fivefold typology of global cultural flows has become a common starting point for theorists seeking to understand the relationship between globalization and culture. It is these ideas about cultural flows and '-scapes' – articulated in *Modernity at Large* – that have thus also received most critical engagement. I want in this section to draw on those engagements but also identify a series of potential limitations with his approach in light of the wider assessment of globalization theories developed through this book.

The first area of limitation I want to identify is the central reliance of Appadurai's approach on the metaphors of the 'flow/fluidity' and 'mobility'. This stems back to the epistemological issue of what culture might be understood to 'be'. It could be argued that cultural artefacts are not so easily conceptualized as mobile because they never have a sufficient degree of 'fixity' (either in territory or practice). At the level of epistemology, it may be difficult to isolate a cultural entity sufficiently in order to establish its motion from local to other scales (and most particularly the global). The 'mobilities' paradigm within sociology (Urry 2007) to some extent seeks to address this problem by shifting anthropological approaches to culture away from territorial-based conceptions, but this issue remains central to debates about how cultural globalization is theorized.

Second, even if we accept they exist, there is also a debate about whether cultural flows can be effectively mapped. Paul Hopper (2007) summarizes this issue succinctly when he asks whether it is possible to map 'the sheer quantity of cultural movements' and evaluate them 'in any meaningful way' (ibid.: 45). Everything from 'billboard and television advertisements selling products from other countries' to 'foreign languages being spoken in a country' are 'all instances of cultures being permeated by other cultural influences' (ibid.). Whilst Hopper reminds us that Held et al. argue such a mapping *is* possible, the task seems monumental. What is more, the problem is that 'focusing upon cultural flows does not tell us how they are being interpreted and experienced by recipients, nor the motives that are generating them' (ibid.) The nub of the issue is thus that in all likelihood 'monitoring the volume, speed and location' of cultural flows 'will reveal little about the nature of the cultural interaction' (ibid.: 46). This would appear to be a serious limitation, since it suggests Appadurai's approach will struggle to provide insight into the future direction and consequences of cultural globalization.

Third, there is the perennial issue of power which again recurs in relation to Appadurai's conception of the global cultural economy. Following on from the limited scope of the 'flow' metaphor for capturing cultural interaction, it also ignores the power relations that underpin cultural interactions. Hopper argues that 'we need to take account whether there are some powers or influences dominating and defining global cultural flows and processes' (ibid.: 46) which is certainly the case, but I would argue that the issue runs far deeper in that cultural entities or artefacts are embedded in power relations. Without the capacity to understand the constitution of power in cultural interaction in the contemporary globalized world, we can only develop a rather limited understanding of the development of new cultural forms.

Fourth, and the final issue I want to identify here, there is also the recurrent problem of the concept of (cultural) 'deterritorialization'. As with the discussion in chapter 2 of Giddens's development of this concept, Appadurai's implementation of the term is similarly caught up in a series of epistemological problems and potential contradictions. If, as Hopper suggests, Appadurai's conception of cultural deterritorialization aligns to the idea of 'a transformation in the relationship between culture and territory', then it remains firmly in a minefield of epistemological problems centred on the 'territorial-ness' (or otherwise) of cultural entities. In short, as I argued with Giddens's use of the concept, to be 'deterritorialized', cultural entities must have some territorial property to their constitution. Without revisiting this critique at length, the problem is that this territorial-ness is very hard to delimit and is enormously complicated by its interaction with ideas of both place and identity.

Conclusion: (the lack of) engagement with Appadurai and cultural globalization

Criticisms notwithstanding, the influence and impact of Appadurai's cultural thinking about globalization has been significant across the social sciences. However, as I suggested at the start of this chapter, much engagement with his work has been at either a superficial level or perhaps more often has been confined to narrow debates about the relationship between globalization and culture. Appadurai's five-fold typology of '-scapes' remains a 'classic' account of the nature of the dimensions that need to be considered when seeking to understand how culture becomes 'globalized' (or not) in the contemporary period. Yet whilst Appadurai clearly sets out this approach in a manner that transcends almost every strand to the globalization debate (economic, political, social, etc.), an appreciation of this tends to be absent from 'mainstream' debates about the global economy or even in the political science literature engaged with effects of globalization on the nation-state and the nature of existing and future supranational institutions.

This is what I mean by suggesting that, despite his high profile in certain areas, Appadurai's thinking, along with that of other cultural globalization thinkers, is marginal to the mainstream debate. For example, many of the issues Appadurai engages with in discussing media and ethnoscapes provide a very different conceptual cut on the nature of Castells's 'space of flows' and the global informational economy. In fact, his analysis of the global cultural economy opens up a series of questions about the relationship between cultural ideas and the transnationalization of financial markets, firms, regulatory environments and business practices. Similarly, although a little more widely engaged with, his analysis of national cultural formation provides a series of trenchant insights into debates about the erosion of national sovereignty, the future of national and supranational entities, and what form new institutions of global governance might need to look like. Whilst various contributors to debates about some of these issues occasionally make reference to his or others' cultural thinking about globalization, for the most part issues of culture are ignored. Even Held et al. in their tour-de-force book, *Global Transformations*, partition off cultural globalization (and their concomitant discussion of Appadurai) into a fairly discrete chapter concerned with the 'cultural' dimension to the debate.

This belies a key problem in globalization thinking in relation to culture. Whilst each chapter of this book has sought to deal with a thematic aspect of globalization thinking in relation to one or a small number of key thinkers, many of these thematic elements – like the aspects of the globalization debate they relate to – are entwined with other 'themes'. Likewise, I argued in the introductory chapter that dividing the globalization debate into different sub-categories may be necessary but remains problematic. Nowhere is this more evident than in dealing with the issue of cultural globalization and Appadurai's interventions in seeking to theorize it. For culture as a concept remains ambiguous insofar as every aspect of social life is imbued with it. Any consideration of cultural globalization thus leads back to difficult epistemological questions about a whole range of key concepts, including social practice, scale, place, identity and territoriality.

It is therefore fitting that we end our journey through thinking about globalization on a cultural theme and with perhaps the classic thinker on this topic. For reaching the difficult issue of cultural globalization at this final stage brings us full circle back to the fundamental epistemological issues identified in the academic thinkers including Giddens, Held, McGrew and Castells. Appadurai's contribution to thinking about cultural globalization illustrates well the inseparability of this so-called 'dimension' to globalization from those such as (neo-liberal) economic globalization that have occupied most thinkers. The fact that many other strands of globalization thinking have yet to fully engage with the implications of this remains one of the most significant challenges for future thought about globalization, and one which leads to the next and final chapter where I seek to draw together some overall conclusions.

Further reading

Works by Arjun Appadurai

Appadurai, A. (1990) Disjuncture and Difference in the Global Cultural Economy. *Theory, Culture and Society* 7: 295–310.
Appadurai, A. (1996) *Modernity at Large: Cultural Dimensions of Globalization.* Minneapolis: University of Minnesota Press.
Appadurai, A. (2001) Grassroots Globalization and the Research Imagination, in A. Appadurai (ed.), *Globalization.* London: Duke University Press, pp. 1–21.
Appadurai, A. (2006) *Fear of Small Numbers.* London: Duke University Press.

Website resources

Appadurai's webpage: www.appadurai.com/

Commentary and critical engagement

Hopper, P. (2007) *Understanding Cultural Globalization.* Cambridge: Polity.
Tomlinson, J. (1999) *Globalization and Culture.* Cambridge: Polity.

13 CONCLUSION: RETHINKING GLOBALIZATION (AGAIN)

Comparing current thinking about globalization

Thinking about globalization is challenging and, at the end of this book, there is no simple conclusion or 'answer' to give about which of the many thinkers we have examined is 'right', or even to offer the definitive perspective for understanding what globalization 'is' and how it needs to be managed. However, in this concluding chapter I end the book with a comparative analysis of the main differences and similarities between the various key thinkers we have met on our journey. The purpose here is to elaborate around the major areas of agreement and disagreement I identified in the introduction, as well as to try to give the reader a clearer overall idea of which arguments are better constructed than others. This will allow me – in a qualified way – to make some cautious general propositions about what we do and do not know about 'globalization' and where areas of dispute and uncertainty remain. However, rather than try to compile the key arguments of every thinker discussed in this book into an abridged (and probably unhelpful) list or table, I have framed the following discussion around seven dimensions to thinking about globalization.

Definition

Despite the acres of published text given to analysing globalization, it should be clear at the end of this book that no final consensus exists as to how globalization might be defined in anything more than the most general terms. It is true that the academic debate largely accepts the generalized definition offered by Giddens as 'the intensification of worldwide social relations which link distant localities' (Giddens 1990: 64). Remember, for Giddens, Castells and Held et al., globalization is a phenomenon that cannot – in one way or another – be understood outside the context of 'modernity' which is producing it (see 'Conceptualization' below). These thinkers are in broad agreement that the condition of modernity is itself 'inherently globalizing'. Held et al. of course offer a more developed definition with their argument that globalization 'embodies a transformation in the spatial organization of social relations and transactions – assessed in terms of their extensity, intensity, velocity and impact' (Held et al. 1999). Dicken usefully develops this processual understanding of globalization in the abstract, arguing that it is 'not a single unified phenomenon, but a syndrome of processes and activities' (ibid.: 8). Importantly, and in contrast to the political science thinkers, he suggests that the processes behind globalization 'must be understood as *spatial*'.

Of course, several thinkers we have discussed offered what amounts to an anti-definition insofar as they are sceptical that the concept has any validity at all. Hirst and Thompson's contribution here is clearly the most sustained in their view that what is being termed contemporary globalization in fact presents 'a myth' and does not correspond to 'a truly global economy' but rather a period of (at best) heightened internationalization. Such a definitional position is also shared by Wallerstein, who in his later work suggests that the current era is one characterized by a transition in the world capitalist economy. And to some extent, Hardt and Negri's concept of 'globalization-as-Empire' has much in common with this sceptical position. Overall, however, the majority of academic thinkers we have considered suggest that the new concept of globalization is warranted.

Yet, beyond the academic debate, it is fair to say that globalization remains defined primarily as an economic phenomenon (although see 'Conceptualization' below) – even if these thinkers gloss over the uncomfortable problems this creates when their ideas about the phenomenon stray into non-economic areas such as culture or politics. Wolf is up front about this, dismissing discussion of globalization beyond the economic realm as subsidiary and less relevant. In contrast, Friedman is more opaque, mixing his economic-centred view of globalization with arguments concerning advances in information and communications. Likewise, radical thinkers like Klein and Marcos largely target their critique of globalization as an economically driven phenomenon, even if it has significant cultural and political impacts as well.

History

The issue of the history of globalization is to a considerable extent bound into the issue of definition. Early on in this book we encountered Wallerstein's argument that 'what is described as globalization has been happening for 500 years'. Such a position is also well established by Held et al. in their near-encyclopaedic assessment of the development of 'global-scale interconnectedness' back to antiquity. It is similarly present, if less explicitly, in both Giddens's and Appadurai's linkage of globalization with modernity. Therefore, using this most general definition of the concept, the long historical existence of globalization appears well established. Nevertheless, several thinkers reserve the concept of globalization for a much more recent phenomenon. Many of the economic-centred thinkers like Dicken, Sassen, Wolf and Stiglitz essentially map the emergence of globalization in its current form to the post-Second World War world, and particularly the period since the end of the Cold War (i.e. since 1989). Many of the sceptical thinkers we have discussed have responded to this periodization, although the arguments of radical thinkers like Klein, Hardt and Negri are notably focused on the period since the end of the Cold War. However, significant differences do exist even within this recent periodization. Castells, for example, links the history of what he refers to specifically as globalization to technological change in the last few decades, pointing to the ICT revolution that began in the 1970s. Friedman is even more temporally focused, referring to phases of globalization, the most recent of which – linked to recent advances in internet technology – began around the year 2000.

Conceptualization

Throughout this book, I have argued that important differences persist in how various thinkers conceptualize globalization. These differences ultimately derive from different epistemological approaches to understanding what globalization 'is'. In concluding this book, I want to suggest four major strands of thinking around its conceptualization.

First there is the difficult issue of causality – that is, what factors have produced past and current globalization. Several common threads are evident in this respect. To begin with, most of the thinkers featured in this book consider economic activity – and the development of capitalism – to be a central factor behind globalization in one way or another. Some of the 'popular' thinkers, including Wolf, Friedman, Stiglitz, Klein and Marcos, place strong causal emphasis on the economy as a driving force. This generally falls short of seeing the development of the global economy as a straightforward cause of globalization (although Wolf and Friedman do come close), but undoubtedly economic processes are given primacy. Amongst academic thinkers, not surprisingly, there is more caution and less of a sense of economic development being the only causal factor. Those of a Marxian persuasion (Wallerstein, Hardt and Negri) tend to place a stronger emphasis on the tendencies of the capitalist system towards expansion and growth being a key driver. However, the social scientific thinkers, including Giddens, Held et al. and Castells, essentially see globalization as having multiple causes, all bound into the ongoing evolution of modernity. Different academic thinkers put different emphases on aspects within this. For example, Castells clearly regards technological change as a more important contributory causal factor whereas Dicken's treatment is more economic in relation to his focus on the organization of production and consumption. As I suggested in chapter 12, it is Appadurai's thinking that complicates the issue of the causality of globalization most. His engagement with the nature of cultural interconnectedness certainly destabilizes the hegemonic view of globalization being primarily an economic-driven phenomenon.

Second, and following on, a number of key academic thinkers make the case for conceptualizing globalization as a singular, novel phenomenon that extends beyond the economic sphere of social life. In this approach, the concept therefore warrants a generalized meta-theoretical framework. Clearly, given the vast array of aspects to human life that the term is used to refer to, this is an ambitious claim that requires a broad concept that can be applied to many different contexts. Giddens, Appadurai and Held et al. all achieve this by arguing that globalization is an expression of modernity, where Castells more cautiously links it to the emergence of a global network society. These thinkers to varying degrees thus share a view that some kind of 'meta-theoretical' approach is both feasible and desirable for conceptualizing globalization. Similarly, within the popular literature, the view that the concept has generalized validity – whilst more implicit – is shared by positive, reformist and radical thinkers alike. In contrast, other academic thinkers like Dicken are more cautious, seeing globalization as a term referring to 'multiple syndromes'. As already referred to above, strong sceptics like Hirst and Thompson argue that the concept is unjustified and does not represent any general or particularly new phenomenon.

The third issue of conceptualization concerns whether or not globalization should be understood as a processual and systemic phenomenon. Amongst the academic thinkers, there is a strong common conception of globalization as one or more related processes. Giddens, Held et al., Castells, Dicken and Sassen all share some kind of processual view, and it is the fact that globalization is reducible in some form to a process of increasing interconnectedness that underpins many of the meta-theoretical claims made for the term. Again, such a conception is not explicitly evident amongst the popular thinkers although it is easy to argue that processual ideas are present in the thinking of Stiglitz, Wolf and Friedman. However, it is worth noting that a number of the thinkers we have considered view globalization more as a systemic phenomenon than as one or more processes (although the two approaches are not exclusive). Broadly, many of the thinkers that adopt a systemic view draw on a Marxian epistemology. This is only loosely evident in Hirst and Thompson's framework for thinking about the international political system, but Wallerstein's proto-globalization approach clearly represents a strongly Marxist systemic conception of global economy and society. Equally, however, the radical and revolutionary thinkers like Klein, Marcos, Hardt and Negri all seek to engage with globalization as something largely produced by the global capitalist system in some manner.

Fourth, and finally, conceptualizations of globalization are marked by differing views of the politics of knowledge. As I suggested at several points in assessing the contributions of thinkers including Wallerstein, Giddens, Castells, Held et al., Dicken and Sassen, academic theorizations of globalization have widely sought (as these authors do) to generate some kind of objective conceptual framework for understanding globalization in the abstract. These social scientific thinkers thus variously share the perspective that such a value-neutral approach is both desirable and possible. However, many of the popular and radical thinkers come from a rather different perspective which sees globalization as much as a political and ideological project about how the world *should* be rather than as a description of some objective reality. Only Hardt and Negri – and to a lesser extent Stiglitz – occupy a middle ground in this dichotomy of approach insofar as their thinking (albeit in very different ways) combines aspects of the objective theorizing with a clear set of subjective political arguments.

Key transformations

The fourth dimension around which it is worth summarizing the major similarities and differences between the various key thinkers are the key transformations (or processes, where applicable) associated with globalization. There are many possible transformations I might list here, but I want to emphasize four strands that are amongst the most significant.

First, and as I emphasized in the introductory chapter, most of the thinkers discussed see the transformation of our experience of time and space as a key element to contemporary globalization. However, a range of different conceptions of how this transformation is manifest is evident. To begin with, much of the thinking we have discussed conceptualizes the spatio-temporal transformation in straightforward territorial and topographical terms – globalization as a process by which different places and peoples are linked across physical global-scale space. This transformation is often conceptualized as being the interlinkage of different scales – the local, regional, national and global. Both academic thinkers (Wallerstein, Hirst, Thompson) and popular thinkers (Wolf, Stiglitz, Klein) fall into this group.

However, in contrast, several thinkers we have discussed adopt what is arguably a more sophisticated and complicated conception of space–time transformation that draws on other spatial concepts. Thus, Held et al.'s fourfold framework – extensity, intensity, velocity and impact – is essentially a development of Giddens's arguments about the process of space–time distanciation. Castells's thinking about the transformation of space and time also shares much common ground here, although he considerably develops the dynamism of this transformation through the concepts of the space of flows and timeless time. Yet Castells's thinking also differs from the other 'transformationalists' in his important emphasis on the network as a spatial concept for understanding the nature of globalization. Castells shares this engagement with how the transformation of space and time might be conceptualized in topological (network) rather than simply topographical terms with – in various ways – Dicken, Sassen and Appadurai. Each of these thinkers makes use of topological concepts as well as adopting a concomitant relational approach to thinking about the spatio-temporal transformation of social relations. Less obviously, similar kinds of ideas are implicit in many of Friedman's less precise arguments about the 'flat' world.

Second, a pervasive transformative process that runs through many of the academic thinkers considered in this book is that of *deterritori-*

alization or disembedding – although not necessarily in explicit terms. Giddens of course defines this process as central to globalization as social relations become 'detached' from their places of origin and transferred to new locales (re-territorialized). Held et al., in following Giddens, make extensive use of this concept in seeking to understand how globalization reconfigures economy and society. Likewise, Castells's argument that social practices which relied on physical places for time-sharing have been superseded by those built around time-sharing over distance – manifest in the space of flows – is a similar kind of transformation. Furthermore, Dicken's application of the concept of disembedding in trying to understand the development of the globalizing economy also grapples with the way in which socio-economic relations and actors are partially detached and re-attached to locales. However, it is in Appadurai's thinking that deterritorialization is most developed in its application to issues of culture, knowledge and identity in the contemporary world.

The third common transformation or process that runs through much thinking concerns the simultaneous production of homogeneity and difference. Such a transformative theme is present in every thinker we have examined, ranging from Wallerstein's concern for how one world system – capitalism – has become global in scope and what implication that has for different territorially contained economies and societies, to the (not unproblematic) implication of radical thinkers like Klein who attack the perceived homogenized cultural and political outcomes of globalization. Whether cast in such simplistic terms, or in the more sophisticated analysis of the complex production of cultural difference in a globalizing world in the work of Held et al., Appadurai and even Friedman, the tension between the production of sameness and/or difference through globalization represents a major theme for many key thinkers.

Finally, many of the thinkers discussed in this book emphasize the way in which globalization is bound into power processes, both in terms of domination and resistance. Important differences of emphasis exist however. Amongst a significant number of the academic thinkers – Giddens, Held, McGrew, Hirst and Thompson – attempts to develop objective understandings of globalization processes mean that the phenomenon is understood in a relatively apolitical manner. These thinkers are undoubtedly aware of the political engagements that underpin the transformations they associate with globalization, but overall their focus is on a more generalized form of understanding globalization *in toto*. Dicken and Sassen adopt a similar social scientific approach that seeks to describe outcomes rather than explain the politics that have produced them. Castells occupies an unusual middle ground here insofar as his social scientific analysis of the network society seeks to understand the rise of the highly politicized anti-globalization movement itself. In contrast, other thinkers adopt a much more subjective stance that expresses a certain political position. Amongst the academic thinkers, Hardt and Negri position their Marxian analysis as a politicized critique of 'globalization-as-Empire', and articulate what amounts to a more theoretically sophisticated but similar argument than the radical thinkers that globalization represents a political project and involves domination. In contrast, Wolf also emphasizes the politicized nature of globalization as an ideological project, but seeks to defend this project against the radical and revolutionary critiques. For Wolf, globalization is producing misguided resistance that is mistaken in its claims that globalization is a regressive phenomenon (and see below on 'Impacts and consequences').

Actors and agents

Trying to summarize all the different actors and sources of agency that have been identified by different key thinkers is beyond the scope of this final chapter. Yet it is hopefully clear that certain actors and agents are recurrent amongst various thinkers. It is therefore worth highlighting some of the most significant ones.

Firstly, every single one of the key thinkers discussed in this book points to the important role of key supranational institutions and organizations in fostering and maintaining globalization in recent decades. Foremost are clearly the supranational post-Bretton Woods institutions – the IMF, World Bank, GATT/WTO and UN. Most thinkers agree on the key role played by these entities in creating the conditions under which a global economy and society have developed. However, clear differences exist in the nature and role of the agency attributed to these organizations. Many of the academic social science thinkers – for example, Giddens, Castells, Dicken and Sassen – place less emphasis on the role of these institutions over societal organizations, corporations or non-governmental actors. In contrast, much of the popular thinking is very much focused on what is seen as a central role for these institutions – notably Stiglitz, Wolf, Klein, Monbiot and Marcos.

With regard to the second group of significant actors in relation to globalization, few thinkers ignore what they see as the agency of trans-national corporations. However, opinion varies considerably as to the nature and degree of agency possessed by TNCs in relation to global-ization. Some thinkers give TNCs a leading, even primary, role in fostering globalization through the development of the global economy. Many of the popular thinkers fall into this vein of argument, with Friedman and Wolf taking a positive view of this agency whereas Klein, Monbiot, Marcos, Hardt and Negri take a negative one. Stiglitz also places strong emphasis on the agency of TNCs, although adopting a more balanced analysis with respect to the positive and negative implications of this. However, among the academic thinkers, whilst the undoubted significance of TNCs as agents of globalization is acknowledged, there is a diversity of more cautious opinion which tends to cast them as one group of important actors amongst several. Held, Dicken and Sassen all qualify their view of TNC agency with an understanding of how TNCs are bound into relations with other actors. Castells shares much in common with this latter group, but again has a different cut at the agency of TNCs in his emphasis on their role in propagating the diffusion of technologies at the centre of his vision of the global informational society.

Third, despite the hyperglobalist rhetoric described by Held et al. in the 1990s' globalization debate, many of the key thinkers discussed in this book also put considerable emphasis on the ongoing signifi-cance of nation-states (and supranational political entities like the EU) in shaping contemporary globalization. As I identified in the introduc-tion, the broad consensus amongst the academic thinkers discussed is that the nation-state has played an important role in shaping globaliza-tion to date, that it is unlikely to become obsolete but that it is likely to have a changed role in the future as globalization proceeds. Castells is perhaps most radical in his vision of how the 'network state' will represent a significantly different territorial-political unit from that which arose during the nineteenth and twentieth centuries. However, differences remain between thinkers in their assessment of how power-ful nation-states will be as actors. Stiglitz, for example, clearly sees a crucial and central role for nation-states if his reform agenda is to be achieved. In contrast, nation-states appear likely to become less rele-vant as new information technologies empower individuals in the glo-balized world that Friedman foresees.

A fourth commonly prioritized set of actors amongst the key think-ers in this book are political movements, in both the formal and non-formal realms of politics. With respect to the former, a number of both academic and popular thinkers highlight the agency of (formal) politi-cal ideological movements in shaping contemporary globalization. This agency is seen in both a positive and negative light, depending on the perspective of the thinker. For example, Wolf charts the role of neoliberal ideology in the post-Second World War period as important in shaping the actions of states and the Bretton Woods institutions. Wolf sees this as a positive shift away from excessive and anti-market collectivism of state socialist and Keynesian interventionist policies. In contrast, of course, Klein and Marcos (and to some extent Hardt and Negri) also emphasize the role of neoliberal ideology as a basis for political actors to adopt undesirable policies that have led to the negative and regressive impacts of globalization (see 'Impacts and consequences' below).

However, other thinkers also place considerable significance on non-formal political movements. From their objective social scientific perspective, for example, Castells, Held et al. and McGrew all see new social movements (such as the environmental movement) as key actors in the development of globalization. Castells of course focuses on the agency of the anti-globalization movement as such an actor par excellence. However, Appadurai's thinking suggests the significance of informal political movements (and all kinds of social movements) beyond a simple binary opposition of their role in either promoting or resisting globalization. His analysis of the complex ways in which cultural flows, ideas and identities are disseminated at the global scale in the contemporary world suggests that the role of political movements in globalization is much more complicated than much of the current literature acknowledges.

Finally, a fifth group of actors that concern many of our key thinkers corresponds to the role of individuals and small groups. Different thinkers cite numerous different actors in this respect, whether US presidents or lobby groups, but several common threads are worth drawing out. First, there is a diversity of opinion about the capacity of individuals and small groups to act and influence the development of globalization in general. Those thinkers influenced by the modern structuralist tradition in social theory (be that Marxian or other forms of epistemology) place very limited emphasis on individuals. In the thinking of Wallerstein, Held, McGrew, Dicken, Sassen, Hirst and Thompson, the role of the individual in globalization is hard to discern amongst larger-scale actors and societal processes or structural shifts. Castells is perhaps an exceptional case in this in that his ideas do identify the significance of key small groups such as NGO leaders, global workers or terrorists. Whilst overall this understanding of where agency resides in today's world may well be justifiable in dealing with such a broad concept as globalization, some of the thinkers we have discussed do point to the crucial agency of certain small groups and even individuals. Radical thinkers like Klein, Monbiot, Marcos, Hardt and Negri see individual political action as the basis for alternative forms of globalization to the current neoliberal version. In fact they all view resistance to this hegemonic form of globalization as being about individuals or small groups taking a stance against large entities like governments, institutions and corporations. Again, perhaps most radically, it is Appadurai who provides the most challenging thinking about how small groups have significant agency in his arguments about the importance of diasporic communities in shaping national identities.

Impact and consequences

Whilst we have encountered many specific arguments in this book about the various impacts and consequences of contemporary globalization, the diversity of propositions made is considerable. These range across debates about whether the contemporary world economy is becoming 'truly global', whether globalization is producing an erosion of national sovereignty or what kinds of impacts it is having on individual lives. Yet many of these impacts – political, economic or cultural – can be associated with the particular set of concerns of a given thinker and all of these cannot be drawn together here. However, one major issue about the impact of contemporary globalization has occupied almost all of the thinkers we have discussed, and does justify some concluding comment. This is the issue of whether globalization overall is a positive (or progressive) as opposed to a negative (or regressive) phenomenon.

Broadly speaking, thinking on globalization tends to fall into one of three general positions on this question of impact and consequences. These positions transcend both academic and popular thinking, and of course individual thinkers do not necessarily exclusively occupy any one position with respect to all their ideas concerning globalization. First, there are those thinkers who regard globalization as a positive, beneficial and progressive development in human society. Obviously, I argued at some length in chapter 8 that Friedman and Wolf view the phenomenon in such a light, although there are differences in emphasis between them. Wolf argues that (neoliberal) globalization is positive because it corresponds to the extension, development and integration of market economies and liberal democracies across the globe which he suggests is producing many positive benefits including a reduction in wars, greater material wealth and more tolerant societies. Friedman adopts a broadly similar perspective but further emphasizes the stimulating and empowering impact of globalization facilitated by new information technologies. However, this positive view is not restricted to these popular thinkers. In various ways, Giddens, Castells, Dicken and Sassen adopt a generally (if more muted) positive view of globalization as a progressive transformation that is bringing a range of economic, political and cultural benefits to society.

Secondly, however, others adopt a more neutral view of the consequences of globalization, arguing that it has both positive and negatives impacts. Amongst the popular thinkers, Stiglitz's analysis most fits this position as he acknowledges the negative consequences of recent globalization and outlines a framework for reforming how to make it 'work better' in the future. However, a number of academic thinkers we have discussed – Held et al., McGrew, Hirst, Thompson and Appadurai – identify both positive and negative outcomes of globalization, although in their social scientific approach this is often more implicitly that explicitly stated.

Third, and lastly, a range of the thinkers we have discussed share a negative view of globalization that in some form associates this phenomenon with regressive or undesirable consequences. Such a position is implicit in many whose thinking draws on a Marxian approach and whose conception of globalization is essentially closely tied to the ongoing evolution of world capitalist society. Wallerstein, Klein, Marcos, Hardt and Negri all occupy such a position in one way or another, and their view that globalization has negative impacts on aggregate runs back to the Marxian arguments that counter the Wolf position – namely that growing poverty, inequality and oppressive forms of power are associated with the operation of the capitalist system. For these thinkers, and in common with a substantial literature (e.g. Hertz 2002; Turner 2008), the consequences of globalization are an extension and amplification of the problems that capitalism has already produced historically.

The key critiques of current globalization thinking

Having drawn out the major areas of similarity between different thinkers, the penultimate task in this concluding chapter is to outline the significant threads of critique that run through the globalization debate. Individual chapters have pointed to the specific problems with each of the key thinkers' ideas, but it is important to add to this an understanding of what criticisms are common to them. This makes most sense when structured around a consideration of academic and popular thinking respectively.

Academic thinking: meta-theory and the postmodern state of knowledge

The first major area of criticism that applies to many of the academic thinkers concerns the viability of generalized 'meta-theoretical' frameworks for understanding globalization. 'Grand' theories of globalization remain vulnerable to the criticism that they are too ambitious and reduce multiple, complex changes in the contemporary world to one, inappropriate conceptual framework. Such a postmodern critique has for some time been levelled at modern social theories and, for example, has been directed at Wallerstein's Marxian world systems analysis since the late 1980s. Whilst the emergence of globalization theories has come in the aftermath of the postmodern challenge, many key thinkers continue within a strong modernist theoretical tradition that seeks to develop generalized social scientific theory. In this respect, Giddens and Castells are both vulnerable to this critique. Furthermore, although Held et al.'s approach evades some of the more direct criticism of producing an inflexible or simplistic 'one size fits all' approach to globalization, when applied to the numerous specific cases or contexts that equate to a 'global transformation', the relevance of their concepts is not always clear. Hirst and Thompson's classic contribution questioning the validity of general claims for the concept of (economic) globalization thus remains a salient reminder of the risks associated with abstract theoretical propositions that do not bear detailed empirical scrutiny. Other academic thinkers we have encountered – notably Dicken and Appadurai – are more sensitive to the limited nature of their theoretical claims.

Second, and very much related, there are significant limits to the kind of systemic and structural epistemological tradition that general theories of globalization tend to be constructed upon. The 'postmodern' shift in the state of social scientific knowledge, whilst by no mean unproblematic in all respects, has left a justifiable legacy of scepticism around the capacity of social theorization to effectively capture the social world with structuralist concepts. Thus, the social scientific thinking of most of the academic thinkers discussed remains strongly wedded to conceptualizing globalized social relations as the interaction of relatively stable structures (states, institutions, social classes, etc.) at the global scale. The post-structuralist challenge has been quite effective at demonstrating the problems with this epistemology, and puts in doubt to what extent it is useful to view increasingly societal interconnectedness at the planetary scale as *systemic* (Goede 2006; Jackson 2003; Peters 2002). Understanding globalization as a systemic phenomenon (at least in the stronger use of this terminology) is at best a deeply problematic and complex question, and the contention is that such an idea needs to be regarded with extreme caution. The contemporary globalized world is not only a far more complex entity than Wallerstein's world systems approach succeeds in capturing, but systemic thinking does not necessarily even effectively conceptualize the nature and form of all the actors involved in globalization. Only a limited number of the thinkers we have considered – Dicken, Appadurai, Hardt et al. and Negri – engage with the challenge of this postmodern critique.

Third, there is a further consequence of the so-called 'postmodern' shift in the nature of social scientific enquiry and academic thinking about globalization: an unresolved and inconsistent recognition of the politics of knowledge. Many of the sociological (Giddens, Castells) and political science (Held, McGrew, Hirst and Thompson) thinkers discussed present theoretical approaches to understanding globalization that present themselves as neutral and objective accounts of the contemporary world. Such a perspective is an inheritance from classical 'modern' approaches to social science that aspires to develop objective accounts of the social world. The postmodern challenge continues to question whether or not 'objectivity' in theorization is possible in this manner, arguing that all forms of knowledge are situated and politicized (Latour 1999, 2005; Seidman 1994, 2008). Such a point appears especially pertinent in relation to globalization theories since the debate about this concept is so heavily and overtly political and subjective in nature. Whether or not it is possible (or desirable) to develop objective theories of globalization thus remains contested (Mittelman 2004).

Fourth, the preponderance of academic thinking about globalization continues to focus on political-economic approaches to defining globalization, with clearly important 'sub-categories' of the debate, such as cultural globalization, remaining marginal and receiving less attention. Given the sheer breadth and number of cultural aspects to global cultural flow, this is problematic. However, and furthermore, it betrays a more fundamental problem with contemporary academic thinking insofar as the classification of globalization (Bisley 2007) into 'sub-categories' appears restrictive and potentially inadequate for understanding all the various phenomena subsumed in the term.

Partitioning off the cultural (or indeed any) dimension of globalization as a separate object of analysis creates a range of difficult epistemological issues. The work of Appadurai and other theorists of cultural globalization (Hopper 2007; Nederveen Pieterse 2004; Tomlinson 1999) demonstrates the entwinement of cultural facets in all aspects of global scale interconnectedness.

Lastly, a common critique of much academic thinking about globalization is that it employs a simplistic and consequently problematic spatial epistemology. In light of the discussion in chapter 7 of the work of Dicken and Sassen, the scope for developing a more sophisticated approach to the spatial constitution of global interconnectedness appears to be substantial. Whilst I argued that neither Dicken nor Sassen present an unassailable approach to their respective objects of analysis (the global economic and global city network), much of the sociological and political science literature on globalization would benefit from a substantial engagement with the implications of their arguments. For example, the international relations literature concerned with state sovereignty continues to develop arguments that utilize a simplistic concept of the relationship between nation-states, 'their' economies and territory that appears highly problematic in light of Dicken's arguments. Even where a leading sociologist – Castells – has developed a far more sophisticated conception of the spatiality inherent in technological globalization, his arguments about the reconfiguration of time and space (whilst often cited in passing) have largely been ignored by much of the globalization literature. Appadurai's contributions about the fluid nature of localities also serve to reinforce this point.

Popular thinking: oversimplification and a lack of alternatives

Most of the popular thinkers considered in this book can be criticized for perpetuating a rather simplistic and narrow conceptual understanding of globalization as an economic phenomenon. In light of the sheer complexity of many of the academic conceptualizations we have engaged with, this appears highly restrictive in terms of its analysis of contemporary globalization. Wolf, Friedman, Stiglitz, Klein and Marcos rarely if ever stray from an understanding of globalization as a wider consequence of the development of a globally interconnected economy. Much of the academic thinking discussed in the chapters of this book successfully demonstrates how the economic realm is inseparable from the social, cultural, technological and political aspects of contemporary social life. Whilst Wolf and Stiglitz come closest to engaging with this more sophisticated view of globalization, popular thinking about globalization remains significantly constrained by this narrow approach.

A second major criticism of popular thinking is that it tends to present caricatured or dogmatic representations of what globalization 'is'. Thus, I suggested academic and popular thinkers alike occupy each of the three general positions often either as a negative phenomenon linked to the (implicitly regressive) ongoing development of global capitalism or as an almost utopian progressive development panacea for human society. Neither position is especially convincing, although the roots of these caricatures are complicated. With regard to the former, I would suggest that the negative 'almost conspiratorial' perspective of thinkers like Klein or Marcos is also present in the more academic but nevertheless still 'popular' thinking of Hardt and Negri. Whilst these radical thinkers on many occasions do make valid and trenchant criticisms in relation to the consequences of neoliberal economic globalization, the implicit assumption is that both capitalism and state or organizational power is bad in all circumstances. The philosophical roots of such ideas have a complex ancestry in Marxian, left-wing and even anarchistic philosophies dating back more than a century but are vulnerable to criticism for developing an overdetermined conception of power and agency. This literature thus appears blind to the complex role of states, institutions and other actors as intermediaries in outcomes from globalization that it regards as both negative *and positive*.

This leads to a third and familiar argument: that, despite the emergence of an increasingly high-profile literature, radical 'anti-' thinking on globalization has largely failed to produce a feasible blueprint for 'another world'. There is almost universal agreement in the most recent review contributions on 'anti-globalization' (George 2004) that the neoliberal global economy needs to be replaced with a different kind of system. By default, most proposals for an alternative system that appears significantly different to a market-based economic system draw on a Marxian-based communist or socialist set of ideas. Aside from the critics who suggest that planned or other kinds of non-market economic system cannot respond to the contemporary expectations of the global population for consumption, Klein, Marcos and Monbiot have few if any concrete proposals of how such an alternative is to be achieved politically. This perhaps explains in part the substantial attention paid to Hardt and Negri's thinking, which at least tackles the latter issue (if ambiguously). Yet, as I argued, Boron's powerful critique of Hardt and Negri suggests that their proposition that the 'multitude' can provide the basis for an alternative form of global democracy is deeply problematic.

Conversely, and fourth, in relation to the popular 'positive' thinking of Wolf and Friedman, there remains a largely utopian faith in globalization as the long-awaited and long-needed extension of free market liberalism (Bhagwati 2004). This is an unbalanced perspective for several reasons. For a start, it misrepresents the complex interaction of political and economic processes that have produced the contemporary global geo-economy (to use Dicken's term), ignoring the politicized history of globalization. However, probably far more important is that it presents a highly utopian conception of the development, extension and functioning of markets. A growing body of social scientific work points to the complex relationship between states and supranational institutions, on the one hand, and firms and markets on the other. As Stiglitz is at pains to emphasize, the notion of the 'pure' market and 'perfect' competition as conceived in neoclassical economics has arguably little or no relevance to 'actual existing' economic globalization, let alone any other dimension to global interconnectedness. Whilst Wolf's erudite thinking in support of free market economies has some sensitivity to this problem, he still presents a rather unsophisticated view of what markets (and market economies) are and how they interact with non-economic phenomena (Slater and Tonkiss 2001). Furthermore, if the radical thinkers are guilty of overstating the power of TNCs (e.g. Hertz 2002) and other economic agents, then thinkers like Friedman certainly also present what is at best a selectively positive perspective on the activities of these actors.

Fifth, and finally, my concluding argument in relation to 'reformist' thinking such as that articulated by Stiglitz is that, whilst it probably offers the most feasible proposals for developing an alternative to neoliberal economic globalization, it still faces several substantial limitations and challenges. The first of these is similar to the problem faced by the radical or revolutionary thinkers: the political mechanism for change. Stiglitz more than most is aware of the obstacles to achieving real political change in world society but his work only lightly engages with the mechanisms that might lead to the reforms he proposes. It is true that the global economic downturn since 2007, and especially the crises experienced by the financial system, creates some political space for change. For example, discussion about some kind of 'Bretton Woods II' system and an abandonment of the US dollar as the global reserve currency are finally on the table at summits between world leaders. Likewise the election of the Obama administration perhaps signals a real mechanism for many reforms, but it still is true that reformist thinkers remain stronger on what needs to be done than how it is to be achieved.

A further issue, however, is the nature of the consensus on what kinds of reform are needed, and in particular around the global institutions and global governance. Stiglitz shares common ground here with a number of academic political science thinkers like Held – and other radical thinkers such as Monbiot – but in their arguments for creating more democratic global institutions and global governance, I would argue all share a need for more detailed proposals. Specifically, much remains unclear in reformist thinking about how the existing framework of (not very democratic) global governance which has evolved through a complex and contested politicized history could be replaced wholesale with a new kind of framework that (by its very nature) is based on an ideal type.

Future thinking about globalization: key research questions

I want to end this chapter, and our journey through globalization thinking, by identifying what I think are the major research questions that emerge in light of the analysis in this book. Such a task inevitably involves prioritizing certain issues over others, but I hope it will provide a thought-provoking endpoint and stimulate further debate.

The first – and probably most pressing – research question in seeking to understand and theorize globalization is whether existing conceptualizations of globalization are adequate to understand the multiple and complex transformations that the term seeks to explain. The analysis of various globalization theories in this book suggests that the issue of whether a sufficient general theory of globalization is possible or desirable is far from resolved. Future thinking about globalization needs both to explore the utility of complex typologies of globalization such as that developed by Held et al., but also to examine the epistemological foundations that underpin such meta-theories. The question of whether 'globalization' as an umbrella-concept is anything more than a description of global-scale interconnectedness remains unresolved. Future thinking needs to develop more sophisticated arguments to support the idea that it is a form of generalized process that is common to many different dimensions of social life.

Following on, a second key set of research questions centre on the relationship between the economic and non-economic spheres. Thinking about globalization has, to date, privileged the economic dimension and ignored the extent to which (globalizing) economic activity is constituted through non-economic dimensions to social life. Whilst several influential academic thinkers including Giddens, Held et al. and Castells have developed much broader theories of globalization, the ideas of cultural thinkers like Appadurai demonstrate how much farther this research agenda can be taken. There needs to be a significant re-evaluation of the epistemological assumption that underlies thinking about globalization, certainly to the point that the possibility of analysing economic globalization without recourse to cultural or political issues is brought under close scrutiny. Future thinking about globalization needs, in short, to transcend the limitations of the narrow epistemological approaches that have framed the ideas of many of the thinkers considered though this book.

Third, and following on from this last point, there is a specific need to reconceptualize the nature of both agency and actors involved in propagating or resisting globalization. Many of the thinkers we have considered have had to confront the difficulty of reconciling existing (and conventional) conceptions of key actors with their new and evolving forms. The key point is that the phenomena being captured in the term 'globalization' is not being shaped by static, unchanging actors that inhabited the world previously. Nation-states, supranational institutions, corporations and political movements are in a state of dynamism that is symbiotically bound into developing global societal interconnectedness. The challenge for future thinking about globalization is to develop better conceptions of these changing actors which escape older, and increasingly inappropriate, understandings of their nature. Both Dicken's and Appadurai's thinking, for example, opens up this agenda in various ways. Dicken's shift towards a relational and topological understanding of transnational firms that interact in complex global production networks calls into question existing assumptions in much of the globalization literature about what capacity TNCs have to act, how they exercise power and how that agency might be regulated. Similarly, Appadurai's cultural-based analysis destabilizes many of the existing assumptions about how culture, identity and political agency are developed and sustained in a globally integrating world.

Finally, the analysis in this book suggests that there is an urgent need for future research to rethink the relationship between conceptions of globalization on the one hand, and the role of politics as well as the politics of knowledge itself on the other. Thinking about globalization has been far too little concerned with the 'messy' detail of how institutions can be changed, or how new structures of global governance might work. This is not to downplay the importance of those academic thinkers like Held and McGrew who have laid out models for new institutional forms or global governance, but the ongoing problem remains the disconnection between proposed models for a different kind of globalized world and the means to reach that situation. In part this might be attributed amongst academic thinkers to the legacy of modern social theory and its goals of producing objective and politically neutral ideas about the world, but I would end by arguing it is more a result of the difficult challenge that engaging with the complex realities of global politics represents for globalization thinkers. If the reticence of many thinkers discussed in this book to provide detailed proposals for *how* institutional transformations and regulatory changes are to be achieved indicates anything, it is that it is far easier to imagine the goals for reform than to map the road to get there. Stiglitz has of course made one of the most significant attempts to do this, but there is need for more thought to be given to this issue by many more thinkers. The debate about what globalization 'is' will certainly continue, but consensus on the parameters of the debate is now well established, and it is time for the enormous energy channelled into understanding globalization to be redirected towards thinking about the (almost certainly less exciting) mechanisms for achieving a better kind of globalized world.

NOTES

1 Giddens provides a much lengthier discussion of *how* trust is disembedded and re-embedded than can be covered here. He draws on the work of Erving Goffman in particular as he seeks to theorize the nature of trust relations under globalizing modernity (see Giddens 1990, pp. 79–111).
2 The concept of space as a social product has much in common with the ideas of Henri Lefebvre (see Lefebvre 1991).
3 With the political science literature, 'minilateralism' is used to refer to preferential agreements between small groups of nation-states (usually over trading arrangements).
4 The terminology comes from 'game theory', as developed within economics.
5 The pauper labour argument is a proposition within classic economic theory that posits if a nation trades with a country with lower wage levels it will reduce domestic wage rates, potentially to the low level of the trade partner.
6 Antonio Gramsci (1891–1937) was an Italian Marxist politician and theorist who co-founded the Italian Communist Party. Gramscian Marxism proposed the concept of 'cultural hegemony', emphasizing the importance of cultural values and norms in the process of class domination. This explained why revolution may never happen as capitalism developed a cultural consensus where the working class increasingly identified with the interests of the bourgeoisie.

REFERENCES

Abouharb, M. and Cingranelli, D. (2007) *Human Rights and Structural Adjustment*. Cambridge: Cambridge University Press.

Agnew, J. (1994) The Territorial Trap: The Geographical Assumptions of International Relations Theory. *Review of International Political Economy* 1: 53–80

Allen, J. (2003) *Lost Geographies of Power*. Oxford: Blackwell.

Amin, S. (2005) Empire and Multitude. *Monthly Review* 57(6).

Anderson, B. (1991) *Imagined Communities: Reflections on the Origin and Spread of Nationalism* (2nd edn). London: Verso.

Appadurai, A. (1990) Disjuncture and Difference in the Global Cultural Economy. *Theory, Culture and Society* 7: 295–310.

Appadurai, A. (1996) *Modernity at Large: Cultural Dimensions of Globalization*. Minneapolis: University of Minnesota Press.

Appadurai, A. (2001) Grassroots Globalization and the Research Imagination, in A. Appadurai (ed.), *Globalization*. London: Duke University Press, pp. 1–21.

Appadurai, A. (2006) *Fear of Small Numbers*. London: Duke University Press.

Barker, C. (1999) *Television, Globalization and Cultural Identities*. Milton Keynes: Open University Press.

Baudrillard, J. (1994) *Simulacra and Simulation*. Trans. S. Glaser. University of Michigan Press.

Beck, U. (1992) *Risk Society: Towards a New Modernity*. Cambridge: Polity.

Bhagwati, J. (2004) *In Defense of Globalization*. Oxford: Oxford University Press.

Bisley, N. (2007) *Rethinking Globalization*. Basingstoke: Palgrave Macmillan.

Boron, A. (2005) *Empire and Imperialism: A Critical Reading of Michael Hardt and Antonio Negri*. London: Zed Books.

Callinicos, A. (2002) The Actuality of Imperialism. *Millennium – Journal of International Studies* 31(2): 319–26.

Castells, M. (1991) *The Informational City: Information Technology, Economic Restructuring, and the Urban Regional Process.* Oxford: Blackwell.

Castells, M. (2000a) *The Rise of the Network Society: The Information Age: Economy, Society and Culture, Vol. I,* (2nd edn). Oxford: Blackwell.

Castells, M. (2000b) *The End of the Millennium, The Information Age: Economy, Society and Culture, Vol. III* (2nd edn). Oxford: Blackwell.

Castells, M. (2001) *The Internet Galaxy: Reflections on the Internet, Business and Society.* Oxford: Oxford University Press.

Castells, M. (2003) *The Power of Identity, The Information Age: Economy, Society and Culture, Vol. II* (2nd edn). Oxford: Blackwell.

Cohen, J. and Sabel, C. (2005) Global Democracy? *NYU Journal of International Law and Politics* 37(4): 763–97.

Dabrowski, M., Gomulka, S. and Rostowski, J. (2000) Whence Reform? A Critique of the Stiglitz Perspective. Available online at http://eprints.lse.ac.uk/20167/

Dawson, T. (2002) Stiglitz, the IMF and Globalization. Text of speech available at www.imf.org/external/np/speeches

Deleuze, G. and Guattari, F. (1972) *Anti-Oedipus: Capitalism and Schizophrenia.* London: Athlone Press.

Deleuze, G. and Guattari, F. (1982) *A Thousand Plateaus.* London: Athlone Press.

Dicken, P. (2007) *Global Shift: Mapping the Changing Contours of the World Economy.* London: Sage.

Falks, R. (1990) Economic Dimensions to Global Civilization. Working paper presented to the Cairo meeting of the Global Civilization project, Center for International Studies, Princeton University.

Flanders, S. (2002) Is Stiglitz Right? *Prospect Magazine* (Aug.).

Flint, C. and Taylor, P. (2007) *World Economy, Nation State and Locality.* Harlow: Prentice Hall.

Foucault, M. (1977) *Discipline and Punish.* New York: Random House.

Foucault, M. (1980) Body/Power. Trans. C. Gordon, in *Power/Knowledge: Selected Interviews and Other Writings, 1972–1977.* Brighton: Harvester.

Foucault, M. (1984a) Nietzsche, Genealogy, History. Trans. D. Bouchard and S. Simon, in P. Rabinow (ed.), *The Foucault Reader.* New York: Pantheon.

Foucault, M. (1984b) *The History of Sexuality,* Vol. 1. London: Penguin.

Frank, A. (1966) The Development of Underdevelopment. *Monthly Review* 18.

Friedman, T. (1999) *The Lexus and the Olive Tree.* London: Harper Collins.

Friedman, T. (2005) *The World is Flat: The Globalized World in the Twenty-First Century.* New York: Allen Lane

Friedman, T. (2007) *The World is Flat: The Globalized World in the Twenty-First Century* (2nd edn). New York: Penguin.

Fukuyama, F. (1991) *The End of History and the Last Man.* New York: The Free Press.

George, S. (2004) *Another World is Possible If.* London: Verso.

Giddens, A. (1990) *The Consequences of Modernity.* Cambridge: Polity.

Giddens, A. (1996) Globalization: A Keynote Address. *UNRISD News 15,* 4–5.

Giddens, A. (1999) *Runaway World: How Globalisation is Reshaping our Lives.* London: Profile Books.

Goede, M. (2006) *International Political Economy and Poststructural Politics.* Basingstoke: Palgrave Macmillan.

Hardt, M. and Negri, A. (2000) *Empire.* Cambridge, MA: Harvard University Press.

Hardt, M. and Negri, A. (2004) *Multitude: War and Democracy in the Age of Empire.* New York: Penguin.

Harvey, D. (1989) *The Condition of Postmodernity.* Oxford: Blackwell.

Harvey, D. (2003) *A Brief History of Neoliberalism.* Oxford: Oxford University Press.

Held, D. and McGrew, A. (2007) *Globalization/Anti-Globalization: Beyond the Great Divide.* Cambridge: Polity.

Held, D., McGrew, A., Goldblatt, D. and Perraton, J. (1999) *Global Transformations: Politics, Economics and Culture.* Cambridge: Polity.

Herod, A. (2009) *Geographies of Globalization: A Critical Introduction.* Oxford: Wiley-Blackwell.

Hertz, N. (2002) *The Silent Takeover: Global Capitalism and the Death of Democracy.* London: Arrow Books.

Hess, M. (2004) 'Spatial' Relationships? Towards a Reconceptualisation of Embeddedness. *Progress in Human Geography* 28(2): 165–86.

Higgins, N. (2005) Zapatista Poetics and Cultural Humanism, in C. Eschle and B. Maiguashca (eds), *Critical Theories, International Relations and 'The Anti-Globalization Movement'.* London: Routledge, pp. 87–102.

Hines, C. (2000) *Localization: A Global Manifesto.* London: Earthscan.

Hirst, P. and Thompson, P. (1999) *Globalization in Question* (2nd edn). Cambridge: Polity.

Hopper, P. (2007) *Understanding Cultural Globalization.* Cambridge: Polity.

Huntington, S. (1997) *The Clash of Civilizations: And the Remaking of World Order.* New York: Simon Schuster.

Jackson, P. (2003) Mapping Post-structuralism's Borders: The Case for Poststructuralist Area Studies. *SOJOURN: Journal of Social Issues in Southeast Asia* 18(1): 42–88.

Jessop, R. (2002) *The Future of the Capitalist State.* Cambridge: Polity.

Jones, A. (1998) Re-theorising the Core: A 'Globalized' Business Elite in Santiago, Chile. *Political Geography* 17(3): 295–318.

Jones, A. (2002) The Global City Misconceived: The Myth of 'Global Management' in Transnational Service Firms. *Geoforum* 33: 335–50.

Jones, A. (2006) *The Dictionary of Globalization.* Cambridge: Polity.

Jones, A. (2008) Beyond Embeddedness: Economic Practices and the Invisible Dimensions to Transnational Business Activity. *Progress in Human Geography* 32(1): 71–88.

Juhasz, A. (2007) *The Bush Agenda: Invading the World, One Economy at a Time*. London: HarperCollins.

Kennedy, P. (1988) *The Rise and Fall of the Great Powers: Economic Change and Military Power 1500–2000*. London: HarperCollins.

Klein, N. (2000) *No Logo: Taking Aim at the Brand Bullies*. New York: Flamingo.

Klein, N. (2002) *Fences and Windows: Dispatches from the Front Lines of the Globalization Debate*. New York: Flamingo.

Klein, N. (2007) *The Shock Doctrine: The Rise of Disaster Capitalism*. London: Penguin.

Krugman, P. (1998) What's New about the New Economic Geography? *Oxford Review of Economic Policy* 14: 7–17.

Latour, B. (1999) *We Have Never Been Modern*. Harvester Wheatsheaf.

Latour, B. (2005) *Reassembling the Social*. Oxford: Oxford University Press.

Lefebvre, H. (1991) *The Production of Space*. Oxford: Blackwell.

Leitner, H., Peck, J., and Shepperd, E. (eds) (2006) *Contesting Neoliberalism*. London: Guilford Press.

Lovelock, J. (1979) *Gaia: A New Look at Life on Earth*. Oxford: Oxford University Press.

Lukes, S. (1974) *Power: A Radical View*. Basingstoke: Macmillan.

Lyotard, J.-F. (1984) *The Postmodern Condition: A Report on Knowledge*. Manchester: Manchester University Press.

MacGillivray, A. (2006) *A Brief History of Globalization*. London: Robinson.

Mann, M. (1997) Has Globalization ended the Rise and Rise of the Nation-State? *Review of International Political Economy* 4(3): 472–96.

Marcos, S. (2002) *Our Word is Our Weapon*. London: Serpent's Tail.

Mittelman, J. (2000) *The Globalization Syndrome: Transformation and Resistance*. Princeton: Princeton University Press.

Mittelman, J. (2004) *Whither Globalization? The Vortex of Knowledge and Ideology*. London: Routledge.

Monbiot, G. (2004 [2003]) *The Age of Consent: A Manifesto for a New World Order*. London: Harper Perennial.

Monbiot, G. (2006) *Heat: How to Stop the Planet Burning*. London: Allen Lane.

Nederveen Pieterse, J. (2004) *Globalization and Culture: Global Melange*. Lanham, MD: Rowman and Littlefield.

Ninkoich, F. (2000) Review of 'Empire'. *Political Science Quarterly* 3: 488–9.

Ohmae, K. (1995) *The End of the Nation State*. London: Harper Collins.

Okur, M. (2007) Rethinking Empire After 9/11: Towards a New Ontological Image of World Order. *Perceptions* XII: 61–93.

Passavant, P. and Dean, J. (eds) (2004) *Empire's New Clothes: Reading Hardt and Negri*. London: Routledge.

Peck, J. and Tickell, A. (2006) Conceptualising Neoliberalism, Thinking Thatcherism, in H. Leitner, J. Peck, and E. Shepherd (eds), *Contesting Neoliberalism*. London: Guilford Press, pp. 26–50.

Peters, M. (2002) *Poststructuralism, Marxism and Neoliberalism: Between Theory and Politics*. Lanham, MD: Rowman and Littlefield.

Porter, M. (1990) *The Competitive Advantage of Nations*. Basingstoke: Macmillan.

Porter, M. (2000) Locations, Clusters and Company Strategy, in G. Clark, M. Feldman and M. Gertler (eds), *The Oxford Handbook of Economic Geography*. Oxford: Oxford University Press, ch. 13.

Rabach, E. and Kim, E. (1994) Where is the Chain in Commodity Chains? The Service Sector Nexus. In G. Gereffi and M. Korzeniewicz (eds), *Commodity Chains and Global Capitalism*. Westport, CT: Praeger, ch. 6.

Rosenberg, J. (2000) *The Follies of Globalization Theory*. London: Verso.

Roy, A. (2004) *The Ordinary Person's Guide to Empire*. London: Flamingo.

Saad-Filho, A. and Johnston, D. (eds) (2004) *Neoliberalism: A Critical Reader*. London: Pluto Books.

SAPRIN (2004) *Structural Adjustment: The SAPRI Report – The Policy Roots of Economic Crisis, Poverty and Inequality*. London: Zed Books.

Sassen, S. (1991) *The Global City*. Princeton: Princeton University Press.

Sassen, S. (2001) *The Global City* (2nd edn). Princeton: Princeton University Press.

Scholte, J. (2005) *Globalization: A Critical Introduction* (2nd edn). Basingstoke: Palgrave Macmillan.

Seidman, S. (ed.) (1994) *The Postmodern Turn: New Perspectives on Social Theory*. Cambridge: Cambridge University Press.

Seidman, S. (2008) *Contested Knowledge: Social Theory Today* (4th edn). Oxford: Wiley-Blackwell.

Shiva, V. (2001) *Protect or Plunder? Understanding Intellectual Property Rights*. London: Zed Books.

Shiva, V. (2007) *Manifestos on the Future of Food and Seed*. Cambridge, MA: South End Press.

Shiva, V. (2009) *Soil Not Oil: Climate Change, Peak Oil and Food Insecurity*. London: Zed Books.

Sklair, L. (2001) *The Transnational Capitalist Class*. Oxford: Blackwell.

Slater, D. and Tonkiss, F. (2001) *Market Society*. Cambridge: Polity.

Smith, N. (2005) *The Endgame of Globalization*. London: Routledge.

Stalder, F. (2006) *Manuel Castells: The Theory of the Network Society*. Cambridge: Polity.

Stiglitz, J. (1985) Equilibrium Wage Distributions. *Economic Journal* 95: 595–618.

Stiglitz, J. (1999) *Globalization and Its Discontents*. London: Penguin.

Stiglitz, J. (2000) The Contributions of the Economics of Information to Twentieth Century Economics. *Quarterly Journal of Economics,* 115(4): 1441–78.

Stiglitz, J. (2003) *The Roaring Nineties: Why We are Paying the Price for the Greediest Decade in History*. London: Penguin.

Stiglitz, J. (2006) *Making Globalization Work*. London: Penguin.

Stiglitz, J. and Greenwald, B. (1992) Information, Finance and Markets: The Architecture of Allocative Mechanisms. *Industrial and Corporate Change* 1(1): 37–63.

Stiglitz, J. and Grossman, S. J. (1980) On the Impossibility of Informationally Efficient Markets. *American Economic Review* 70(3): 393–408.

Storey, J. (2008) *Cultural Theory and Popular Culture: An Introduction* (5th edn). Harlow: Pearson.

Thrift, N. (1990) Doing Regional Geography in a Global System: The New International Financial System, the City of London and the South-East of England 1984–87, in R. Johnson, J. Hauer and G. Hoekveld (eds), *Regional Geography: Current Developments and Future Prospects*. London: Routledge, pp. 180–207.

Tomlinson, J. (1999) *The Globalization of Culture*. Cambridge: Polity.

Turner, G. (2008) *The Credit Crunch: Housing Bubbles, Globalisation and the Worldwide Economic Crisis*. London: Pluto Press.

Urry, J. (2007) *Mobilities*. Cambridge: Polity.

Wallerstein, I. (1974) *The Modern World-System, Vol. I: Capitalist Agriculture and the Origins of the European World-Economy in the Sixteenth Century*. New York/London: Academic Press.

Wallerstein, I. (1979) *The Capitalist World-Economy*. Cambridge: Cambridge University Press.

Wallerstein, I. (1989) *The Modern World-System, Vol. III: The Second Great Expansion of the Capitalist World-Economy, 1730–1840s*. San Diego: Academic Press.

Wallerstein, I. (2000) Globalization or the Age of Transition? A Long-Term View of the Trajectory of the World System. *International Sociology* 1(2): 251–67.

Williams, R. (2005) *Culture and Materialism*. London: Verso.

Wolf, M. (2004) *Why Globalization Works*. Yale: Yale University Press.

Yeung, H. and Peck, J. (2003) Making Global Connections: A Geographer's Perspective, in J. Peck and H. Yeung (eds), *Remaking the Global Economy*. London: Sage, ch. 1.

INDEX